the
Baseball Drill Book

AMERICAN BASEBALL COACHES ASSOCIATION

BOB BENNETT, EDITOR

Human Kinetics

Library of Congress Cataloging-in-Publication Data

The baseball drill book / Bob Bennett, editor.
   p. cm.
   ISBN 0-7360-5083-3 (soft cover)
   1. Baseball--Training. I. Bennett, Bob.
   GV875.6.B35 2003
   796.357'2--dc22

                                   2003019592

ISBN-10: 0-7360-5083-3
ISBN-13: 978-0-7360-5083-8

Copyright © 2004 by Human Kinetics, Inc.

Developmental Editor: Leigh LaHood; **Assistant Editor:** Ragen E. Sanner; **Copyeditor:** John Wentworth; **Proofreader:** Coree Clark; **Permission Manager:** Toni Harte; **Graphic Designer:** Robert Reuther; **Graphic Artist:** Francine Hamerski; **Photo Manager:** Dan Wendt; **Cover Designer:** Andrew Tietz; **Art Manager:** Kareema McLendon; **Illustrator:** Roberto Sabas; **Printer:** United Graphics

Human Kinetics books are available at special discounts for bulk purchase. Special editions or book excerpts can also be created to specification. For details, contact the Special Sales Manager at Human Kinetics.

Printed in the United States of America   20   19   18   17   16   15   14   13   12

The paper in this book is certified under a sustainable forestry program.

Human Kinetics
Web site: www.HumanKinetics.com

United States: Human Kinetics
P.O. Box 5076
Champaign, IL 61825-5076
800-747-4457
e-mail: humank@hkusa.com

Canada: Human Kinetics
475 Devonshire Road, Unit 100
Windsor, ON N8Y 2L5
800-465-7301 (in Canada only)
e-mail: info@hkcanada.com

Europe: Human Kinetics
107 Bradford Road
Stanningley
Leeds LS28 6AT, United Kingdom
+44 (0)113 255 5665
e-mail: hk@hkeurope.com

Australia: Human Kinetics
57A Price Avenue
Lower Mitcham, South Australia 5062
08 8372 0999
e-mail: info@hkaustralia.com

New Zealand: Human Kinetics
P.O. Box 80
Torrens Park, South Australia 5062
0800 222 062
e-mail: info@hknewzealand.com

the
Baseball
Drill Book

Contents

Introduction

Drills are the life blood of any practice. They provide the setting and opportunity for growth, improvement, and maintenance. They create an environment that prepares the athlete and his team for game competition. When done properly, drills excite, invigorate, challenge, and encourage. Through repetition of drills and within drills, skills are perfected. This allows the athlete and his team to execute difficult maneuvers more efficiently.

Some of the best baseball coaches in the country have combined their wisdom to put this book together. If you're a beginning coach, this book will help you gain the foresight you need to select drills that suit your team both as individuals and as a unit. If you're an experienced coach, this book promotes wise and practical use of your precious practice time and will improve your ability to match your drills to the precise needs of each member of your team.

Many time-tested drills are clearly described and diagramed and are readily available for any coach or player. There are also new drills, shown for the first time. Step-by-step guidelines for performing and conducting the drills are suggested, as well as ways to modify the drills for greater variety and customization.

The coaches who have put this book together are happy to give back to the game what the game has given to them. Passing it on is the cornerstone of the baseball coaching profession. We thank and pay homage to the many pioneering baseball coaches who generously passed along their gift of knowledge to us.

Key to Diagrams

Path of ball	- - - - - ->
Path of player (running)	———————>
CH	Coach
F	Fungo hitter
B	Batter
C	Catcher
P	Pitcher
R	Runner
Ⓡ	Relay/cut-off man
X	Any player
1B	First baseman
2B	Second baseman
3B	Third baseman
SS	Shortstop
CF	Centerfielder
RF	Right fielder
LF	Left fielder

PART

I

Effective Applications

Chapter 1

Incorporating Drills Into Practices

Bob Bennett

Practice has several purposes. Learning to perform, developing, maintaining, and perfecting skills are the basic objectives of a beneficial practice. In the pursuit of these objectives, such areas as discipline, teamwork, persistence, timing, mental toughness, responsibility, organization, and gamesmanship play important roles during practice.

Coaches should ensure that learning, developing, maintaining, and perfecting skills are included in each practice. A good practice session also invigorates, enlightens, teaches, develops, excites, encourages, and promotes teamwork among team members. Your ability to select the best drills to match your practice goals often determines the success or failure of your practice sessions.

Three familiar quotes succinctly describe the importance of practice. The saying "practice makes perfect" has often been used to illustrate the need to do things repetitively while pursuing excellence. The value and importance of practice sessions is expressed even more strongly by the commonly heard saying, "perfect practice makes perfect." An even more precise and descriptive way to point out the importance of practice is "practice makes permanent." Choose any, all, or none of these sayings but realize that most would agree that practice sessions directly relate to the final results.

We practice to prepare for each game. If that practice is productive, the results will show. A well-designed practice in which players repeat and diligently try to perfect fundamentals is a big step toward success. A poorly designed and sloppily executed practice likely produces chaos and leads to failure in games.

Drills are an important part of teaching and coaching. Some coaches use drills without knowing it. I once had a coach tell me, "I'm not big on drills. I seldom use them." Then I watched his team practice and noticed the skill and precise rhythm and timing of his players. I further noticed that his team's batting practice was very well organized and that outfield and infield practice was impeccably orchestrated. Of course, what his players were doing was running

Well-organized practices that contain effective drills lead to good playing on game day.

drills. Their pepper games (a drill), their hitting in the batting cages (a drill), and even their playing catch (another drill) clearly showed the results of fine teaching techniques through drills.

What Is a Drill?

A drill is a means of teaching and training through repeated exercise or repetition of an act. Fielding a series of ground balls, playing catch, practicing footwork, hitting, running the bases, or doing any other activity that is repeated can be called a drill. These kinds of activities make up a practice schedule. Among the many practice activities are both productive repetitions and unproductive, even harmful, repetitions.

It's virtually impossible to conduct a practice without using drills. However, it is not difficult to conduct a practice using drills that do little toward achieving team or individual goals. Obviously, the most effective practices incorporate proper drills that help players pursue excellence in the skill being taught. This is where sound teaching begins. Sound, effective drills are among a coach's key assets.

The Value of Drills

Muscle memory is important in accomplishing any athletic endeavor. Throwing a baseball, hitting it, and running the bases properly are activities that require freedom of movement. To perform these activities successfully, the performer must be able to react without having to carefully tell each muscle group what to do. His reactions are seemingly automatic. Muscle memory is the result of teaching the muscles how to perform a specific activity and repeating that activity until it can be done freely without methodical thought. Throwing, for example, requires some thought in where to throw and how hard to throw, but the mechanical part of throwing (getting the proper grip, bringing the arm into throwing position, and releasing the ball) should be routine. In order to get to the automatic stage, the muscles are trained to react quickly to each competitive situation.

Either the athlete is already gifted with the ability to make a mental command and have his muscle groups react and perform, or the athlete must train those muscle groups to respond to his mental commands. Most baseball skills must be methodically practiced before the body is able to react freely and without conscious thought to each part of the activity. This is muscle memory. Mental toughness and concentration are also necessary. Learning the proper techniques and methods and then repeating them correctly form an avenue toward success.

You can incorporate drills into practice in many ways. Some coaches use the "machine gun method," which employs several kinds of drills to improve a single skill. The theory here is that someone will benefit from something. In other words, if enough different kinds of drills are executed and enough different kinds of approaches are used to explain the skill, something from these drills will stick to some of those who participate in them.

It's true that some players are astute and skillful enough to get the most out of even an ill-conceived, poorly conducted practice session, but these are the rare ones. Most players need the help that carefully chosen and orchestrated drills can provide.

Drills used wisely and correctly dramatically improve skills. There are many roads to success. Some coaches do most of their teaching with a few well-planned drills. They select drills that fit the lesson plan and repeat them with precision. Others use many different well-thought-out drills to accomplish the same end. Some coaches are clever enough to design on-the-spot drills that fit perfectly into the lesson plan for the day. Successful coaches and teachers have, or develop, an ability to know exactly where they are going and how they will get there. They can identify the areas that most need work and select the proper drills to address them. Coaching with concern and passion, they stay focused until they get results.

Along with selecting the proper drill, it's also important to choose the best length of time to do the drill and the number of times to repeat it. Appropriate drills performed several times in short spurts usually work better than lengthy drill sessions with long intervals between them.

Drill Categories

Drills can fall into several categories, but for convenience I'll use just three: individual drills, position drills, and team drills. To make the most of each practice, incorporating drills that precisely fit each situation is a key, and the selection of such drills is the responsibility of the coaching staff. Quality repetitions produce the best results. Anything else is unacceptable.

Individual Drills

Individual drills pertain to specific traits, strengths, and weaknesses of single players. They address the needs of an individual rather than a team. Sometimes it is necessary to develop special drills that address a player's unusual circumstances or problems. Fortunately, pioneering coaches have left a legacy for the coaches of today. We have at our disposal hundreds of well-designed baseball drills to suit most of our needs. Good coaches take the time to discover and explore the many resources available to them.

A player might have a rare or unusual throwing problem. Another might have developed a serious and detrimental flaw in his batting swing. Other individual players might repeatedly make the same kind of fielding, running, or mental mistake. Good coaching requires the coach to use the information available and match a problem with its solution. In most cases, a well-designed drill that addresses a specific problem done with diligent repetitions is a sound approach to meet the challenge.

Position Drills

Each position in baseball has its own demands. Some skills are common to all positions, whereas other skills are unique to a position. For example, rotation and grip of the ball are common to all positions, but the arc of the throw and the trajectory it should take vary among positions. Pitchers and outfielders both need a longer arc on their throws. The pitcher, however, needs to bend his front leg more than the outfielder does because of the trajectory of his throw. Each player should practice position-specific drills.

Infielders and catchers have some similarities in throwing, but each position creates unique demands that must be addressed through drills. Footwork and clearing from the hitter are both unique to the catching position and should be specifically addressed. Footwork around the bag and feeds are specific to infielders and need proper attention.

Some position drills will be similar to those for another position, so positions might do them together. Other position drills will benefit only a particular position and would be a waste of time for others. Most good coaches develop staple drills for each position that help improve, maintain, and perfect the skills of that position. I suggest devoting at least 15 minutes a day to these drills with total concentration. Here are a few examples:

Pitching

1. Balance on pushoff foot drill
2. Balance on stride foot drill
3. Grip and rotation drill
4. Target catch drill
5. Pickoff move drill

Catching

1. Proper stance drill
2. Receiving drill
3. Grip drill
4. Footwork drill
5. Blocking drill

Infielders

1. Glove drill
2. Grip and rotation drill
3. Quick hands drill
4. Short hop drill
5. Agility drill

Outfielders

1. Isolated feet drill
2. Footwork drill
3. Grip and rotation drill
4. Straight-line, long-toss drill
5. Outfield agility drill

Hitting falls under all three categories—individual drills, position drills, and team drills. Staple drills for the hitters can be done with a mixture of dry run or shadow drills and off the batting tee.

Hitters

1. Soft stride drill
2. Walk away from the hands drill
3. Back hip to target drill
4. Ball toss drill
5. Batting tee drill

Select five drills for each position, make sure your players understand them, and then perform them with diligence and concentration. Such practice pays great dividends. Drills require self-discipline from players and proper encouragement and supervision from the coaching staff. When done right, coaches are needed only to add to or change the drills in order to challenge, evaluate, or encourage players. Players assume responsibility for the drills they're executing. Those who take charge of more responsibility than others often become team leaders.

Team Drills

Alignments, bunt defenses, infield and outfield procedures, base running, first and third situation, pop fly priorities, batting practice, and other defensive and offensive situations fall into the category of team drills.

Teamwork, discipline, timing, and confidence are all by-products derived from team drills. To develop the teamwork necessary to compete successfully, you need to select team drills that develop skills, enhance timing, create communication, and help players perfect skills. Here are some team drills I recommend:

1. Bunt offense drill (at least 45 minutes per week)
2. Bunt defense drill (at least 45 minutes per week)
3. Pop fly priorities drill (at least 45 minutes per week)
4. Alignment drill (at least 45 minutes per week)
5. Around the infield with pitchers drill (teams the pitcher with each infield position and includes covering third base on throws from the outfield and covering home plate on passed balls and wild pitches; at least 45 minutes per week)
6. Infield and outfield procedure drill (daily)
7. Base running drill (at least 45 minutes per week)
8. First and third situations drill (at least 45 minutes per week)
9. Batting drill (daily)
10. Ground balls, fly balls, ground balls drill (daily)
11. Stretching drill (daily)

Time-Tested Drills

Baseball has a great history. Many outstanding coaches have given back to the game they coached with a passion. Their gift of knowledge and a wealth of time-tested information can be found on library shelves and Web sites. Hundreds of excellent drills exist on every facet of the game. Drills on the basic bunt defenses, alignment of plays, double-play footwork for infielders, defending the first and third double steal, batting tee, ball toss, pepper, and short hop are a few examples. Furthermore, there are fundamental drills for each position. Many of these drills are demonstrated at the American Baseball Coaches Association Annual Coaches Clinic. Many time-tested drills are described and illustrated in this book, such as base-running drills on turns and leads, bunting drills, grip and rotation drills, and a variety of team drills. All we have to do is find them to take advantage of the sweat and tears of great coaches past.

A legacy of time-tested throwing, fielding, hitting, running, and gamesmanship drills is available. Properly used, these drills fill the needs of most players, coaches, and teams. They also extend an invitation for us to improve or add to them, or even create new drills.

Employing some grip and rotation drills at the outset of teaching youngsters proper throwing technique will pay great dividends. Systematically repeat these drills to promote maintenance and then excellence. Such drills are fundamental for young players, as they allow and encourage players to become self-sufficient.

Introducing a few well-considered drills for a balanced batting stance works wonders for young hitters and helps them develop a fundamental base that lasts a lifetime. A solid drill that develops a soft stride while preparing the hands to get into a load position is valuable to every young hitter.

A balanced fielding position is important for each infielder. Drills that include proper foot position, body positioning, and glove presentation are all important for developing a good fielding position. A drill that repeats correct movements and positions makes the balanced position routine.

Drills that promote competition help players and teams develop and perfect gamesmanship. Drills that simulate the bunting game or the base-running game hone and perfect competitive skills.

Each drill should have a purpose. No drill should be used just to fill time. Poor use of a drill renders the drill useless and promotes bad habits because of the lack of care in performing it. A few purposeful and meaningful drills that zero in on a target are much more effective than many drills done to fill practice time.

The length of a drill should depend on the skill level and age group performing it. Short drills done with intensity are generally more effective with younger, less experienced athletes. The same can be said for older age groups that lack experience or skills, although this group's attention span is somewhat longer than the younger age group. The length and purpose of the drill directly affects the excitement with which it's executed.

On-the-Spot Drills

Some of my most productive drills are those I developed on the spot during practice. Such drills are often effective because they're born of necessity. They fit the problem like a glove. I often use whatever's available to help solve a problem. For instance, a rubber mat or a piece of carpet has helped me cure overstriding in pitchers. I place the mat at a distance that gives the pitcher enough room to stride properly. If his stride is so long that his stride foot lands on the carpet, or rubber pad, he knows his stride is too long.

A paper cup or small plastic bucket may be used to help pitchers with their pushoff and follow-through with their pushoff leg. I put the paper cup about two feet to the right of the pitcher's pushoff foot and a few inches toward home plate. The pitcher pushes off and back with his pushoff foot, then lifts that foot and forms a circle to the right and over the cup and lands on the toe of the pushoff foot. As he completes the braking action of his throwing arm and completes the follow-through, he turns the heel of the pushoff foot over, completing the throw with the least amount of stress.

These are examples of creating on-the-spot drills. As a coach learns more about the position he is teaching and gains appreciation of good teaching techniques, his mind opens to unlimited possibilities. Necessity and passion develop wonderful remedies.

Selecting Drills That Fit

As I said earlier, practice has many purposes. One purpose is to introduce and learn new skills and techniques. These drills should target a very specific goal and be allotted plenty of time. They require patience from all parties involved. When introducing skills or techniques, repeated, focused work on a single fundamental is much more productive than trying to cover several things at once.

Improvement should occur during each practice session. Players start at their level of competency and practice with commitment to execute more efficiently. Constant improvement requires persistent effort. Drills with this purpose in mind should be more intense than introductory drills, and expectations should be elevated. Sometimes improvement drills are aimed at a single fundamental; other times they take a broader approach. In any case, they demand a lot from both players and coaching staff. Accountability is crucial when improvement is the goal. Hard work and willingness to spend quality time on the task are imperative if improvement is to occur.

Maintaining the level of skill that each player and the team have reached requires drills that repeat, illustrate, evaluate, and measure execution. Maintenance drills are skills and plays being repeated in a gamelike manner. Repeating each drill correctly is the only way to maintain the high performance level in game conditions.

Dwight Evans, former right fielder of the Boston Red Sox, illustrated how maintenance drills can pay off. Evans was known as one of the most consistent players of his time. One of my coaching friends observed him practicing base-running techniques during pregame batting practice at Fenway Park. Each time Dwight finished his turn in batting practice he ran hard to first base, then took a good lead, read the pitcher's move to the plate, and reacted with precision to get a good jump on stealing second base. After reaching second base, he again took his lead, but this time he read the pitch to the plate and timed his lead according to the pitch. If the ball was hit to the weak side of the infield on the ground, he advanced to third base with the hustle of a player in a real game. If the ball was caught by the catcher, he returned to second base. On a fly ball, he tagged on normal or deep fly balls and went halfway on short fly balls. When the ball was hit on the ground to the strong side of the infield, he returned quickly to second base. On line drives, he froze until he saw the ball go through the infield or else returned quickly on balls hit directly to a fielder. After reaching third, he went through it all again, always with great concentration and effort, as if playing a real game.

Evans practiced base running with such unusual fervor that a coaching friend once asked him why. Why was he so diligent with his base running during pregame batting practice? Evans answered that running the bases with keen, focused concentration and effort was the only way he could stay sharp as a base runner throughout the season. The way he practiced was the way he played his games, and vice versa. This is a great example of how maintenance drills can work.

Pursuit of excellence is another integral part of each practice session. Perfecting any skill or activity requires much preparation and commitment. Drills in this context are quite demanding. Timing, communication, accuracy, and consistency are all required. Every aspect of the drill must come together perfectly to achieve a perfect result.

Repetition

Drills are made to be repeated. The manner in which they are repeated is of utmost importance. The skill level, age group, and interest level of your players should determine the kinds of drills you use and how long they last. A drill should have the undivided attention of those performing it. A wise coach matches his drills to his players and their needs. Several short drills done with intensity are much more productive than one long drill that sees the players fade as it continues.

Repetitions help to improve and perfect; they make movements and execution of an action routine. It is extremely important for repetitions to be done correctly. If they aren't, bad habits can be developed. Repetition also develops self-discipline and persistence, which in turn improve concentration level. It is through repetition that players learn to do mechanical exercises routinely, without needing to think about each step along the way. Being automatic, or routine, frees the mind and body and allows players to play their best.

Summary

For our purposes, we have divided drills into three categories: individual drills, position drills, and team drills. For all drills, it's important to match practice drills to game situations. Here's a rundown of the tips we've reviewed in this chapter:

- Organize drills to fit your players' needs.
- Make drills productive to produce better game results.
- Employ drills that provide opportunities to improve skills.

- Use well-executed drills that build mental toughness and teamwork.
- Find, study, and adapt time-tested drills to fit the team's needs.
- Learn to develop drills on the spot to help players with unusual problems.
- Repeat drills to make skills routine.
- Perfect practice makes perfect performance.

Chapter 2

Performing and Conducting Drills

Bob Bennett

Those who perform drills determine whether the drills will be successful. Properly organized drills encourage performers to succeed, but organization and selection of drills cannot assure success unless performers put forth committed effort. On the other hand, poorly organized drills discourage players and make practice much more difficult. But the performers are still the key. With the right kind of effort, players can overcome poor organization.

With all the drills and information available, coaches have no excuse for organizing practice sessions improperly. Practice organization requires planning and concern for the players and the program. If players are to grow and attain success, they should have the opportunity to become their best. To create a solid teaching environment, coaches must plan the practice schedule carefully and adapt to the needs of the team.

Setting the Stage

Organization, knowledge, and attitude set the stage for learning. The coaching staff should conduct drills with patience, urgency, accountability, and enthusiasm, with the intent to execute each part with success. A coach must believe in the drills. His belief and ability to persuade others to believe are essential to the success of the drills.

The organization and methods of performing each drill are the responsibility of the coach. These set the stage. The coach sends important messages to players. If, for instance, the coach organizes only a few drills for outfielders, he implies that defensive outfield play is not a high priority. Each position requires work in several areas. Proper emphasis of these areas fosters and promotes good teaching and good learning skills.

Establishing a Good Work Place

Developing and maintaining a sound work place enhances learning. The people involved produce the work place. If equipment is necessary to conduct the drill, the coaching staff is responsible for seeing that it is in place, operable, and safe. If any of these conditions are not met, organization is lacking.

Wherever drills are performed, the surface should closely match the surface where the game activity will take place. A well-groomed infield gives the infielder the best opportunity to be successful in repeating sound fundamentals. A tamped and solid mound affords the pitcher the best setting to achieve consistency. Grass cut to match the length of grass on game day is the proper surface for the outfielder to practice his fielding. The catchers' and hitters' practice areas should match the game surface as closely as possible. These objectives are desirable but not always attainable. Every effort should be made to match the conditions of the practice setting to the conditions of the game setting.

Safety

With all drills and with the practice session in general, the safety of participants should be a top priority. The coaching staff should provide water breaks, avoid overstressing the body, and give particular attention to the care of the arm. Fatigue creates mistakes and causes lapses in concentration, but that doesn't mean that players should not be pushed. They should, but they should not be driven to the point of total fatigue during the course of drills. If players become fatigued, expect them to suffer a loss of timing, concentration, and success. If the purpose of the drill is conditioning, this kind of intensity may be acceptable if all the prudent guidelines are followed.

Most players need to have some guidelines drawn concerning their safety. Younger players, for instance, often pay little attention to where and how they play catch. Even older players are sometimes guilty of playing catch haphazardly. They have to be reminded to play catch in parallel lines, with enough room between pairs to allow for errant throws.

In drills that require communication, coaches should conduct a predrill instruction in safety. Serious injuries may occur in pop-fly priority drills, alignment drills, base-running drills, and any other team drills. In long alignments, for example, the two middle infielders are in danger if the fungo hitter does not give them enough time to get out of the line of fire. Specific instructions are necessary regarding sliding and getting out of the baseline in certain situations. A good dose of common sense and a few seconds devoted to thoughtfulness will be enough for most coaches and players.

Baseball is unique in that every player throws the baseball in most of the drills. In conducting each practice, a good coach organizes the drills with that factor in mind. Running drills, nonthrowing drills, and throwing drills must be carefully sprinkled throughout each practice.

Proper conditioning should have preceded each drill. If players' arms are not in shape, few throwing drills should be in the practice schedule. Stretching and warming up for baseball activities should take place before any drills. Coaches should allow adequate time for loosening and warming up the arms before each drill that requires throwing.

Organization

The proper use of time starts with organization. Practice time is precious. Each moment arrives only once. How that moment is used may decide the success of a drill. Putting drills in the proper order and organizing them so that they connect the various pieces of practice creates a worthwhile learning environment. Orderliness sets the wheels in motion to make each drill profitable.

Keeping the drill organized and exciting requires the cooperation of all who participate in it. With awareness and understanding of the importance of time, players will be able to maximize the benefit of each drill. Organization does not end with preparation; it continues throughout the practice.

Every action in a drill should contribute to attaining successful results in the game setting. Every drill should incorporate timing—a major component in making practice as gamelike as possible. Later we will discuss the steps to take in learning how to do each drill properly. During the first steps, the actions are purposely slower, but that unhurried pace lasts only until players learn the process. Taking these initial steps at a slow pace will speed up the learning process and help players graduate to the competitive environment where action occurs at full speed. Full speed with proper timing is the performance goal for each drill.

Wise Use of Time

Organization depends on many factors. Time is one of the factors that plays an important roll in each drill. A well-conducted drill does not drag or have long dead periods. Participants are made aware of the importance of time. Drills should start and finish on time unless extenuating circumstances intervene. Both the coaches and the players are responsible for ensuring that time is not wasted. All it takes to break the rhythm of a drill is for one coach or one player to disregard the importance of time.

When each player operates under a time frame, with real concern for himself and equal concern for his teammates, the work place is productive. Each player should have his day in the sun, a time when he has a chance to shine. When each player learns to honor and respect each of his teammates' turns, drills begin to take wings. A player can do this only after he has learned to respect his own turn. Time and space on the athletic field are never permanent, and no individual owns them. We must learn to share that time and space.

The coaching staff and players should be mindful of the rhythm of practice. If one player is out of rhythm, or if the coach stops a group drill to have a lengthy coaching session with one player, the drill is disrupted. Coaches can dispense corrections and special advice to an individual by continuing the drill with all other players while pulling the counselee out of the line to discuss the points to be made.

Coaches who fail to pay attention to time can sap the attention of players. A nine-hour practice is probably an act of futility. Several shorter sessions with rest and food breaks that add up to the same amount of time spent in practice would be much more fruitful. To run productive drills, the players and coaches must be physically and mentally alert. Long, drawn-out activities may satisfy the need to claim that the activity, or fundamental, has been covered, but long sessions do not mean that players have learned the skill and can use it efficiently.

Players can make time almost appear to stand still. For some players the two-minute drill in football is plenty of time to run enough plays to succeed. Yet for other players the two-minute drill is an exercise in watching the hands of the clock race to an unsuccessful end to the game. Some use time with great skill. Others act as though the clock doesn't exist. Time is a huge factor in the success of a drill. A perfect throw is negated if it takes too long to reach the target. Both time and timing are necessary ingredients to producing good practice sessions that lead to winning games.

The wise use of time is vital to the learning process. Time used properly keeps interest alive and gives participants a chance to execute efficiently without the feeling of being in a hurry or having to rush through the situation. Wise use of time makes things neater. Things feel like they fit and belong.

When participants have little or no concept of time, strange things begin to happen in drills and games. Players throw to the wrong base, runners steal without being challenged, players take poor routes on ground balls and fly balls, and other mistakes continue to pop up. We have learned by experience that one throw does not fit all occasions and that the same lead does not work for all situations.

Prepractice Preparation

A practice schedule should be posted the morning of each day of practice to help the players prepare for the session. A schedule also teaches the players the coaching language of the program. A thoughtful and interested player will use the posted practice schedule to prepare himself for each drill in the practice session. He will be able to remind himself what duties his position requires to make the drill successful. The posted practice schedule should evoke conversation, questions, and answers among the members of the team.

Before any given drill, instruction should occur. Some drills will require only a few seconds of instruction, whereas others will require distribution of in-depth information. Some drills will require strict guidelines.

To get the most out of each drill, players should have clear understanding of how the drill operates, what purpose it serves, how it benefits each position and the team, and how it connects to game situations. If the players see the importance of the drill, understand that they can benefit from it, and recognize that it will make them more efficient in game conditions, they will cooperate more fully.

Procedure

Sound fundamentals must be sold and bought. Participants must dissect the drills, work on a single part, add parts, and then work on the whole drill. Each drill can be broken into several drills, each highlighting one or more fundamentals. A good coach notices details and impeccably commits to see that each part contributes functionally and efficiently to the whole.

The following is a good procedure for conducting drills. Explain the drill. Describe the assignment of each position. Set guidelines for execution. Discuss commitment. Evaluate, encourage, and correct. Review and evaluate after each drill.

Explain

Explain the drill. Make sure that each player understands what the drill entails. Describing the importance of the drill to the game setting encourages players to practice the drill with the intensity required in a game situation. The purpose of the drill should be a major point of emphasis.

Describe

Describe the duty of each position and emphasize the need for teamwork. Make sure that each player understands his assignment. Emphasize the key factors in the drill. Pinpoint the speed and manner in which the drill is to be performed. Declare the purpose, expectations, and value of each drill.

Set Guidelines

Guidelines concerning the execution of the drill are necessary. If the drill is to be performed at game speed, announce that to the players. If the drill is being done for the first time, a walk-through may be appropriate. The guidelines of that drill would be different from those of the full-speed drill. The players should know what is expected of them and how they are being evaluated. The guidelines establish the standards for each drill.

Discuss Commitment

The importance of the drill should be reiterated, and a reminder concerning the importance of commitment is appropriate. If a drill is worth doing, players should do it with enthusiasm and interest. Commitment starts with the coach. How he reacts to the drill and how much he stresses its importance are vital to its success.

Evaluate

Evaluate, encourage, and correct. Throughout each drill, the coach should be busy evaluating. The coach should understand the talent of his players and hold them accountable for the level at which they are able to perform. Coaches must learn to look at drills and players with different eyes, evaluating some drills and some players with rough eyes and others with fine eyes. Coaches may want to judge a group and a drill with rough eyes at one point and fine eyes at another. Developing the ability to look with different eyes elevates the coach to the highest level of teaching.

The rough-eye look is for the less skilled athlete, the younger, inexperienced athlete, or the skilled athlete who is learning a new task. The fine-eye look is for athletes who are highly skilled, competitive, and capable of excelling at the assignment given. A good coach shifts from using rough eyes to using fine eyes according to the situation. Further, he moves back and forth by making all kinds of adjustment in between. Focus, interest, and passion are necessary to acquire this evaluative technique.

Encourage

Encouragement is an important part of coaching. The act of coaching invites us to talk about mistakes and errors. The goal of much of our practice, once the season starts, is to repair mistakes. The tendency is to criticize more than encourage. A good part of the evaluative process should be to find positive contributions. When you find such performances, highlight and praise them. Encouragement creates excitement and interest. Positive input results.

Correct

A vigilant coach sees details. The coach has the duty and obligation to help correct what is wrong. His expectations should match the skill level of his players, their knowledge of the activity, and the degree of difficulty of the drill. Patience, intensity, persistence, concern, vigilance, and coaching knowledge are all helpful in making the needed corrections.

Review

Reviewing drills is sound teaching technique. A review gives players a perspective on their progress, provides a forum for positive reinforcement, and allows the coach an opportunity to point out areas that need improvement. A short evaluation after each drill is useful because the work is still fresh. Using this procedure will pay long-term dividends.

Attitude and Body Language

An excited, focused group can make any drill profitable. Positive attitude is essential. If the coach has properly explained the drill, emphasized its importance, given careful attention to its goals, and made sure that the players understand them, then the attitude of the participants should be excellent. For any drill to be successful, participants must be interested in it. They must see the need for doing the drill. They need to understand that the drill will be beneficial to them and that it relates to the game.

Because attitude is important, good communication is essential between the athletes and coaching staff and among players. Words encourage or discourage. Actions do the same. What and how things are said are important on the practice field. Sarcasm and personal criticism are counterproductive and have no place on the practice field or the playing field. They are harmful and hurtful, and players seem to remember them longer than they do positive statements. Encouraging words invigorate and inspire. They invite and include. These words should be spoken often in each drill.

Positive body language is uplifting. It demonstrates a cooperative contribution and invites good relationships. Players seldom misread positive body language, whereas negative body language often sends inaccurate information. A simple thumbs-up, a smile, or a look of approval by a coach or fellow teammate after a successful play can speak volumes. A nonresponse or a look of "So what?" also sends a powerful message. One encourages. The other indicates lack of concern.

Some simple rules of courtesy do wonders for relationships. Eye contact by all parties involved in any exchange of information is helpful. Maintaining a look of interest when dispensing information encourages open ears. An acknowledgment that information has been received verifies sustained interest and receipt of the sender's gift of information or knowledge.

Learning Sequences

Interchange of ideas and thoughts is extremely important to any learning environment. Questions should be invited, and answers should be given respectfully. For some, learning is difficult, particularly the learning of some drills. Others seem to assemble and use information quickly and successfully. Patience and understanding are staples in the learning process. Find a way to encourage the free flow of information to and from players. Their questions often provide the coach with the directions for the rest of the journey.

A specific sequence of learning steps maximizes both teaching and learning. Each step has a purpose, and each of the early steps is designed to prepare for execution at game speed.

Step 1. Explain or diagram. Each drill should be carefully explained, using diagrams when needed. This step is the time to communicate fully by inviting and answering questions. A misunderstood drill is difficult to perform and usually becomes an act of futility. The coach should emphasize the importance and purpose of the drill and show its connection to the game and to players at this time.

Step 2. Walk-through. The walk-through allows each player to become accustomed to the various responsibilities that are required, of not only his position but also all other positions involved in the drill. Steps, spacing, coverage, and timing issues can be properly addressed in the walk-through. Communication and teamwork for each part of the drill can be emphasized as well. The purpose of this step is to make sure that each player knows his assignment and understands positioning, timing, and spacing as well as the need for teamwork.

Step 3. Live at half speed. The third step should become closer to gamelike execution. Care should be taken to see that each player knows his assignment and is capable of carrying it out. The first three steps will take a little more time at the outset but will pay dividends in the end. The drill will run more smoothly and allow each player to execute more efficiently. This process helps players develop confidence in the drill and in themselves. The first three steps purposely include no opposition, but they prepare the players for heated competition later.

Step 4. Full speed without opposition. If players have successfully performed the first three steps, they are ready to run the drill at full speed. Each player should know his assignment by now. To solidify the learning process, run the drill without opposition. Remember, a drill merely perfects parts of the game. Players must understand what and how to do something before they can do it with precise execution.

At this juncture dummy opponents may be used. This method may involve placing a hitter at the plate who just stands in but is not live, or active. Runners may be used to aid in spacing and positioning. The dummy opponents are not there to deceive or challenge at this point.

During this step, the intensity level should rise and emphasis on timing, communication, and successful fluid movement should increase. The drill should begin to take shape.

Step 5. Full speed with restricted opposition. The drill is now progressing to gamelike execution, except that some restrictions should still hold back the opposition. For instance, on difficult timing plays such as bunt defenses and the first-and-third play, the runners should be live but have a specific assignment. On the first-and-third play and plays with a similar degree of difficulty, learning and confidence will be enhanced if the pressure is applied in increments. If a player has not yet perfected all the intricacies of a difficult defensive play and must deal with tasks that overwhelm, setbacks will be likely. A well-planned approach to learning can prevent some of those setbacks from occurring.

Step 6. Full speed with complete competition. Now the players should be ready to run the drill effectively and compete fully. The goal in teaching drills is to get to this step as quickly as possible.

Players should be expected to operate under game conditions. Communication, teamwork, timing, and execution of throws and catches should be done with the speed and efficiency required in game situations. Each drill represents part of the game. The purpose of the drill is to practice that part of the game until players can perform it successfully.

Step 7. Review and evaluate. An evaluation or review should follow each drill. The evaluation need not be a long session, although it may be necessary to spend some time drawing attention to positive and negative contributions made in the drill. A good evaluation may be as short as saying, "Well executed, good job," or as long as offering a complete list of things done well or a list of things lacking.

Every step is important to the learning process. Each step may require a large amount of time or may be done very quickly. If coaches have taught the first five steps and players have learned them, each successive drill may start at step six. Making that choice is the responsibility of the coach. When players display a high degree of confusion or misunderstanding, backtracking through the steps is necessary to provide a good learning environment.

A good coach demands perfection. A good coach understands the learning process and uses his knowledge and experience to make sure that the players have been provided the proper information, time, and understanding to apply that information.

Following these seven steps in teaching drills improves the learning process, provides continuity to the practice, and maps out the details of each drill. A player who knows his assignment is on his way to successful execution of that assignment. A few minutes spent at the outset to walk through and explain will save time later and make the drills more productive.

Summary

- Organization and attitude of the coach sets the stage.
- Safety should be carefully considered.
- Both coaches and players are responsible for establishing a good work place.
- Time used wisely creates and fosters good rhythm.
- Teamwork is a major factor in producing a gamelike setting.
- Sharing time and space is important to teamwork.
- The coach evaluates and manages each drill.
- Posting a practice schedule before each practice is helpful to the learning process.
- Explain, describe, evaluate, encourage, correct, and review.
- Develop free flow of information to and from the players.
- Follow the seven steps of teaching drills.

Chapter 3

Making Drills Gamelike

Bob Bennett

The object of any drill is to improve the skills and execution of the players during the game. To be beneficial, the drill should be practiced with the speed, timing, positioning, spacing, and communication that occur in game situations. A good deal of discipline, teamwork, interest, enthusiasm, commitment, and hard work is necessary to make drills gamelike.

Repetitions are important in the learning process. The closer that drills come to game conditions, the greater will be the benefits derived from the practice. Competition has a way of upgrading the energy level and interest level. Some athletes innately compete both in games and in practice. These athletes compete to improve on their own performance and to pursue excellence. Practice for them is exhilarating and offers a chance to excel.

Other athletes need a stimulus. These athletes may have good intentions but allow the rigors of day-to-day activities to lower their interest level. Adding degrees of competition to a drill often refurbishes the wayward athlete's energy and interest. Competition ignites the fires of ambition.

Making the drills competitive generally improves the practice setting and better prepares the team for game competition. Keen observation and sound judgment are required, however. To make the competition gamelike, competitors should be evenly matched.

With the help of good judgment, competition in practice is an asset. It challenges, lifts, encourages, inspires, motivates, disappoints, and tests the athletes, as it does in the game. We play better when we are encouraged, challenged, inspired, motivated, and evaluated fairly after the test.

During the game, we confront disappointment and failure. When we experience these things in practice, we can better learn how to accept, use, or deal with them. Competition in practice mimics the environment of competitive games.

Simulating Game Conditions

To make drills gamelike, you can adjust several components of the drill, including speed, timing, rhythm, positioning, and spacing. Try to make every detail match the situation that would be present in a game. Following are some practical ways to carry out drills in gamelike fashion.

Full-Speed Actions

After players have properly honed all segments of a drill, it is essential that they practice it at game speed. They must incorporate both speed and accuracy into the drill session. Some plays require absolute accuracy but allow adequate time to get the body positioned properly to hit the target. Other plays require both speed and accuracy. With little time to perform an action, the activity becomes more difficult. Each player must practice in this setting to be able to perform consistently under game pressure. To get the most out of practice, these parameters must be the standards

Practicing rundowns, alignments, pop-fly priorities, base running, or any other defensive or offensive drill at less than game speed will result in inconsistent play. Operating at half speed, giving only minimal effort, and making halfhearted throws in practice are foolish endeavors. These kinds of actions tend to show up on game day. Generally, one of two things happens on game day because of poor practice habits. Either the sloppy habits continue, or players attempt to make a quick adjustment, under pressure, to execute with precision. Most athletes are not good enough to make these kinds of adjustments without working hard in preparation for game situations.

Unless they are learning the steps involved to carry out the drill, participants must put forth full effort to produce consistent successful results in competition. Even with full-speed action from all participants during practice sessions, operating consistently and effectively during games is difficult.

In base running, for example, getting a lead, being able to react quickly to the pitcher's move to first or home, and beating the catcher's throw to the base are all important components of stealing a base. Quickness, proper running technique, and superb reactions are all important factors in successful base running. Practicing these skills at half speed will not benefit the base runner.

To perform with precision in the heat of battle, players must have seen the heat of battle in practice. The battlefield should be brought to the drill situations.

Timing and Rhythm

Timing on any play is the key factor. Timing between the pitcher and middle infielders is essential for holding runners, for picking off runners, and for allowing the infielder to be able to retract and get into good fielding position. Timing comes into play on cutoffs, leads, pickoffs, base running, hitting—virtually every aspect of the game. To ignore it is foolish, so timing should be one of the focal points of the drills.

Good rhythm accommodates both the individual and his team. Body movements are successfully activated when they occur in sequence and flow rhythmically. Whether running, throwing, hitting, or fielding, rhythm is vitally important.

The team's rhythm helps it gain and maintain momentum. Defensive players are more efficient when they are in sync with the rhythm of the pitcher. A pitcher with erratic patterns tends to break the rhythm of his defense.

If drills are to be gamelike, the rhythm of each participant should be of great concern. Players at all positions involved in each drill should flow as a unit.

© Human Kinetics

The pitcher's rhythm, especially with relation to the fielders, is important to practice in a gameline manner in drills.

Spacing and Positioning

How and where each player positions himself is vital to each play. If a player cheats to get into better position to cover a base, he gives up space in one or more other directions. Conversely, if a player gets in a position that enables him to cover more area in which to field the ball, he will have more difficulty covering the base in a steal situation. Positioning is extremely important in each drill.

During drills players have a tendency to cheat because each play occurs repeatedly. Players tend to cheat in one direction or the other, depending on the consistency of the repetitions. In repeating the activity, adding all the potential challenges that may occur is more competitive and more in line with what happens in the game. Live situations provide a more realistic approach.

When working on alignments, teamwork on ground balls, fly balls between outfielders, pop flies, bunt defenses, double plays, and so forth, spacing becomes a key ingredient. When players are too close to each other during a drill that involves communication or teamwork on fly balls or ground balls, the drill is of little value and does not mimic the game situation. The same is true of most other game-situation drills.

On alignment of plays, spacing is critical to the outcome. Correct spacing furthers the progress of each player and improves the communication and decision-making process. Each player should assume his game position, which means that the spacing between players and the distance from home plate to each player is the same as it is in the actual game.

When players position themselves too close to each other or cheat in the direction the ball will be hit during the drill, the practice becomes unrealistic. On alignment of plays, the outfielders and infielders often pre-position themselves according to the direction in which the ball will be hit. Good discipline prevents this sloppiness from happening.

Implementing Gamelike Qualities

Besides adjusting the mechanics of drills to make them gamelike in speed, timing, positioning, and so on, coaches should recognize the intangible qualities and attitudes that help a player get the most out of gamelike drills. You can make the drill as gamelike as possible, but if the players aren't focused on learning and working together, they won't reach their potential. The intangibles to focus on include communication, discipline, commitment, interest, enthusiasm, and teamwork.

Communication

The success of a play often depends on sound communication. A forceful call, recognition of the call by the players involved, and support or help are the components needed to get the desired results. Communication during each drill should have high priority.

A well-communicated play runs smoothly and eliminates most of the hazards when two or more players are involved. A ball near the outfield fence or a pop fly near a dugout or backstop requires not only a firm decision about who should catch the ball but also confirmation from the other player or players involved and help with the fence or any other obstruction.

On bunt plays the action is fast. Players must make quick decisions. A failure to call for the ball or a delay in covering a base often results in a misplayed bunt. Part of making the bunting drills similar to game situations is placing a premium on proper communication. To make bunting drills gamelike, pit a live offense against a live defense.

Make sure that the spacing between the players and the fence or dugouts is the same as that which occurs in the game. The positions of the players should also match their respective positioning under game conditions.

Whether working on double-play feeds, pitchers' covering first base, or any other part of the game that requires communication, positioning and spacing are extremely important.

Discipline

Adhering to sound fundamentals takes discipline. Both self-discipline and team discipline are necessary to execute drills repeatedly and maintain the energy level and mental alertness that the game demands. The natural adrenal flow created by the game's environment is missing in the drill setting. Although this gamelike atmosphere cannot be precisely simulated, many of the game elements can be implanted into each drill. For a drill to be beneficial, the team and each player must adhere to the high standards necessary to perfect it.

All parts of the drill should be executed with precision to simulate game conditions. Moreover, pressure should be created. The more closely the pressure matches the game situation, the more valuable the drill is. Doing this takes discipline. Discipline guides the team through the daily workout and provides the impetus to commit to excellence in carrying out each drill.

Repeating details with precision is necessary to obtain the desired results in game situations. Players should persist until they are familiar with all movements and can execute them automatically.

Team discipline provides a shield against dropping to the lowest common denominator. It promotes responsibility and commitment. A premium is placed on hustling, coordinating coverage, backing up, and communicating well. Teamwork is required to get the most out of practice, and team discipline is needed to have the perseverance to pursue excellence on a daily basis.

Commitment

To make drills productive and gamelike, the players and the coaching staff must be committed. With commitment, the rough edges can be honed to a fine edge. If each player, the team, and the coaching staff devote themselves to the pursuit of excellence, each drill will come alive and produce positive game results.

When athletes and coaches are dedicated to a common cause, magic seems to happen. Communication is excellent, awareness increases, urgency and the need to excel develop, enthusiasm is in the air, and great progress results.

Interest

Interest is the key to learning anything. Interest starts with the individual. Many factors play a role in maintaining or increasing our interest—organization, cooperation, challenges, contributions, teamwork, friendships, relationships, and the environment. The practice setting and all that goes with it are of paramount importance in keeping interest alive and thriving.

A well-organized drill that offers specific challenges invites cooperation and teamwork and develops relationships and trust. Good drills challenge, excite, encourage, and produce positive results.

Enthusiasm

Enthusiasm, like interest, starts with the individual, but poorly organized drills that have little to do with game situations can easily dampen it. Undue criticism or abject failure can also deplete or even kill enthusiasm. Positive input by coaches and fellow players, improvement, and well-organized practices that match game situations can build and maintain enthusiasm.

A coach should be aware of the signs that show lack of enthusiasm. If he does not notice the red flags, the practice will dwindle to a dull, monotonous repetition of poor habits that stand a good chance of showing up on game day, especially in the late innings of a long game or when the score is lopsided. Good drills done with enthusiasm create good habits that show up in game situations, particularly in tough ball games.

Teamwork

Working together is essential if drills are to be fruitful. Cooperation is a staple of teamwork. Without cooperation, communication, timing, and concentration are lacking. Through teamwork, drills can be competitive and made to resemble the situations that occur in games.

Coach's Motivation

The manner in which the coach emphasizes the drill greatly influences the players' interest in it. Players usually copy the coach's interest. A highly motivated coach generally produces a highly motivated drill session. The coach plays a major role in how players will run drills.

The coach needs to be forceful and sell each drill that he presents to his team. A clear explanation, with body language that projects a belief in the practice session, sets the stage for a well-executed drill. The manner in which the coach makes corrections and encourages his players and the persistence he exhibits in carrying out the drill are further actions that demonstrate his level of interest.

Information successfully imparted by the coaching staff is essential to the learning process. The key is persisting until players do the work correctly. Patience and persistence set an example and promote competition throughout each drill.

When breakdowns occur, encourage and lift but do not lower the bar. We naturally tend to become discouraged when parts of the drill break down or when some players fall short of our expectations in grasping the concepts of a drill. This is where we need to apply good coaching techniques.

Coach's Vigilance

The coaching staff must show vigilance in directing each drill. The team should reach the goals for each drill. Success, as always, is in the details. How those details are executed is what causes success or failure in the game. If the persistence level does not match the importance level, the lesson will likely fall short of its mark. When something is important, there is urgency about it, tenaciousness, and incentive to do it. Interest is wrapped around it. The coach and leaders of the team demonstrate the importance and urgency of the activity through their statements and body language. Good game results depend on sound fundamentals and precise execution.

Connecting Drills to the Game

When expectations are high and standards are upheld, drills will be productive. Any drill executed with intensity, great concern, and interest will be beneficial. The drill must relate to game situations. Often, drills are run that do not connect to the game strategy being employed.

Rarely used strategies require less practice time. Fundamental skills are always useful, so practice them often. Practice and perfect what you will use in competition. The things done in practice should match the things done in the game. If a team is defensive minded with great pitching, the practice should focus on ground balls, defensive situations, alignments, pop-fly priorities, holding runners, and so forth. Because this team's major weapon is defense, practice of those skills should dominate the practice session.

Gamelike Execution

The tenacity to see a drill through is an important key. Persistence is probably what separates the successful coach from the unsuccessful one. Good coaching calls for prodding, pushing, and guiding. It calls for correcting, evaluating, and reviewing, and then correcting, evaluating, and reviewing again. This process continues until players do the drill properly. Each time players perform the drill correctly, their confidence will grow.

There is nothing like persistence and patience to help you see a job through, get a lesson plan done, produce a practice schedule, or run and complete a drill. For a drill to be productive, players must learn it and practice it well. The timing, execution, intensity, communication, and overall efficiency of the participants measure the degree of success of each drill.

If these things are done well and the drill is designed for what it is supposed to accomplish, marked improvement will occur in game situations.

Practical Ways to Make Drills Competitive and Gamelike

1. Mental pressure situations. Set up imaginary situations and assign a goal to the player or players. Players compete to reach the given goal.
2. Challenges. Present the player or players with a challenge (for the catcher, blocking a number of balls consecutively; for fielders, fielding a certain number of balls in a row; for pitchers, throwing an assigned percentage of pitches to a specific target; and so on.)
3. Head-to-head competition.
   a. Set up a situation that requires two offensive players or two defensive players to compete against each other. The situation must be the same for each player. Examples include two catchers throwing to second base for accuracy, two outfielders hitting a target from a prescribed position in the outfield, or two hitters target hitting to the opposite field.
   b. Set up a situation that requires one offensive player to compete against one defensive player. For example, a pitcher can compete against a batter, a catcher can compete against a base runner, and so forth.
4. Controlled intrasquad games.
   a. Set up a game situation and have a defensive team compete against an offensive team several consecutive times in a specific situation.
   b. Make each inning of an intrasquad game the ninth inning with the game on the line.
   c. Set up intrasquad games with each inning having a specific score (1 to 1, 2 to 0, 2 to 1) or put runners on base, assign a score, and limit the number of innings to finish each game. Several games can be played in one practice, with a winner and loser declared in each game.
   d. Bases-loaded drill. Each pitcher is challenged to pitch in one of these situations for one inning:
      • No-out situation
      • One-out situation
      • Two-out situation
5. Intrasquad setting with point system. Assign and record points for positive results. For example, award 5 points for an RBI with two outs, 3 points for an RBI with less than two outs, 1 point for steal, 1 point for a base hit, and so on. Design a point system for defense as well. A negative system can also be incorporated, with –1 point for an error, –2 points for a mental error, and so on. Done consistently and used properly, the point system will lift the competitive level in intrasquad games.

6. Stopwatch. A wonderful tool for providing incentive to a competitor is the stopwatch. Time infielders on double-play attempts, catchers from reception to the catch at second base, pitchers on their moves to home plate, base runners on running to first base, and so forth.

7. Radar gun. Use the radar gun in the bullpen or intrasquad games to chart and measure the variation in speed of pitches. This method can help you judge whether a pitcher is changing speeds enough to destroy the timing of a hitter. Use of the radar gun improves the concentration of the pitcher and helps establish goals.

8. Simulated game. Set up an offensive situation and place a team on defense. Challenge both teams with various game situations through one or more innings of play. An entire offensive team is not necessary. Groups of four offensive players at a time are ideal.

9. Timed batting practice drill. Set up several batting practice stations and change hitters every two minutes. Because each hitter has a set amount of time, teammates must work efficiently. This approach encourages a more organized and energetic batting practice, promotes better shagging, and puts a premium on throwing strikes.

10. Game on the line drill. For both the defense and the offense, this type of drill challenges players to perform as they would in an actual game.
    a. Bring a pitcher in from the bullpen in a bases-loaded situation.
    b. A batter hits in that situation.
    c. The score is tied. Either the batter or the pitcher wins.

11. Target hitting. For right-handed hitters to hit to the opposite field, set up cones on the edge of the outfield side of the infield approximately 15 feet from second base and 15 feet from first base. Do the same on the opposite side of the field for left-handed hitters to hit the opposite way. Each hitter has five swings to hit the ball on the ground between the cones. If after five swings the batter hits the ball between the cones on the ground, he is rewarded with another swing. As long as the hitter continues to hit the ball within the stated parameters, he stays in the batter's box.

12. Team and individual evaluations by each drill participant. Some drills are conducive to having the participants evaluate each other, their competitive counterparts, or the group or team. This method of evaluation tends to elevate the performance of the drill and enhance learning. For example, a pitcher can evaluate another pitcher, a position player can evaluate another position player, and each player can evaluate the execution of the drill.

By elevating the following aspects of play in drill sessions, players will experience a competitive setting that closely resembles the environment found during games.

- Hustle
- Pressure

- Urgency
- Focus
- Intensity
- Observations
- Teamwork

The coach is responsible for seeing that drills are run for the purpose for which they were designed. A competitive drill should be executed sharply and crisply. Participants should finish each drill with a feeling of accomplishment.

Summary

- The goal is to operate drills at game speed.
- Sound fundamentals should form the basis of each drill.
- Discipline guides the team through the rough spots.
- Interest and commitment are necessary to achieve success in drills.
- Timing is vital to the practice and execution of each play.
- Competition lifts the drill, creates a challenge, and helps mirror game conditions.
- Competition improves the practice setting.
- The coaching staff and leaders of the team play important roles in each drill.
- Success is usually found in the details. Each detail is important.
- Being vigilant and persistent will ensure that the drill is done precisely.
- Finish each drill with a feeling of accomplishment.

Physical Training

Chapter 4

Conditioning Drills

Ed Cheff and Bruce Madsen

Baseball is an explosive sport. Hitting, throwing, and running are short-duration, high-speed, explosive activities. In this chapter, coaching staff and players are asked to spend valuable time and energy on conditioning. In case you're unsure about the value of conditioning in baseball, we'll begin with a clear and logical explanation of the rationale behind the conditioning process. Our goal is your players' enthusiastic commitment toward baseball excellence through conditioning—not just grudging compliance in the face of authority.

During rest and inactivity, 80 to 85 percent of a person's blood (the body's primary heating agent) pools in the core organs of the brain, rib cage, and abdomen, making for a diminished blood supply in the body's muscles and connective tissue. As a consequence, muscles and tissue are cool at the start of a practice. These cool muscles and connective tissue lose their flexibility and elastic properties; they move sluggishly, like licorice in the refrigerator.

A rich blood supply in the muscles and surrounding tissue is unnecessary during times of relative inactivity. But if you don't allow adequate time and movements for blood redistribution before transitioning into high-force activities, you greatly increase the risk of muscle and connective tissue damage.

Any aerobic activity that exclusively employs the legs (biking, stair stepping) will not lubricate and warm up the torso and upper extremities. While the progressive speed increases in walking to jogging to moderate-speed running are adequate to begin the warm-up process, alone they aren't enough.

In baseball, the pitching arm moves backward (externally rotating the humerus) to a frighteningly extreme range of motion. Then it violently reverses directions, moving forward (internally rotating the humerus) at up to 100 mph. This explosion is sometimes repeated up to 140 times per game. Think of racing full speed in reverse and then slamming the transmission in drive and immediately accelerating up to 100 mph. The preparation for explosively violent activity must be progressive, task specific, and executed with precision.

Photo by Kyle Mills of the Lewiston Tribune

*The extreme range of motion and speed required for throwing are just one example
of why specific conditioning is important.*

An average baseball game lasts about two and a half hours. Some go much longer. How much of that time is spent sitting and standing around? The cardiovascular training in our program is strictly encouraged for players with excessive body fat. If fat inhibits a player's performance, it's then treated as a problem.

Our conditioning drills must be sport and task specific to fully prepare our team for injury prevention and maximum sport performance. Our focus is on high-intensity explosive activities that trigger fast-twitch muscle fibers. Our training protocol is biomechanical and baseball specific; it includes drills for flexibility, strength, speed, agility, quickness, and muscular endurance.

Focus   To lubricate joints while moving blood out of the core organs and into the joints, muscles, and connective tissue.

Setup   All players participate at once. You need an open area, either indoors or outdoors, to complete these drills. After the jogging, line up players for stretching; it's recommended that five players are in each line. This creates less rest time and more consistent moving and agility.

Procedure   Begin the activity with 8 to 10 minutes of low-intensity jogging with a gradual increase in stride length. Now that the muscular tissue is warm dynamically, stretch all of the major muscle groups. Then have players line up in groups of five or fewer. Our goal is to have each player perform all of the exercises two times at the distance of 90 feet, down and back being counted as one repetition.

1. High knees. Stay on toes and jog forward, touching the ground as many times as possible while moving forward. It should take about 10 seconds to travel 90 feet.
2. Power skips. Lift one leg up at a time while exploding upright with the other. The knee should explode up, stretching the hamstring, during this exercise. See figure a.
3. Side bursts. Begin with feet together. Stay low and explode in the direction you're headed by accelerating one leg. Hop out and land on one foot followed by the other. Maintain balance and stay low.
4. Backward run. Run backward with big strides. Stretch the legs back as far as they can reach. See figure b.
5. Sprint. Sprint 90 feet at about 85 to 90 percent maximum effort.

a

b

Coaching Points   This drill includes gradually increased effort because the exercises are designed to stretch, lubricate, and prepare players for high-intensity activity. Players should start at 70 percent of their maximum effort, then progress to 85 percent, and then 90 percent. If you're dealing with injured or deconditioned players or if the weather is cold, you'll need to adjust these percentages downward.

2   TIMED BASE RUNNING

Focus   To create maximum effort every time a player runs the bases.

Setup   All players participate at once on any regulation-size baseball infield. You'll use all three bases and home plate.

Procedure   Note that all base-running drills are timed and logged. Line up all players at home plate. They'll run first to first base. The object in this drill is to simulate beating out a routine ground ball. After three repetitions to first, players move to the next base and progress to home plate.

Players run from home to second base, as if they have hit a double. Once all players have reached second base, have them score from second immediately afterward.

Now that the players are back to home plate, have them simulate hitting a line drive base hit. The simulation involves running to first base and taking a hard turn, then going back to first base. Allow enough time for a runner to get back to first before starting the next runner. Do this activity twice for each player.

The next simulation is hitting a ball into the outfield gaps. The goal here is to set up a coach in the third-base box and make the runner pick up the coach three-fourths the distance to second base so he has to react to the coach's decision (whether that be staying at second or going to third base). Do this activity twice for each player.

Next, line up all players at third base and have them simulate tagging up. Say, "Go!" or clap your hands as a signal that the ball has been caught.

Coaching Points   Make sure it's clear, before and after each drill, what you expect from your players. Our goal is to focus on base-running details: giving maximum effort, hitting the inside part of the bag, leaning in when taking a turn at the bag, and picking up the coach at the right location.

The number of exercises in this drill is more than enough to develop fast-twitch muscle fibers. You often hear coaches say, "Yeah, I worked their butts off today!" You don't need to do that. If a player runs an average of 4.15 to 4.25 seconds to first base, and his times at maximum effort increase to 4.35 to 4.45, he's doing enough work for now. If you have him do much more, you risk compromising his explosive speed development.

Modifications   All explosive activities are to be performed at 90 to 95 percent of perceived maximum effort. Our focus is to keep the player from antagonistic muscle firing, inhibiting peak performance. For example, if a player is running with his fists clamped tight, his pectorals are firing when they should be completely relaxed.

3   BAT ROTATIONS

Focus   To recruit and develop muscle fibers using lateral leg drive and hip, torso, and abdominal rotation; to stretch abdominal, hip, and torso by resisting full-body turn using a bat.

Setup   Pairs of players do this drill with one bat for each pair, outdoors or indoors.

Procedure   The bat rotation exercise is performed by standing in a hitting stance, then placing the bat behind the back horizontally, holding it with both elbow creases firmly to the body. The head of the barrel is located on the player's dominant swing side. For example, if the player swings the bat right handed, the barrel should be in his right elbow crease. If the player with the bat is right handed, the partner begins by standing behind and to the right of the dominant swing side; for left-handed players, the partner stands behind and to the left of the player. The partner creates resistance by holding the bat barrel with his right hand. His left hand should be on the player's right shoulder. The left hand is for stability only.

The player with the bat visualizes hitting a fastball up and in. He then strides or gets into the loaded position to address this pitch, staying "stacked" (chest perpendicular to the ground). The lower half of his body accelerates with a pivot. A hard turn of the hips and abdomen rotates against the resistance created by the partner. As the partner creates resistance against the force behind the bat, three things occur: stride, pivot, and strong follow-through. The partner creating resistance is responsible for correcting tilt or lean and for making sure the player is focused and concentrating on staying balanced.

Each repetition should last about 5 seconds one way. If it takes 5 seconds, it's not fast! After the player has rotated as far as he can go (through the hitting zone), the partner creating resistance holds and stretches the player for three seconds. The player then rotates back for another five seconds the same way he came, finishing in the upright position he began in. Each repetition takes about 13 seconds.

Coaching Points   Make sure the right leg and hip rotate first (for right-handed players). This is followed by a hard pivot along with good upright posture as the exercise is completed. The most important part is the first movement. If the player tilts, lunges, or leans forward, he's doing the exercise wrong. Our focus is to challenge hitters to stay "stacked" and on top of hard fastballs thrown up and in. If the hitter tilts or leans, his success rate of hitting this pitch diminishes further with every inch he leans.

To clarify the drill, point out the distance a hitter's barrel has to travel to reach a high inside fastball if he's "stacked" as opposed to if he's leaning. The importance of rotating back is to prevent an imbalance of muscles in the abdomen.

Focus To force hitters to hit pitches inside while knowing the next pitch is coming within a matter of seconds; to increase muscular endurance by challenging hitters to maintain good balance, good routes to each toss, lateral leg drive, and proper hip, torso, and shoulder rotation.

Setup Players work in pairs with one bat and 10 to 20 baseballs. You'll need a cage or soft-toss net.

Procedure One player lines up on one knee at an angle of 45 degrees, facing the hitter. The feeder stands in front and to the left of a right-handed hitter.

Feeders need 10 to 20 baseballs on the ground in front of them. Before the drill begins, the hitter is in the loaded position. His stride or load is complete. The feeder gathers as many balls in hand as he can and repeatedly underhand tosses balls into the batter's hitting zone, hard and inside. Tell tossers to aim their tosses 12 inches in front of the hitter's front knee and below his belt. They should toss a ball about every two seconds (exact time depends on the strength, quickness, agility, and balance of the hitter).

The hitter tries to consistently put the appropriate stroke on each toss. He focuses on getting back into hitting position before the next ball approaches.

Coaching Points   Soft toss is a good warm-up technique for any hitter. The drill is also a great conditioning tool. We try to end our hitting workout with this exercise. Completing four sets of 15 repetitions is plenty for most college hitters. As always, assess a player's strength, quickness, agility, and balance before deciding on the number of sets and repetitions.

While the drill is going on, give the hitter feedback. Tell him what he's doing right and wrong so that he can adjust during the drill or retain specific actions.

Modifications   To increase difficulty, reduce the time between tosses.

5   TORSO ROTATION

Focus   To create resistance against the torso and abdomen while standing in the hitting position; to recruit fast-twitch muscle fibers that accelerate the torso.

Setup   You'll need one piece of surgical tube for each player and a pole or fence with plenty of space around it. Tie the tube around the pole or fence belt high. Five feet of tube left over and hanging loosely is a good length to work with. Red, blue, or black surgical tubing with moderate to heavy thickness is required.

Procedure   Each player uses only one tube during this exercise. The player sets up in hitting position with the end of the tube held in both hands as if he's holding a bat. Make sure the tube is tight before beginning. The tube creates resistance when the hitter strides and accelerates his back leg into hitting position. His hands stay close to his body, with emphasis on leg drive and torso rotation.

The exercise is complete after the player pulls the tube through the zone. It's not necessary for the player to extend his hands past his body to finish his follow-through with a swing movement. Once the tube reaches a simulated point of contact, the movement is complete.

Coaching Points   Players should do this exercise on both sides of the body to prevent muscle imbalance in the abdomen. Three sets of 8 to 10 repetitions on both sides is a good beginning workout. As the players gets more conditioned, increase the number of repetitions and sets. But no more than 15 repetitions should be done per set. Once the body slows down we're no longer effectively working the batting speed-specific fast-twitch muscle fibers.

Focus   To recruit ballistic explosion from the rectus abdominis and obliques in a simulated throwing motion.

Procedure   Each player has a piece of tubing. Begin with the tube six inches above shoulder height. Players start with slight slack in the tubing and take a crow hop to pull through with their abdominals in a simulated throwing routine. Green or red tubing is usually appropriate resistance.

a   b

Coaching Points   Players rest 5 to 10 seconds between reps and complete 8 to 10 repetitions per set. Start with a slow speed and ensure precision of movement and safety. Gradually increase the speed and resistance as the player masters the activity. The leg drive and overhead abdominal pull are emphasized in this drill. Full extension of the arm is inappropriate—it creates too much pull and leverage against the vulnerable shoulder and elbow joints. Players gradually work up to full-speed explosions.

Focus To build strength, flexibility, muscular endurance, and explosive power of the external rotators.

Setup Each player has one surgical tube tied at waist or shoulder height (depending on the movement). This is a progression exercise. Start with the surgical tube tied at the waist. As the player increases the warm-up, move the surgical tube and tie it to the shoulder. Light-resistance yellow surgical tubing is initially appropriate. Never progress past green tubing.

Procedure Begin with the tubing tied waist high to a fixed object. Stand with the exercising elbow at the side and bent 90 degrees. Hold the tubing in the hand to be exercised; the palm of that hand rests on the belly. The working shoulder will be farthest away from the fixed object; grasp the handle with hooked rather than clamped fingers to ensure blood flow. Stand with tubing just tight enough that there's no slack.

Keeping the forearm tight to the side, slowly move the hand out away from the belly. Some portion of your forearm should always contact your abdomen. The forearm pivots around the torso, starting at the wrist and finishing at the elbow. Stay within a pain-free range of motion; full range of motion differs for each player but should be increased gradually to 150 to 170 degrees. There should be a slight warm sensation in the upper shoulder and warmth and fatigue around the back of the shoulder blade. If there's discomfort in the arm, this is joint pain; the exercise should be stopped. There should be no pain during the exercise, after the exercise, or on the next day. If pain occurs, back off and work within your pain-free range the next day.

Start with two sets of 20 reps; increase range of motion and resistance on the second set. Add one repetition every other day up to 25. Then increase resistance by moving six inches farther away from the fixed object. Reduce reps back to 20 and gradually increase.

Coaching Points *Caution:* The best throwing players don't exceed six pounds on this exercise even with a healthy shoulder. The rotator cuff muscles are tiny, joint-stabilizing muscles 1/15th the size of the biceps. The speed of movement should begin allowing two seconds in each direction. Gradually increase speed to approach game velocity.

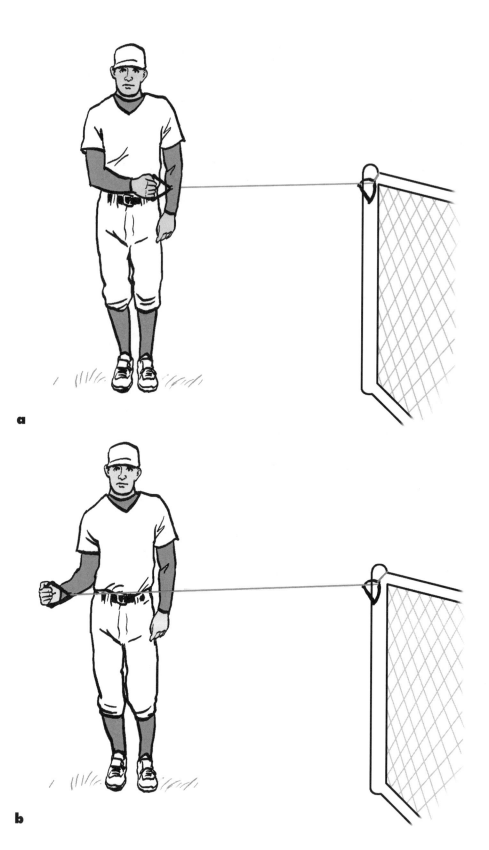

a

b

Focus   To build strength, flexibility, muscular endurance, and explosive power of the internal rotators.

Procedure   This exercise is the same as external rotation except here the tension is applied while pulling toward the body. The working shoulder is on the same side as the tubing. The internal rotator muscles, including the pecs and lats, are stronger than the external rotator muscles, so players will have substantially more muscle strength in this drill. Given this additional strength, players begin 12 to 18 inches farther from the tubing tie-off spot than in the external rotation drill. All other procedures and coaching points are identical to those described in external rotation.

a

b

9   EXTERNAL ROTATION WITH ELEVATED ELBOW

Focus   To build strength, flexibility, muscular endurance, and explosive power of the external rotators.

Procedure   With the elbow elevated, this drill more closely approximates the mechanics of throwing than the previous drills did. However, in this position the shoulder is less stable and more prone to rotator cuff injuries, so do these exercises only after the other rotator cuff exercises.

Instead of standing sideways, the player faces the tubing tie-off spot. The elbow is elevated to shoulder height and bent 90 degrees, with the forearm parallel to the ground. The player slowly rolls the forearm back while the humerus remains stable and in a direct line with both shoulders. The forearm should continue back as far as comfortably possible. The finish position closely approximates the full wind-up position for the arm and shoulder.

There should be no pain during the exercise, after the exercise, or on the next day. If pain occurs, back off and work within your pain-free range the next day. Start with two sets of 20 reps; increase range of motion and resistance on the second set. Add one repetition every other day up to 25. Then increase resistance by moving six inches farther away from the fixed object. Reduce reps back to 20 and gradually increase. Speed should slowly increase to approach game velocity.

Coaching Points   During the learning phase of the exercise, be sure to stabilize the shoulder and humerus so that only external rotation occurs. When players are first doing this exercise, their muscles are on average 25 to 50 percent weaker in the elevated position. Adjust tubing tension accordingly.

10   INTERNAL ROTATION WITH ELEVATED ELBOW

Focus   To build strength, flexibility, muscular endurance, and explosive power of the internal rotators.

Procedure   The player stands with his back toward the tubing tie-off spot. The elbow is elevated to shoulder height and bent 90 degrees, with the forearm perpendicular to the ground. The player slowly rolls the forearm forward until it is parallel to the ground.

There should be no pain during the exercise, after the exercise, or on the next day. If pain occurs, back off and work within your pain-free range the next day. Start with two sets of 20 reps; increase range of motion and resistance on the second set. Add one repetition every other day up to 25. Then increase resistance by moving six inches farther away from the fixed object. Reduce reps back to 20 and gradually increase. Speed should slowly increase to approach game velocity.

a   b

Focus   To work the fundamentals of fielding techniques at maximum effort.

Setup   All infielders and outfielders participate. Use infield and outfield fungo bats.

Procedure for Infielders   Make sure the fungo hitter is creating the closest angle to a gamelike ground ball. For instance, if he's hitting a ground ball to the third baseman, he should be aligned as close to home plate as possible before starting.

Hit a variety of ground balls and hard and soft choppers. Ground balls that make infielders take two to three hard steps to the right and left of their body are very effective. All ground balls hit at infielders are hit to maximize lateral explosion toward the baseball left and right. Ground balls hit to infielders also need to be simulated as double-play situations so that all players practice turning a double play.

Procedure for Outfielders   When working with outfielders, we try to maximize their effort and response to hard-hit line drives and fly balls.

Line outfielders up in the outfield. The goal is to hit a fly ball or line drive at least 10 steps to each player's right or left or 10 feet behind him. To work on different angles, line your players up accordingly. To work on balls to their left (your right), line players up to the right of the first participant; to work on balls to their right (your left), line players up to the left of the first participant. Make sure balls are fielded with the right form—glove always open, running in stride with the glove, not reaching for the ball until the last step has been taken before closing in on the ball.

Coaching Points   Infielders can field ground balls during scrimmage games between innings while the pitcher warms up. Double plays can also be turned while the pitcher warms up. Using time efficiently is our goal. The purpose of conditioning players while they work on technique is to create as many gamelike situations as possible during practice.

Outfielders need tough chances in order to improve. Routine fly balls won't do the trick. In outfielder practice, our goals are as follows: (1) a first step explosion in the direction the ball is traveling, (2) stay in stride, and (3) make a great catch. Pursuing the ball with the correct route to catching it becomes rigorous and hard after 20 or more repetitions. When players begin to tire is when the endurance element of the drill begins and focus needs to increase.

For efficiency, hit fungos to outfielders between innings of a scrimmage. Line outfielders up in centerfield and work on balls to their right and left and over their heads. Try to get at least three or four hard line drives or fly balls to each outfielder between innings. Over the course of a nine-inning scrimmage that's 27 to 36 fly balls for each outfielder.

Modifications For increased conditioning, increase the number of ground balls fielded in each exercise. For versatility and different challenges, incorporate hard ground balls and simulated throws to home plate in the outfielder part of the drill.

12   OUTFIELD PASS PATTERNS

Focus To work fast-twitch muscle fibers to develop quicker direction change.

Setup Only outfielders do this drill. You'll need balls, cleats, gloves, and a large open space.

Procedure Set outfielders up in a football format, facing the line of scrimmage. The coach is the quarterback; the outfielder is the receiver. The distance between the outfielder and quarterback depends on the pass pattern being run. Two pass patterns we use are the 12-yard post and the 5-yard out. Figures a and b show what the pattern routes look like and where the ball should be thrown.

- The 12-yard post pattern (figure a) is designed to have the outfielder take off, run 12 yards, angle in at 45 degrees while staying in stride, then picking up the quarterback and receiving the pass.
- The 5-yard out pass pattern (figure b) is designed to make the receiver run 5 yards past the line of scrimmage, explosively turn at a 90-degree angle, head toward the sideline about 5 to 8 yards, then receive the ball.

In this drill, you don't want to make perfect throws to your receiver. Throw the ball behind the outfielder to make him turn around and adjust. Throw it far in front of him to make him dive. Make the pass pattern routes longer and farther to match receiver success.

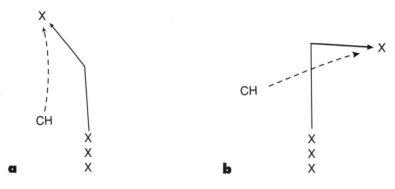

Coaching Points   After players run 10 to 15 pass patterns (depending on the condition of each player), you're no longer developing fast-twitch muscle fibers. Try to maximize the effort that each player has to put forth to catch the ball. Many times, outfielders take incorrect routes to catch fly balls and need to change direction quickly to recover lost ground and time. This drill practices that skill. Use a variety of pass patterns to challenge them. Forcing outfielders to divert their vision from where the ball is coming creates a gamelike fly ball that requires full-body turns. Regaining location of the ball, continuing pursuit, and making a great catch take practice; some players will need more work on this drill than others.

Modifications   Create variety by mixing up several pass patterns for outfielders to run.

13   SIDE TO SIDE WITH GLOVES

Focus   To work on infielder explosiveness using lateral movements while focusing on good fielding technique.

Setup   Only infielders do this drill. You can run this on the infield dirt area or on the warning track.

Procedure   Set up any number of players facing you on an infield or similar surface. First have them simulate a preliminary movement ("prelim"—small steps taken before the pitch is made); this helps the player achieve a balanced posture with emphasis on lateral movement.

Next, focus on the player's first step, which will depend on what kind of ground ball he's fielding. The first step, open, and then crossover are most important to work on when beginning. The second and third steps are the next most important. After completing these two steps, the infielder should be in a balanced position to make his throw. If a right-handed infielder is working on backhanding a ground ball, his right foot will be to the right of the ball and his glove will be positioned in front of his body, showing the inside leather of the glove to the ball. The left elbow is down; the eyes and head are focused behind the glove.

As the previous steps occur, the infielder appears to be in almost a lunge position with about 80 percent of his bodyweight beneath his right leg. If a right-handed infielder is reaching for an open-hand ground ball, he takes two to three hard steps and simulates picking up a ground ball. In this case a higher percentage of body weight is on the left foot.

a

b

Coaching Points   Complete three sets of 15 repetitions with a minute rest between. Make sure the elbow stays down, the face stays behind the glove, and the body is in a good fielding position. In this drill, consistency is the key to success.

Modifications   Carry over these techniques into fielding fungo ground balls and live ground balls.

Focus　To recruit fast-twitch muscle fibers that enhance first-step lateral explosion.

Setup　This drill can be done indoors or outdoors.

Procedure　Set players up facing one direction and exploding to the right. Players begin with knees slightly bent, on their toes, and ready to explode. Players stay low and drive through the hips, leaping out in the direction they're going in. They eventually land in the same athletic position they started in. Work at about 90 feet distance. Players do two complete sets down and back.

a

b

Coaching Points　The side burst improves first-step lateral explosion. Focus on making players stay low and drive at the hip. They should give maximum effort. Remind them to stay down; they want to feel a burn in their legs.

Focus   To develop front, back, and lateral explosion to all angles as well as hip and torso upward explosion.

Setup   One player stands in a 10-foot radius circle with cones (or tape, paint, or chalk) designating different angles every 45 degrees.

Procedure   The player begins in the middle of the circle. Starting at the space directly in front of him, he takes two hard steps; once his second step lands, he hops into the air as high as he can. The activity is highly explosive and quick.

In each circle the cones indicate every 45-degree angle stemming out from the middle; use these marks to designate the direction the player is to explode toward—go down each line around the circle. The drill can be done differently each time. Each day's workout might consist of going strictly around the circle for intervals; or have players focus on one direction only. When going sideways, perform a lateral shuffle. Perform a backpedal when moving backward. Each movement angle should represent a different muscle fiber recruitment.

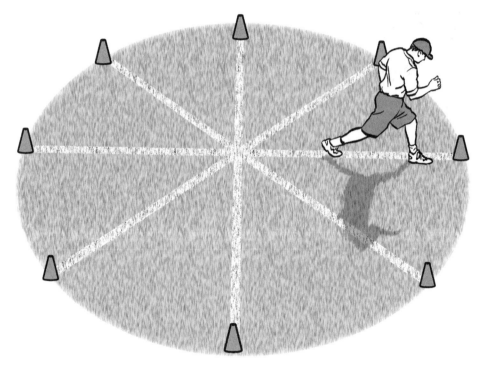

Coaching Points   We're looking for two explosive steps taken toward the designated cone and maximum effort put into the hop into the air. To start with, do three sets of 10 to 15 reps. As conditioning improves, have players do three sets of repetition for one minute. This activity is very useful in recruiting forward, lateral, backward, and upward explosion.

Modifications   Try setting up players at each cone and have them randomly yell out one at a time. The player in the middle takes two hard steps toward the player who called and then hops. Then he immediately responds to the next voice he hears, moving in that direction and hopping, and so on until every player at every cone has called out. In this activity, the player in the middle has no idea which way he'll have to explode next, which makes the drill more gamelike.

Chapter 5

Warm-Up Drills

John Savage

A proper warm-up is important to performance. Warm-up drills should always precede the activity. Players who seriously want to increase their flexibility spend 45 to 60 minutes a day on the task. Baseball demands strength, endurance, power, balance, and core strength. Our goals for our players include the following:

- Injury prevention. A fit player is less likely to be injured; if he is injured, he recovers more quickly if he's fit.
- Improved work capacity. An ability to handle high-quality work and recover quickly allows players to repeat that work in their next workout.
- Balanced muscular development. By "balance" we mean between the front and back of the body and right and left side of the body, with muscles strengthened as needed for optimal performance in baseball.
- Improved range of motion at the joints without compromising joint integrity.
- Improved core strength. Strength of the abdomen, low back, and hips allows more effective transfer of the force generated by the legs to the shoulder and arm for force application.
- Improved understanding of the strengths and weaknesses that help accelerate their development.

Our recommended warm-up is an active warm-up that must be done in sequence for maximum benefit. There are three basic warm-ups, each with its own objective and emphasis:

- Warm-up 1: Dynamic running
- Warm-up 2: Flexibility stretching (legs and back; upper body)
- Warm-up 3: Lateral speed and agility

Do two sets of each exercise over the recommended distance.

1. High knees. Run forward, bringing knees up close to the chest; emphasize arm action (20 yards).
2. Butt kick. Run forward, bringing heels as close to the buttocks as possible; emphasize arm action (20 yards).
3. Knee-to-chest skip. Skip forward, bringing one knee to the chest. Keep the head up and work the arms as if running. Repeat on the other leg (30 yards).
4. Strides. Emphasize arm action (60 yards).
5. Strides. Emphasize hips-tall posture (60 yards).
6. Backward skip. Lean forward at the waist, skip backward, bringing heels to buttocks. Keep the head up and emphasize arm action (20 yards).
7. Backward run. Lean forward at the waist with knees bent; run backward while pumping the arms and reaching as far up and back with the foot as possible (20 yards).
8. 100-yard run. Do two at 80 percent, two at 85 percent, and two at 90 percent.

17 QUADRICEPS STRETCH (LEGS AND BACK)

Focus   To stretch the front part of the leg (above the knee).

Procedure   Lie on the left side, resting the side of the head in the palm of the left hand or on the left arm. Hold the top of the right foot with the right hand between the toes and the ankle joint. Gently pull the right heel toward the right buttock to stretch the ankle and quadriceps (front of thigh). Hold for 10 to 15 seconds. Never stretch the knee to the point of pain. Switch legs and repeat.

Modifications   Lean against a partner or wall with the right hand. Reach behind and grasp the right foot near the toes with the left hand. Pull the heel toward the buttocks and hold for 10 to 15 seconds. Switch legs and repeat.

18   BUTTOCKS STRETCH (LEGS AND BACK)

Focus   To stretch the upper hamstrings and hip.

Procedure   Hold onto the outside of an ankle with one hand. Place the other hand and forearm around the bent knee. Gently pull the leg as one unit toward the chest until there's an easy stretch in the back of the upper leg. This stretch might be best done while players rest their back against something for support. Hold for 15 to 20 seconds. Make sure the leg is pulled as one unit so no stress is felt in the knee. After this, slightly increase the stretch by pulling the leg a little closer to the chest. Do both sides.

19　HIP FLEXOR STRETCH (LEGS AND BACK)

Focus　To stretch the front of the hips, hamstrings, and groin.

Procedure　From a standing position, move one leg forward until the knee of the forward leg is directly over the ankle. Make sure the front knee doesn't move beyond the ball of the front foot. Push the left hip forward, keeping the right (back) leg straight. From the lunge position, kneel on the right knee. Place both hands on the floor, keeping the head and trunk upright. Slowly slide the right knee backward and hold for 15 to 20 seconds. Switch legs and repeat.

Coaching Points　This stretch helps with lower back problems.

20 BUTTERFLY GROIN STRETCH (LEGS AND BACK)

Focus To stretch the groin.

Procedure Sit up tall in a butterfly position with the soles of the feet together and chest up. Grasp the ankles and push the knees toward the floor with the elbows. Stretch until there's tension in the inner thigh.

Focus   To stretch the upper back, lower back, side of hips, and rib cage.

Procedure   Sit with the left leg straight. Bend the right leg, cross the right foot over, and rest it on the outside of the left knee. Bend the left elbow and rest it on the outside of the upper right thigh, just above the knee. During the stretch, use the elbow to keep the leg stationary with controlled pressure to the inside. With the right hand resting behind the body, slowly turn the head to look over the right shoulder; at the same time, rotate the upper body toward the right hand and arm. While turning the upper body, turn the hips slightly in the same direction. This should cause a stretch in the lower back and side of hip. Hold for 15 seconds. Do both sides. Breathe easily and do not hold the breath.

Coaching Points   This stretch helps in the trunk rotation.

22 STANDING SHOULDER STRETCH (UPPER BODY)

Focus To stretch the triceps and rear deltoids.

Procedure Stand with feet shoulder-width apart and knees slightly bent. With arms overhead, hold the elbow of one arm with the hand of the other arm. Gently pull the elbow behind the head, creating a stretch. Go slowly. Hold for 15 seconds. Do both arms.

23 FOREARM AND WRIST STRETCH (UPPER BODY)

Focus   To stretch the muscles of the lower arm.

Procedure   With the right arm extended in front of the body and parallel to the ground, point the right hand and fingers to the sky. Place the left hand at the base of the fingers of the right hand and gently pull back toward the body. Hold for 15 seconds. Pointing the fingers toward the ground, gently pull back on the fingers with the left hand and hold. Follow the same procedure with the opposite arm.

a   b

Focus   To work the lower and upper back.

Procedure   Stand with feet shoulder-width apart and knees slightly flexed. Keeping the torso upright, turn and slowly twist to the left and then back to the right. Make sure the arms are out to the side and with palms down. Repeat movement for 15 seconds.

a

b

Focus   To stretch the rotator cuff and forearm.

Procedure   Stand near a fence or gate with one elbow to the side; bend the elbow to 90 degrees. Place tubing or a resistive band in the hand with the other attached to the fence or gate. Rotate the hand toward the belly. Return slowly to the start position and repeat. Do for both arms.

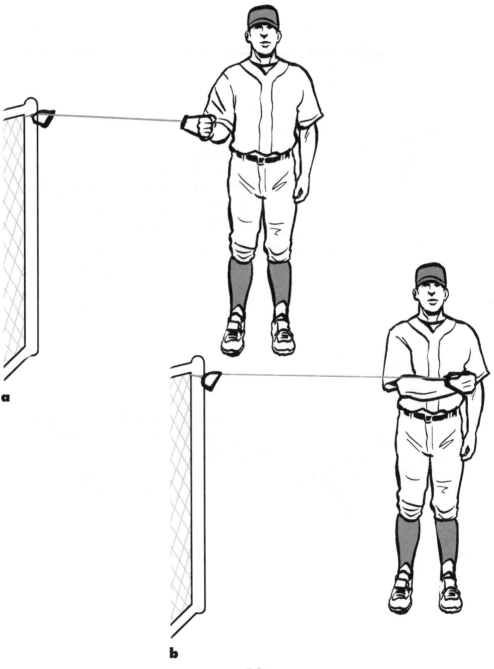

a

b

Focus   To loosen up the rotator cuffs.

Procedure   Lie on one side on the dugout bench. Hold a two-pound weight in one hand and rest the other arm on the side of the body. Bend the elbow of the arm with the weight to 90 degrees. Rotate the hand toward the sky, keeping the arm and elbow to the side. Return slowly to the starting position and repeat. Do for both arms.

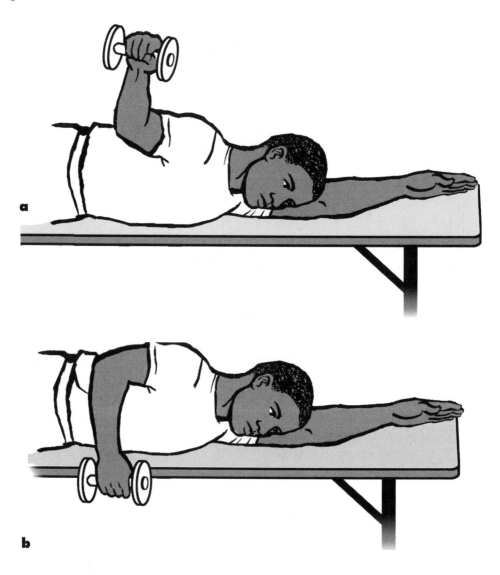

a

b

Focus   To improve lateral speed and agility.

Procedure   Follow the steps in the order described.

1. Carioca. Run laterally 10 yards, crossing one leg over the other. Go in both directions.
2. Forward and back. Run backward 10 yards, forward 5 yards, and backward another 10 yards until covering 30 yards. Repeat twice.

3. Zig-zag run. Run at a 45-degree angle, planting the right foot and driving off to the left for 5 yards. Repeat, alternating driving off the right and left foot for 30 yards.

4. Four-corner cone drill. Starting at the back right cone (cone 1), sprint 15 yards and touch cone 2; shuffle to the left and touch cone 3; run backward and touch cone 4; shuffle back to cone 1; shuffle laterally across the box to cone 3; run backward to cone 4; sprint out of the box past cone 2. A full rotation should be done in 30 seconds.

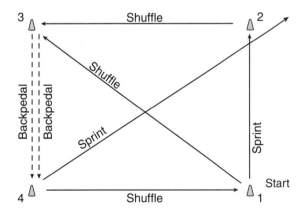

Fundamental Skills

Chapter 6

Catching Drills

Jack Smitheran

As children, one of the first baseball phrases we learn is "play catch." The first baseball-related skills that a young player learns are the primary defensive skills of catching and throwing. These two skills are the cornerstones on which sound defensive teams are built. Teams that take care of the ball—that is, teams that catch and throw the ball consistently well—are teams that play good defensive baseball.

If defensive skills are the first baseball skills learned by a young player, why are they the skills least practiced? Just because throwing and catching are learned first, this doesn't mean they are the easiest to master. But many times these skills are overlooked—which can have disastrous results because winning teams are nearly always strong on defense. Teams that win know how to take care of the ball.

In baseball, the true meaning of the word *team* is exemplified in the club's ability to play defense. Only on defense can all nine players function as one unit. Each player has a personal responsibility on every play. There's nothing more unifying than a team that comes together to make plays day after day. Conversely, nothing is more destructive to a team's unity than booting routine plays. A team's sense of pride and unity is directly affected by its ability, or inability, to play sound defense. Only on defense can a team ensure itself of never losing—because you can't lose if you don't get scored on.

The drills in this chapter are designed to improve a player's ability to catch the ball through coaching, technique, and repetition. Never confuse repetition with success. Focused repetition with attention to detail allows improvement to occur. Remember that practice doesn't make perfect—practice makes permanent. Work on making your practices perfect, and that carries over onto the field.

Focus   To develop hand-eye coordination, footwork, and timing with fielders' feet and hands.

Setup   You'll need one handball per player and a wall.

Procedure   The fielder tosses a ball against a wall about three feet away. When the ball returns, the fielder taps the ball off the bounce to the wall again, using his glove hand only. The fielder taps the ball back and forth to the wall with his palm up, as if the hand is the glove and in the proper receiving position to field ground balls. As the fielder is tapping the ball, he moves his feet to keep the ball in the center of his body and develop a rhythm. The fielder's goal is to keep the ball moving for 25 to 30 taps in a row.

Coaching Points   Focus on the infielder tracking the ball into his palm, working to get under the ball with his glove hand, tapping the ball out in front of his body, and developing a rhythm with his feet and hands.

Modifications   When fielders are doing this drill for the first time you might want them to focus on just tapping the ball against the wall without moving their feet and tapping the ball out in front of their body. The hardest part of this drill is the hand-eye coordination part of it.

Focus   To maximize the number of ground balls and throws to the proper bases in the infield.

Setup   Infielders take their positions on the infield. You'll need three players (coaches or pitchers) with fungo bats and three catchers.

Procedure   Do three rounds of 4 minutes each, totaling 12 minutes. In the first round, fungo 1 hits ground balls to the shortstop, who throws to first base. Fungo 2 hits ground balls to the second baseman, who works on double-play feeds to second base. Fungo 3 hits to the third baseman, who is playing in and throws home. All hit balls are returned to the fungo from which they were hit. (See figure a.)

In round 2, fungo 1 hits to the shortstop, who works on double-play feeds to second base. Fungo 2 hits to the second baseman, who is playing in and throws home. Fungo 3 hits to the third baseman, who throws across to first base. All hit balls are returned to the fungo from which they were hit. (See figure b.)

In round 3, fungo 1 hits to the shortstop, who is playing in and throws home. Fungo 2 hits to the second baseman and throws to first base. Fungo 3 hits slow rollers to the third baseman, who is charging in to work on fielding bunts and throwing to third base. (See figure c.)

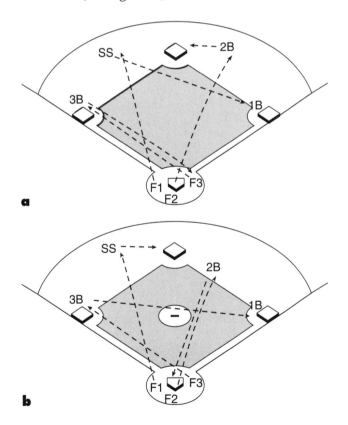

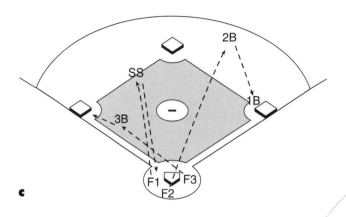

c

Coaching Points   As infielders are fielding ground balls, remind them not to sit back but to attack the ball, field it from the bottom up, and make a good, accurate throw or feed. For balls being hit to infielders playing in, remind players to field the ball and get their feet quickly into throwing position to get the runner at home.

Modifications   If you don't have enough catchers, have infielders field the ball, get into a good throwing position, and then lob the ball back to the hitter. If you have more than one infielder at each position, have them rotate in and out or have them field five grounders and then switch. For plays going to the second- or third-base bag, infielders can catch for a partner who is fielding the ball (e.g., on feeds to second or bunts to third).

Focus To work on proper routes to the ball, fielding ground balls properly, and throwing accurately.

Setup Infielders and outfielders work together in groups of four. Groups form a square of players about 10 yards apart. You'll need one ball per group.

Procedure Player 1 rolls a ground ball directly at player 2. Player 2 fields the ball properly and throws the ball to player 4. Player 4 rolls a ground ball directly at player 1. Player 1 fields the ball and throws to player 3. Player 3 rolls a ground ball directly to player 4. Player 4 fields the ball and throws to player 2. Player 2 rolls a ground ball directly to player 3. Player 3 fields the ball and throws to player 1. The format is repeated for backhands and for balls fielded on the fielder's glove side.

Coaching Points Pay attention to the route fielders take to field balls that are being rolled directly at them. Fielders should be getting to the right of the ball or around it (for right-handed fielders). Focus on proper fielding techniques: fielding the ball from the ground up, getting under the ball with the glove, and good throwing mechanics.

Modifications Another way to run this drill is to put infielders in one group and outfielders in another. This is a good drill to run indoors on a basketball court on rainy days.

31   PANIC DRILL

Focus   To teach players to pick the ball up off the ground without putting it back into their gloves and set their feet in a proper throwing position toward the intended target.

Setup   Set up position players in groups of four. Players take one of the four infield positions. Coach is at home plate with a fungo bat and a ball.

Procedure   Hit a ground ball to each player at the infield positions. As the fielder is fielding the ball, he purposely boots it. He retrieves the ball as quickly as he can by getting over the ball so that it's between his feet. He needs to make sure that his feet and shoulders are aligned with the base he will throw to. He picks the ball up by pushing it into the ground to get the proper grip and then moves into throwing position. He does not put the ball into his glove. As he throws the ball, he shuffles his feet in the direction he's throwing toward to gain ground. Hit four balls to each fielder.

Coaching Points   Remind fielders not to panic when they boot a ball. Encourage them to get over the ball so that it's between their feet. They should not waste time putting the ball into their glove. Check that they align their feet in the direction they're throwing to.

Modifications   Vary the base that fielders throw to. Have them make throws to each of the four bases.

32   TRIANGLE FLY BALL COMMUNICATION

Focus   To work on player communication on fly balls and pop-ups.

Setup   Three groups of four to five position players can do this drill together. Two groups align themselves 15 yards apart from each other, facing the coach about 20 yards away. The third group is about 5 yards in front of the coach, also facing him. This creates a triangle of players. The first player in each group goes first.

Procedure   The group in front of the coach represents the infielders. The group to the coach's right represents the centerfielders and the group to his left the left fielders. The coach tosses a ball high into the air between all three groups. The fielders work on communicating with each other on who will catch the ball and on catching the ball properly. A call should be made as to who is going to try to catch the ball. Do this drill until all players are comfortable with fly ball communications and everyone has performed the drill perfectly.

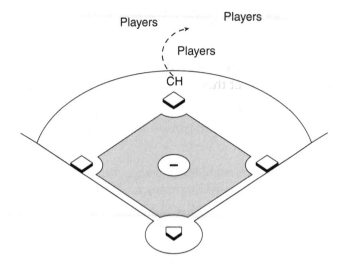

Coaching Points Remind players about who has priority on fly balls: outfielders over infielders, centerfield over left field and right field, middle infielders over corner infielders, corner infielders over catcher, and catcher over pitcher. Tell fielders not to call for the ball or yell "I got it" until the ball reaches its highest point. Teach fielders to catch the ball properly by getting behind the ball, facing the infield (except for catchers), and catching the ball with two hands off their throwing-side ear slightly above their head. The outfielder not catching the ball backs up the fielder who is catching it. The infielder pulls up and starts to back off so that he doesn't startle the fielder making the catch.

Modifications You can use a fungo bat to hit balls to the three groups. If so, spread the groups out a little wider and deeper. You can also break the three groups into outfielders and infielders, with infielders and catchers playing shallower than outfielders.

Focus   To help players improve in tracking and fielding ground balls hit directly at them, to their backhand side, to their glove side, and on short hops.

Setup   Infielders work in partners with one ball per pair. Players face each other three to five yards apart. You can do this drill on the infield dirt or outfield grass.

Procedure   Infielders face each other and get into good fielding position: knees bent, butt down, and hands out in front of the body. Fielders roll ground balls to each other. In round 1, they roll ground balls right at each other. In round 2, they roll ground balls to the backhand side. In round 3, they roll ground balls to the glove side. In round 4, they roll short hops. Each round has 10 rolls. Fielders should not move their feet but should stay in good fielding position, track the ball with their glove, work to get their glove under the ball when fielding it, and catch the ball in the web of the glove. Every third ball an infielder fields he should flip back to his partner straight from his glove. This way the fielder learns to feel the ball in the web of the glove.

Coaching Points   Focus on fielders fielding balls out in front of their body, tracking the ball into their glove, and catching the ball in the web of their glove. Don't let players get sloppy with their fielding position. Remind fielders to work hard to stay under the ball with their gloves and to field the ball from the ground up.

Modifications   Have the infielders increase the distance to 7 to 10 yards apart. This allows them to roll the ball a little harder and makes the drill more gamelike.

SHOESTRING CATCH

Focus To work on catching low line drives and fly balls falling right in front of them.

Setup Infielders and outfielders do the drill in groups of four or five. Players are in a single-file line facing the coach about 15 yards away. Run this drill in the outfield grass. You need two baseballs.

Procedure Players run toward the coach at 75 percent speed on his call. Coach throws a low line drive at the player running toward him, aiming for the knees. The player tries to catch the ball before it hits the ground. Run this part of the drill at least twice through. In the next part of the drill, the coach calls for players to run at him and then points to his right or left. The player then breaks in that direction at a 45-degree angle. Once the player breaks, the coach throws a low line drive for the player to catch. Run three rounds at each direction for each player.

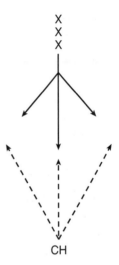

Coaching Points Focus on players trying to catch the ball properly. They should catch the ball with one hand and on the run. Teach players to adjust their glove according to the height of the ball. They should turn the glove so that it's facing either upward or slightly downward, depending on the height of the ball. For balls to the midsection or higher, players should get under the ball with their glove and glove-arm elbow.

Modifications To make the drill more gamelike, fungo the ball to players instead of throwing it. Throwing goes much quicker, and you're much closer to the players to correct them and slow down the drill. If you fungo the ball, you'll need to be 25 to 30 yards from your players.

Focus To work on proper drop steps, catching fly balls on the run, and tracking the ball into the glove.

Setup Outfielders and infielders do this drill. Players line up in single file about five yards from a coach. The coach and players face opposite directions. Each player needs his glove and a ball.

Procedure The first player up tosses his ball to a coach. On the coach's call, the player takes a proper dropstep and runs in a straight line as fast as he can, but under control. As the player is running, the coach tosses the ball to the player so that he has to catch the ball with his glove extended out and on the run. The ball should be caught with one hand only. Once all players have done the drill three times, they switch to the other side of the coach to do it again from the opposite side and at a different glove angle.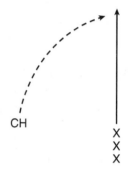

Coaching Points Check the fielders. Make sure they take proper dropsteps. The dropstep should be done with the leg closest to the ball stepping back into a straight line and getting the head and shoulders turned as quickly as possible. Focus on fielders tracking the ball into their glove with glove arm extended.

Modifications You might need to split your group in two. If so, the coach stands in the middle of the two groups and alternates throwing balls to each line.

Focus   To practice infield foot work and proper fielding techniques.

Setup   Infielders set up at their positions. You'll need two fungo bats and a catcher for each hitter.

Procedure   Fungo 1 hits to the shortstop and first baseman. Fungo 2 hits to the third baseman and second baseman. The ball is always returned to the fungo it was hit from. Each infielder fields the ball with his nonglove hand in his back pocket or behind his back. Balls need to be hit right at the infielder for this drill to work. Catching the ball one-handed forces infielders to get their feet in proper fielding position to catch the ball.

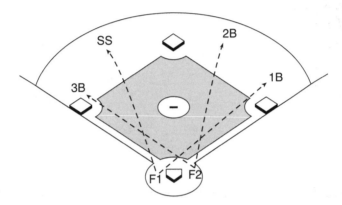

Coaching Points   Focus on the routes infielders take to the ball. Infielders (if right handed) should be getting slightly to the right of the ground ball and then making their approach to the ball. Watch for fielders getting their feet set down on time to field the ball, fielding the ball out in front of them and from the bottom up, getting their glove under the ground ball, and keeping their head down.

Modifications   Put the infielders in a single-file line and roll the ball to them. This a good method to introduce the drill. They should be at the back of the infield; the coach should be on the infield grass. This allows the coach to keep the drill under control and to help players struggling with foot work and routes to the ball.

Focus   To practice fielding the short-hop ground ball.

Setup   Infielders partner up and face each other about three yards apart. Each pair needs one ball.

Procedure   Fielders get into a good fielding position: knees bent, butt down, hands out in front of the middle of their body. One fielder tosses a short hop in front of his partner, about 6 to 12 inches in front of his glove. The partner fields the ball on the short hop, working on fielding it from the bottom up or getting under the ball with his glove. Fielders do 10 to 12 short hops each.

Coaching Points   Remind your fielders to catch the ball out in front of their bodies with arms slightly extended and wrists flexed down. They are to field the ball from the bottom up, working on keeping their glove under the ball and keeping their head down.

Modifications   If players have trouble throwing each other short hops, you might want to line up your fielders in a single-file line and give them short hops one at a time. This allows you to give fielders a proper short hop and correct them as needed. You can also slow the drill down for players who are struggling.

Chapter 7

Throwing Drills

Jim Brownlee

Throwing might not be the most glamorous task in baseball, but it's as valuable as any skill on the diamond. Consider that with runners on base and fewer than two outs in an inning, no defensive play can be completed without a throw. And, particularly at the youth and high school levels, many late-inning close games are decided by a player's ability to make an accurate throw.

While throwing might be an underappreciated skill to the casual fan or the occasional player, it's an important measuring stick for coaches and scouts. One of the first skills to evaluate when looking at players who aspire to higher levels of baseball is throwing.

A good throwing arm involves much more than talent. Excellent throwing results from the ability to throw with accuracy and velocity. Any player can improve accuracy and velocity by practicing the right skills in the right way. It takes more than a good arm to throw well—the skills involved range literally from head to toe.

Coaches should remember that proper throwing mechanics involve the whole body. The throwing drills recommended in this chapter are a progression designed to develop accuracy and arm strength through everyday repetition, which sharpens the skills. Throwing skills frequently fail to develop because players don't spend enough time throwing.

Drills on throwing should focus on helping players improve accuracy and velocity.

Photo courtesy of Illinois State University/Dennis Banks

Throwing can be the determining factor in whether a player gets the opportunity to compete at the next level. Professional scouts and college coaches value players with good arms. Developing a good arm is all about the proper practice of appropriate fundamentals. There's work involved for players and coaches, but the results are easy to measure.

38   SITTING DRILL

Focus   To keep a loose wrist and perform proper rotation on the ball.

Setup   You can do this drill with 2 to 30 players. After a proper warm-up, players pair off by position—catchers with catchers, pitchers with pitchers, and so on. Players sit cross-legged about 8 to 10 feet from their partner.

Procedure   With a proper grip, index and middle fingers should stay behind the ball through release. Rotation on the ball should be from a 6 o'clock position to a 12 o'clock position. Think *6 to 12*. Proper fundamentals in grip and release of the ball are important. The throwing hand should be above the thrower's head; the throwing elbow should be at least shoulder high. Directing the forearm and hand toward the partner, the thrower should follow through, making a fishhook with the throwing wrist.

Coaching Points   Make sure the wrist is loose on the follow-through. Check for proper grip on the ball and make sure rotation is from 6 to 12. Players throw about 20 times each.

a   b

Focus   To exhibit proper throwing mechanics beginning with the grip hand and progressing through the rest of the body.

Setup   You can do this drill with two or more players; for large groups, there should be one coach for every 10 players or so. Players position about 30 feet from a partner with one knee (throwing-arm side) on the ground.

Procedure   Step 1: The arm comes back from the glove extending downward with fingers in front of the ball.

Step 2: As the arm extends behind the body, fingers remain in front of the ball.

Step 3: As the arm comes forward above the ball, fingers are behind the ball.

a   b

Coaching Points   Ensure that the thrower's front shoulder is pointed at the target in a motion similar to shooting an arrow from a bow or firing a gun at a target. During release of the ball, the front shoulder should be pointing at the target. The arm action should be with a smooth rhythm, which includes drawing the arm down and back, extending before coming forward, and reaching above the head while advancing the arm toward the release point. Check for players wrapping their arms behind their backs rather than straight back. Also check for proper follow-through.

Focus on hand position on the ball. During steps 1 and 2, a coach standing in front of the thrower should be able to see the back of the throwing hand. In step 3 the throwing hand should be behind the ball. As the ball is released, make sure players' backs are parallel to the ground. Players throw 15 or 20 times each.

40   STAND-UP DRILL

Focus   To execute proper arm action.

Setup   Partners stand about 30 feet apart. Allow enough space for errant throws.

Procedure   Each player should use proper throwing mechanics. At this point in the drill progression, accuracy becomes a factor. Throwers aim for their partner's midchest area.

Coaching Points   Check for proper arm action plus these points:

1. Upper-body rotation
2. Shoulder pointing at the target
3. Loose arm action
4. Back parallel to the ground on follow-through
5. Proper rotation on the ball

41   CROW HOP

Focus   To use appropriate footwork in throwing.

Setup   Partners start about 30 feet apart and begin to move back with each throw as they warm up. Depending on the age group, players might spread as much as 60 feet apart.

Procedure   This drill emphasizes footwork. Players move farther apart as their arms warm up. The crow hop is simply a step with the back foot toward the target and then a hop while starting to stride with the front foot toward the target.

a   b   c

Coaching Points Proper footwork increases arm accuracy and throwing strength and reduces stress on the throwing shoulder and arm. Make sure the action of the crow hop and stride are toward the target to prevent players throwing across their bodies. Check that the stride and body motion flow toward the target on a straight line. To emphasize the straight line, have throwers line up along a foul line, facing home plate, and do the crow hop drill down the foul line.

Modifications A player can do this drill alone by throwing a ball against a wall.

Focus   To increase arm strength and velocity as well as throwing distance and accuracy.

Setup   Partners pair off by position (catchers with catchers, pitchers with pitchers, and so on). You need enough room for players to throw 200 to 300 feet, depending on their age group. Start with partners about 30 feet apart.

Procedure   All fundamentals from previous drills apply. Use the proper grip and pay attention to footwork (including crow hop).

a   b

Coaching Points   Check for proper grip and footwork. Each throw should be made on line. Players continue to throw until the ball bounces to their partner.

Day 1: 80 percent of maximum throwing distance

Day 2: 60 percent of maximum throwing distance

Day 3: Short toss

Day 4: 80 percent of maximum throwing distance (begin cycle again)

Modifications   Every arm is different, so adjust the drill accordingly. Some players can long toss every day.

c   d

Focus   To ensure the arm slot is proper for overhand, three-quarters, or sidearm.

Setup   Use up to 30 players. Split the team into two single-file lines about 150 feet apart.

Procedure   After proper arm warm-up, players long toss to the first person in line, then go back to the end of the line after one toss. Each player makes 15 to 20 tosses.

Coaching Points   The primary checkpoint is the arm slot. Some players will throw overhand, some three-quarters, and some sidearm. Since every shoulder is different, every player will have a slightly different arm slot that's comfortable for him. It's fine that all players don't throw from the same arm slot.

Modifications   Players can follow their throws and sprint for conditioning as part of the drill.

44   **GRIPPING THE BALL**

Focus   To ensure the grip of the ball is across the wide seams.

Setup   You need at least two players. You can run this drill effectively with large numbers as long as you have one coach for every 10 players or so. For best results, do the drill by positions, with infielders in one group, catchers in another, and so on.

Players pair off in two parallel lines with no other players behind either partner. With younger players particularly, ensure they have plenty of space to throw in.

Procedure   Each player drops to a knee (throwing-arm side) and assumes a stride position with his other leg. It's a good idea to pair players by skill level. Players start about 25 feet apart, which is the distance of each throw.

Partners begin the drill by playing catch, trying to get both hands in the receiving area. As soon as the ball makes contact with the glove, the receiver of the throw starts the throwing process by gripping the ball with his throwing hand. The ball should be gripped across the wide seams with the index and middle finger about one finger-width apart and the thumb under the ball and directly between the index and middle fingers. Many times the initial grip will be correct. If it's not, players should correct their grip before throwing. Correction takes no more than a quarter turn of the ball. Consistent use of the proper grip can be perfected through playing catch with proper focus. Players should learn to feel the two fingers across the wide seams.

In the time it takes to first touch the ball and take it out of the glove, proper grip can and should be attained. Proper grip makes for a more accurate throw with good rotation.

Players do the drill on one knee to isolate part of their body movement so that the focal point is getting the proper grip and creating good rotation.

Coaching Points   Carefully watch the rotation of the ball in flight between the partners. Help players use the proper grip, develop proper rotation on the ball, and perform the drill without stopping or delaying their throwing motion. Movements should be fluid.

45   RELAY DRILL

Focus   To improve ability to field or catch a ball and relay it to a target.

Setup   Players space 50 feet apart from each other in a line of three or more.

Procedure   Thrower 1 relays the ball to thrower 2. Thrower 2 works on moving feet into proper position to relay the ball to thrower 3, and so on. When the ball reaches the end of the line, the drill goes in reverse order.

Modifications

1. Throw ground balls.
2. Throw fly balls.

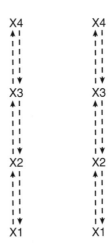

Focus   To improve throwing accuracy for catchers.

Setup   Position a catcher at each base and home plate. Catchers work on throwing from home to all three bases.

Procedure   The ball starts at home plate and can be thrown to any base. The second throw should be to another base. Have catchers make 10 throws to each base.

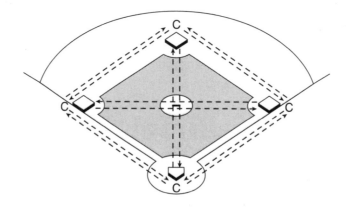

47   FOUR-CORNER PICKOFF

Focus   To improve pickoff moves to first base, base-stealing reads off pitchers, moves to first, and throwing accuracy to first.

Setup   Four pitchers on the dirt part of the mound, each in a stretch position facing a different base, as if that base is home plate. Each pitcher's back shoulder points to a coach standing on the rubber. Position one pitcher at each base and home plate. One runner is at each base, simulating a lead off first base.

Procedure   When coach calls, "Pickoff" or "Pitch," each pitcher either throws to his designated first base or pitches to his home plate.

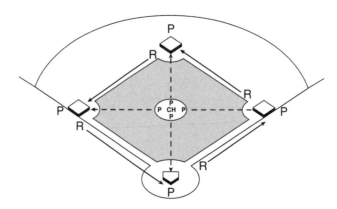

Focus To improve throwing accuracy and communication during rundown plays.

Setup Base runners are on first and third. Position players are behind each base. Players at first and third have a baseball ready to throw.

Procedure Players should also try to run a runner back toward the base he started at. The player receiving the throw must be on the throwing side of the player making the throw. Players call for the ball by saying, "Now!" They keep the ball in a throwing position, not in their gloves. They follow their throws to get in line at the next base.

Coaching Points Avoid making more than two throws on any rundown. Encourage players to minimize the number of throws.

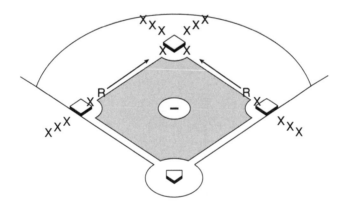

Chapter 8

Sliding Drills

Bob Warn

"Down, get down!" "Hit it!" "Down, in!" "Down, out!" You hear these and other commands from base coaches at every level of baseball. The problem is that players are often given these commands without any previous instruction. Even experienced players injure themselves because of poor sliding techniques. Sliding should be taught as soon as players start running the bases.

When you ask a player to slide, you're asking him to fall with body control. A slide should resemble the landing of an airplane on a runway, not a helicopter landing on a building top. Players should not jump at the base but break down early and greet the base. Beginning a slide early makes for less chance of sliding past the base, less chance of being tagged out, and less chance of injury.

Photo courtesy of Indiana State University Athletics Media Relations Department

Since sliding is essentially falling with body control, players need to learn how to slide properly and thus avoid injury.

The slides used in the drills in this chapter are the bent-leg slide, the headfirst slide, the hook slide, and variations of the three. The bent-leg slide is the easiest and most popular. This slide is used to beat a throw or break up a double play. It's the quickest and safest way to the bag. The bent leg is a good first slide for the younger player to learn. You see the headfirst slide more often today because of the aggressive style of baseball being taught to young players. You also see more close "safe" calls because of the difficulty of putting down a tag on a headfirst slide. The hook slide is a more difficult slide but is excellent for giving minimal tag area to the defensive player. If executed correctly, the hook slider offers only part of his foot as a tagging target.

The drills are designed to help teach the various slides to young players, but a previous knowledge of how to approach each slide is extremely helpful. See table 8.1 for a summary of the advantages and disadvantages of each type of slide.

TABLE 8.1 — Advantages and Disadvantages of Different Slides

Type of slide	Advantages	Disadvantages
BENT-LEG	Easiest to learn Most popular Quickest and safest slide to the bag Good for younger players Runner will use base to pop up, so less chance of going beyond the bag	Can't avoid tag Bigger target for defense Slower getting back to feet unless pop-up is used
HOOK	Avoids the tag best only a few inches of the foot touching the base Has more variations, such as changing to the side away from the ball Has a strong balance for runner during the slide	A bit more challenging to teach and learn Some extra distance required because sliding beyond the base occurs
HEADFIRST	More natural type fall Can move body away from ball during slide More aggressive method Tags are difficult to apply Quickest way to the bag	Hands are more prone to injury Vision may be diminished Slide will not be effective if the fall is too abrupt (must be leaned into) Getting to the feet is much slower after completing the slide Cannot use when ball is waiting for runner
	Advantages of sliding early	**Disadvantages of sliding late**
ANY SLIDE	Safer Softens impact Better read of the play	Injury prone Less understanding of where the tag will be Very hard landing

Focus   To learn to perform a controlled fall for a bent-leg slide.

Setup   Do this drill with four players. Use small rugs (three feet by three feet) on a four-inch foam rubber pad four feet square. A player is positioned on each side of the falling player (who must wear a helmet); the fourth player positions in front of the faller.

Procedure   The front player pulls the rug out from under the faller. The side players are there for safety. To execute this drill properly, the faller throws his arms and head back when the rug is pulled out. One leg should bend underneath to cushion the fall, which should leave the faller in a sitting position at the end of the fall. The top leg, slightly flexed, remains four inches off the floor.

a

b

Coaching Points   Have players use each leg as the bent leg so that they learn to slide on either side with confidence. Give fallers batting gloves to hold rolled up in their hands to remind them not to use their hands to break their fall. Remind players to use the bent leg's thigh and buttocks to absorb the fall. The sole of the bent-leg foot should face the outside. The top leg should be semiflexed and held about four inches off the floor. For safety, ask players to take off their shoes.

50   AIRPLANE LANDING

Focus   To avoid jumping at the base when sliding.

Setup   Position five or six players (sliders) in a line 90 feet from a base. Position two players (as spotters) on each side of the baseline 20 feet in front of the base. Sliders line up wearing socks, sweat pants, and padding to soften their fall.

Procedure   Each player takes a turn running easily toward the base. The two spotters extend their arms toward each other (three feet off the floor) to form a bridge for the slider to slide under without making contact. Emphasis is on an early breakdown of the body to ease the fall. The base is not a goal here but rather an alignment tool. The slider should not reach the base in this drill.

Coaching Points   After they have done the drill a few times, players can leave their shoes on. Don't let speed or reaching the base become the focus; emphasize the slider landing on the runway after clearing the spotters' arms. All techniques of sliding could be practiced here regarding the lower leg's underside thigh and buttocks absorbing the shock of the fall, hands and head thrown backward, and preventing the knee from hitting the ground first. Tell spotters to keep their arms low to the floor the first few times so that sliders are less apt to begin their slides late. You can use a bat as a guide instead of player's arms, as illustrated in the figure.

Modifications   You can also use this drill for the headfirst slide or hook slide.

51   HOOK SLIDE KIP-UP

Focus   To learn proper final position for the hook slide.

Setup   All players participate as base runners on a wrestling mat or other soft surface.

Procedure   Players begin on their backs with knees to their chests. With a rocking motion back and forth, the body moves forward, the legs coming out front together. The final hook slide position is assumed as the body comes forward. The hooking foot from the collapsing leg is arched and pointed, with weight leaning on the collapsing leg's underthigh and buttocks.

a   b

Coaching Points   Remind players to focus on becoming familiar with the final position, not on the slide itself. The hook position at the end of the slide should show only four or five inches of the bag being used, allowing the foot to avoid the tag.

Modifications   Use the finishing hook slide position with the actual slide to execute the entire movement.

52   93-FOOT SLIDE

Focus   To learn how wide to slide while still holding the base.

Setup   Players form a line of base runners directed at a base; one player positions as baseman at a base. An infielder has a glove awaiting a throw from the outfield.

Procedure   Base runners slide wide of the bag, with the ball being at the base ahead of them. As the runner slides several feet past the base, he rolls over toward the base, reaching out to grab it with his outside arm. The defensive player enacts the tag to make the drill as gamelike as possible. Sliders use a headfirst slide or hook slide to practice avoiding the tag.

Coaching Points   Don't do this drill until players can do all slides consistently well. Make a mark on the floor or in the dirt to show each runner his location when the tagging of the bag took place. He can use this information to guide his future slides.

53   HYDROPLANE

Focus   To become adept at all types of sliding.

Setup   Your entire team can participate in this drill at once. You'll need a fire hose or other source of water for this drill. Place four bases on the far edge of a 150-foot square tarp. Line up four lines of players (one for each base) 80 feet away, dressed in shorts only. Assign each base to a coach (barefoot), who critiques each slide.

Procedure   The hose must be manned at all times to ensure a half-inch of water on the tarp. Each coach signals the front player in his line to run toward the base to execute the assigned slide into the base. After being critiqued by his coach, the player returns to the end of his line, careful not to pass in front of the other groups. Players perform bent-leg, headfirst, and hook slides.

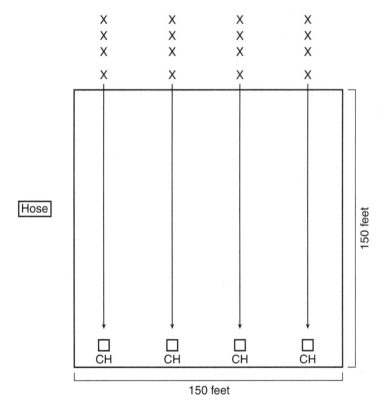

Coaching Points   This drill is perhaps the best approach for teaching young players. Teach each type of slide separately until players perform them all successfully, then use a combination of slides to build confidence and promote spontaneous selection during games. Be warned that enjoyment might override education during this drill—remind players to stay focused. Keep lines far enough apart to ensure safety.

54   SITUATION SLIDE

Focus   To react to a play, using the appropriate slide.

Procedure   Half the players are outfielders; the others are infielders and base runners. As a coach hits balls into the outfield, the defense sets up in proper formation to throw out the runner. The runner chooses an appropriate slide according to the defense's alignment and location of the ball during the tag. If the ball beats the runner to the base, the player tries a backside hook or head-first slide. If the tag man is still awaiting the ball, the slider does a bent-leg or bent-leg, pop-up slide. After a set time has elapsed, switch the two groups.

Coaching Points   Remind players to begin their slides a distance of two body lengths in front of the base. Sliders can choose to mark this spot on the field (or floor) to indicate their takeoff location. Tell players to practice sliding on both sides of their body. Start base runners at all bases so that plays at each base are practiced by base runners and fielders.

Modifications   Use base coaches at third base and first base to make for a more gamelike situation.

Focus   To slide into one base and get a great jump to advance to the next one.

Setup   Your entire team participates in this drill at once. Put a defense on the field, and the rest of the squad runs the bases and slides. Switch halfway through the drill so all players get to slide.

Procedure   With a full defense on the field and half the team as runners, a coach hits a ball to the outfield, setting up gamelike situations. The runners advance to bases using a bent-leg, pop-up slide at second and third base. A second coach stands out in shallow outfield and at times rolls a ball past the player, allowing runners to advance. Players use either leg for the bent-leg slide (though we've seen faster times to the next base when players use their left leg). During this bent-leg slide, the top foot pushes against the bag, allowing the slider to pivot or roll on his bent-leg knee. The momentum from the slide pushes the runner to his feet.

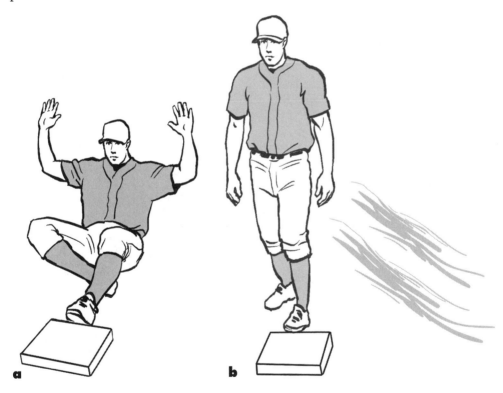

Coaching Points   Have runners keep their hands up and look with the head during the slide. Work with runners to find the baseball upon reaching base. Tell runners to work both sides of the body when sliding.

Modifications   If you're low on players, you can run this drill without a defense on the field. The coach can roll balls in the direction he chooses.

Focus To use a headfirst dive back to first base from a maximum lead.

Setup A pitcher takes the mound; a runner leads off first base with his maximum lead, using a one-way lead to first base. Three more bases lined up toward right field all have runners. All work off the pitcher getting back to their base. There are no first basemen for the last three bags.

Procedure Runners work from their maximum lead, using a crossover step to get back when the pitcher throws over to first. They are diving from a maximum lead. Start runners about two body lengths off the bag, adjusting a bit as need for each individual. The first runner is challenging the pitcher's move. The three other runners are reacting back to their "first" base as if there is a play on them. Give each runner three or four tries at the real first base, then rotate so that all get a turn "going live."

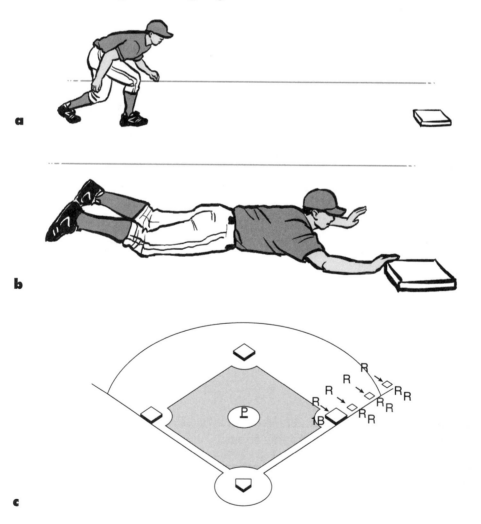

a

b

c

Coaching Points   Runners should wear helmets. If a runner can get back to first without sliding, he doesn't have his maximum lead. Rotate pitchers to give runners different looks.

57   BETWEEN THIRD AND HOME SLIDE

Focus   To block the catcher's view of third base or get tangled up in the catcher's feet.

Setup   Put an infielder at each position and a catcher and pitcher at their positions; a line of additional pitchers wait their turn. The rest of the team are base runners. A coach stands at the plate with a bat. The infield plays in with the assumption that the bases are loaded.

Procedure   The pitch is delivered; the coach hits a ground ball, misses the pitch, or takes the pitch. The runner breaks for the plate if the ball is hit or goes back to third if the ball isn't hit. If the ball is not hit, the runner steps back into the base-line as the ball is caught by the catcher and goes back to third base hard, using a bent-leg, pop-up slide and looking for a possible wild throw. The pop-up is important in the potential of scoring on a poor throw because it's the fastest way to get back to your feet. If the ball is hit, the runner breaks for home, sliding to the front of the plate (about 1-1/2 feet), trying to upset the footwork of the catcher to prevent a double play. The runner should use a bent-leg slide.

Coaching Points   Although sliding is the focus, several other skills are being worked in this drill. Switch the defense and the offense so all players can slide. Switch pitchers on every pitch. The pitch should be a straight change. Instruct runners to lead off at third in foul territory, moving toward the plate.

Modifications   You can do this drill without a defense on the field. The coach rolls ground balls in the direction he chooses.

Offensive Skills

Chapter 9

Hitting Drills

Rick Jones and Mark Kingston

The longer I coach, the more convinced I am that the key to player development is total practice commitment to the key fundamentals of throwing, catching, base running, bunting, and hitting. Consistent player development is the most important contributor to team success.

During practice, we try to focus at least 90 percent of our time on the basic skills of baseball. We try our best to make each practice as gamelike and competitive as we can. We also strive to stay fresh in our approach and use many different formats to accomplish our goals.

Our hitting coach, Mark Kingston, is always incorporating drills into our hitters' routines. These drills emphasize the absolutes of a consistent swing. In doing so, Mark keeps our hitters in competitive gamelike situations. Additionally, he has had great success in developing drills that pertain to each hitter's individual needs.

Our goals each day are the same: Get better as hitters in every phase, including consistency in the swing, weight transfer, pitch recognition, and situational hitting. We don't believe in cloning hitters. Our challenge is to take each hitter and develop his swing understanding. We want him to know the absolutes of a great swing. In working on drills, we create an environment that's as close to gamelike as we can get it.

Drill work is the foundation on which our hitters develop and refine their swings. Drills also provide a point of reference for each hitter. Every hitter, no matter how talented, struggles at times. Drill work can help hitters refind their swing and return to form. We don't believe any hitter can reach his full potential relying solely on batting practice and intrasquad games. Proper technique needed for a consistent swing requires quality repetitions properly executed.

The hitting drills in this chapter are among the many that Mark Kingston has developed for our team. Each drill is based on the needs of each hitter. These drills have made our hitters much more aware of all the factors that play a part in success. We have seen positive strides in our hitters' abilities to recognize and correct problems while displaying a heightened awareness with less anxiety during games. This chapter features 20 drills, the first 10 of which are designed to aid the hitter in the development of his swing; the next 10 emphasize the art of situational hitting and all it entails.

We hope your hitters benefit from these drills as much as our Tulane hitters have. It's our pleasure to share them with you.

58   BEHIND SOFT-TOSS

Focus   To reinforce the importance of staying inside the baseball.

Setup   A coach works with individual hitters. Set up home plate about seven feet from one end of the cage. The coach sets himself up four feet directly behind home plate, either sitting down or taking a knee. The hitter takes his customary position in the box; only his head position changes during this drill. The coach has a bucket of balls, preparing to soft toss.

Procedure   The drill is done in short-toss form, but change the angle of flight from the side to the back. The hitter must turn his head around to see the toss of the ball. The coach tosses each ball as in a normal soft-toss drill. The ball should be delivered from the middle of the plate to the outside corner. The hitter then takes his normal swing, attempting to drive each pitch to the back opposite corner of the cage.

Coaching Points   Most young hitters tend to let their hands get away from their body in an effort to pull the ball. To build a more complete hitter, this drill emphasizes exactly how to "stay inside" the ball, giving instant feedback on each swing. Proper swing is felt on each repetition. The hitter keeps the front side of the body closed for as long as possible, both before and during the swing. Any incorrect movement of the front shoulder makes the hitter reach for the pitch and hit it weakly. Continuous repetitions help the hitter keep his barrel inside the pitch until the moment of contact. This allows him to feel what "staying inside the ball" means.

Focus   To help hitters feel the effects of keeping the front elbow down in the swing.

Setup   A coach works with individual hitters. Use a bungi cord about two feet long with a hook on each end. The batter loops the cord around his torso, placing his front arm inside. The cord should be snug enough to hold the arm in place without restricting the load-up.

Procedure   No ball is needed for this drill. The hitter takes natural, short, efficient, powerful swings with a bat. After many repetitions, remove the bungi and have him take normal swings. He will now feel any inefficient movements in his swing.

a   b

Coaching Points   When the front elbow leaves the body, the most efficient path to the ball is impeded. A properly placed bungi cord forces the front arm to work correctly, thus teaching correct muscle memory. We suggest when using the cord for the first time to also use a tee because this allows the hitter to get comfortable with the new feel. At first the hitter will feel he's too restricted and can't finish his swing. As he takes more swings, remind him that any movement in the elbow only slows his swing down. Emphasize a full, complete swing. Otherwise, hitters tend to cut off their swing, limiting power.

60   CLOSED-OFF CENTER

Focus   To work on hitters staying closed until the last moment to reinforce a short, quick stroke.

Setup   A coach works with individual hitters. The drill requires a pitching screen and can be done in the cage but is best done on the field. Set up the screen so that the coach is throwing from about five feet to the left or right (depending on the side of the hitter) of the pitching rubber. The hitter takes his usual stance in the batter's box.

Procedure   The pitcher (coach) throws a normal batting practice, except that he's throwing from a new angle. He focuses on throwing each pitch on the outer half of the plate. The path of this pitch simulates a well-thrown slider, crossing the plate from the front inside to the back outside. This forces the hitter to stay inside the ball and drive each pitch toward the opposite gap. Attempts to hit these pitches while pulling the front shoulder off the ball result in very weak hits.

Coaching Points   The key to this drill is the hitter keeping his front shoulder closed until the last possible instant. Many hitting faults occur because the front shoulder pulls the hands off the path of the pitch. The front shoulder should remain in place so that the hands can take a direct path into the pitch from near the body. Pulling the front shoulder out causes the hands to make an adjustment going away from the body, which leads to long, slow, ineffective swings. This drill reinforces a short, quick stroke. It's a tough drill to master but teaches very good habits.

Focus   To teach hitters to use hips and hands correctly and help them feel how deep the ball can get in the contact zone.

Setup   A coach works with individual hitters who hit from a tee. Set up home plate at one end of the cage. The plate should be set up differently for right- or left-handed hitters. For right-handed hitters, make the back of the cage an imaginary first-base line with home plate. For left-handed hitters, make the back of the cage an imaginary third-base line. This distance gives hitters instant feedback on every swing.

Procedure   Set up the hitter so that the tee is aligned with the instep of his back foot. The hitter takes full swing to make solid contact toward the rear of the cage or in the direction of the opposite field.

    a   **b**

Coaching Points   The key to this drill is hitters getting a feel for making contact with their hands in front of the ball. Hitters learn the concepts of staying inside the ball and starting their swing with their hips—both essential in successful hitting. The ball placement won't allow the hitter to use an upward swing plane. Any loop in the path of the hands makes contact impossible. This is a great drill because it forces the hitter to do many things correctly without thinking about them.

Focus   To emphasize the importance of controlling body weight during the stride and reducing the tendency to lunge.

Setup   A coach works with individual hitters. Set up home plate at one end of the cage. The hitter takes his normal position in the batter's box in relation to home plate. The coach is on the other side of the plate, either on a knee or sitting down.

Procedure   This drill is very similar to the traditional soft-toss. The difference here is that the coach can "hold" a toss when he wants to. As the coach begins his toss, the hitter loads up and prepares to swing. The coach randomly holds some pitches instead of throwing, observing the stride and body control of the hitter. On the "hold," the batter will feel any time his weight shifts too early or too quickly. This helps eliminate unnecessary movement in the stride. Following each "hold," the coach then tosses the ball after a three count. The hitter takes his swing from whatever position he was in following the stride and holds. A backspin line drive off the back net is the goal.

Coaching Points   Make the hitter take many swings out of his hitting position. Hitters might initially have to take less than ideal swings from a weak-hitting position, but they'll quickly feel the importance of proper balance at the completion of their stride. Quality of swing directly relates to quality of stride.

Focus   To teach proper hitting mechanics.

Setup   A coach works with individual hitters. This drill can be done anywhere anytime. All you need is a bat for the hitter, a ball for the coach, and a home plate. There are no real swings taken; the ball never leaves the coach's hand. The amount of space needed is minimal.

Procedure   The hitter sets up in his normal stance at home plate. The coach stands in the opposite batter's box. Once both are in position, the coach holds the ball in any area of the strike zone. The batter then begins his swing at a very slow pace and stops at the point of contact. All check points are observed to make sure the hitter understands the correct position at this point in the swing. Once the hitter has held his barrel against the ball for a three count, he's instructed to drive through the baseball while the coach offers resistance. This teaches the hitter the importance of retaining a strong position through contact and into the follow-through.

a

b

Coaching Points   By slowing down all the movements in the swing, a hitter can feel what his body should do on every pitch. The coach watches the action of the stride, hips, and hands and the contact point. Because no balls are batted, hitters can concentrate on perfect muscle memory. This way the body learns perfect mechanics, feeling any variation from their best swing on live pitches.

The key to this drill is that the hitter feels his ideal position at contact. He understands the inefficiency of upper cutting or lunging. Making hitters follow through after contact (still at a slow speed), helps them feel which muscles should do the majority of the work and at which point the top hand will actually roll over (late). Constantly change placement in the strike zone to allow hitters to feel the various depths the ball should travel before contact, depending on the location.

Focus To put hitters in a position of instant feedback so they can interpret the result of each swing and adjust as necessary.

Setup A coach works with individual hitters who hit from a tee. Set up home plate at one extreme end of the cage. Set up the tee in the middle of home plate to simulate a ball that will be hit to the middle of the field.

Procedure Align hitters so that the front foot at completion of the stride is even with the tee. The hitter then takes a swing to hit a line drive to the back net at the opposite end of the cage. The goal for the hitter is to consistently square the baseball at contact and avoid pop-ups or ground balls.

Coaching Points The traditional practice of hitting off a tee into a net does not give a hitter an accurate read on how well the ball was hit. By watching a full flight of the ball, the hitter learns when flaws have occurred. Any slight flaw in a swing results in a less-than-perfect backspin line drive. The hitter learns that watching the action of the ball tells him what went right or wrong with the swing. Consequently, he learns the art of making adjustments.

Focus   To build quick hands and bat speed.

Setup   Set up home plate at the extreme end of the batting cage. The coach sets up across from the hitter in order to toss each ball into the hitter's strike zone. The coach prepares to toss five "pitches," holding one ball in the toss hand and four in the other. Once again we like to use the full length of the cage in order to watch the flight of the ball.

Procedure   Hitters need to feel how fast their hands and body can work. This drill forces them to work at their highest rate of speed. The drill also reinforces that a short stroke is the most efficient path to the strike zone. Driving the swing back and forth over the plate shows that the hands are quick as they stay close to the body, slowing down as they stray from the body. Bat speed and efficiency are the main objectives. Once the coach and the hitter are in position, the coach begins to toss one ball after another, forcing the hitter to swing short and quick. The coach should toss the next ball as the hitter has begun to recoil his swing. Once mastered, the drill should have rhythm and pace. Each toss should be in a different part of the strike zone so that the hitter doesn't groove a swing in one area.

Coaching Points   Daily use of this drill builds short, quick swings. Efficiency of movement is learned by each hitter as he feels what helps his swing to get quicker. The body finds its best way to create bat speed through short, quick movements. Again, use of the full cage is recommended to promote line drives. To teach good lead arm action, you can also do this drill with only the bottom hand. As the hitter gets quicker, toss faster.

Focus To teach hitters the importance of getting to a consistent hitting position for every swing. Every hitter, regardless of stance or size, must get to this position to begin a swing.

Setup A coach works with individual hitters. Do this drill using soft toss at one end of a cage. Set up the stance for the middle of the plate. The hitter's goal is to drive the ball to the back of the cage.

Procedure Complete this drill in three steps: the stance, stride, and swing. The hitter begins in his stance and loads up to begin the swing. At the instant his front foot hits the ground, the hitter pauses. He holds this position for a three count, noticing his checkpoints during this pause. Following the pause, the hitter then takes his normal full swing, aiming for a hard backspin line drive off the center of the back net.

Coaching Points One major difference between successful and unsuccessful hitters is the ability to get in the best possible position to explode into a swing. The hitting position is reached after the hands and body have loaded and the stride foot has hit the ground. Look for these traits in the hitter:

1. An equilateral triangle formed by the legs and the ground
2. Shoulders almost level with a slight tuck of the front shoulder
3. Hands over the back foot at shoulder or slightly above shoulder level
4. Level through the belt line
5. Level eyes on the pitch
6. Closed front foot
7. Slightly flexed lead arm
8. Hands holding the bat at a 45-degree angle

Once again, the hitter should gain instant feedback from each repetition. The hitter should learn that starting a swing from an imperfect hitting position affects consistency and strength. Once a hitter feels the difference between correct and incorrect positions, he'll improve rapidly.

67 HIGH-SPEED, CLOSE-PITCH

Focus   To gain repetitions swinging at high-speed fastballs.

Setup   A coach works with individual players. Set up home plate at one end of the cage. Set up a pitching screen about 25 feet in front of the hitter. A coach will then be in a position to throw consistent strikes into the hitting area. Throwing from this position permits more accurate pitches.

Procedure   The hitter sets himself in the batter's box in normal position. The coach, from his sitting position, throws balls with good velocity into different part of the strike zone. The hitter focuses on hitting hard line drives to all parts of the cage. As the hitter gets more advanced, add velocity to the pitch to further challenge him.

Coaching Points   The only way to consistently catch up to and square good fastballs is with a quick, short stroke. This drill teaches hitters to swing hard, yet under control. Trying to lengthen the swing makes it impossible for the hitter to catch up.

All good hitters can hit the fastball. We want to develop hitters who can catch up to any fastball regardless of the speed. Giving the hitter a short amount of reaction time is essential to the drill. This speeds up the hitter's reflexes and forces short, compact strokes. The coach throwing pitches should be sure to use a long arm stroke to allow hitters time to load up and take a normal stride. Only the swing should be quick.

Focus To teach hitters that their approach at the plate varies depending on the count. Many counts are covered so that hitters are prepared for any they encounter in a game.

Setup Players work one at a time on a field or in the cage. Set up home plate at one end of the cage. Place the pitching screen about 45 feet from home plate.

Procedure Begin the drill with the coach calling out the count. The categories of counts are hitters' counts, even, and two strikes. Hitters' counts are 2-0 and 3-1, even counts are 0-0 and 1-1, and of course two strike counts are 0-2, 1-2, and 2-2. We recommended starting with even counts. Each count is done for five pitches before progressing to the next. The hitter tailors his batting approach based on the count.

Coaching Points Hitters must understand the difference between a 3-1 swing and a 2-2 swing. They should learn in which counts to be aggressive and in which to be protective. When hitting in hitters' counts, the hitter learns to adjust the timing of his load-up and stride. A hitter should not be late when he's sitting on a fastball. If he receives any other pitch, the pitch should be taken. Only strong, aggressive swings should be taken in a hitter's count.

In counts that favor the pitcher, the hitter must learn to adjust. He should still prepare to take short, quick swings but must wait longer to commit, refusing to be fooled. Batters will come to understand the importance of developing the mental side of hitting.

Focus   To work on two-strike hitting, face an assortment of pitches, and gain a better understanding of the strike zone.

Setup   Hitters work individually with a coach or pitcher. Set up a home plate at one end of the cage. Set up a pitching screen about 45 feet away. The pitcher prepares to throw a blend of pitches.

Procedure   Each pitch will be on a 3-2 count on the hitter. The hitter earns a point for each hard hit ball or for taking a walk. The pitcher receives a point for a strikeout or a weakly hit ball. Score is kept until either the hitter or pitcher reaches 20 points. The pitcher should be as hard as possible on the hitter. Facing a variety of fastballs, curveballs, change-ups, and other pitches will sharpen the hitter and help him develop into an effective two-strike hitter.

Coaching Points   To be a complete hitter, a hitter must be a tough out with two strikes. This is a great way to create a competitive environment in which the hitter can be challenged. Weaknesses should be identified and exploited. If a hitter is struggling with off-speed pitches, throw a majority of pitches off speed. Before long, you can develop a weakness into a strength. A competitive hitter does whatever it takes to reach 20 points before the pitcher does. This is the type of attitude a great hitter should possess. Becoming an advanced two-strike hitter begins with the right attitude. Stress the importance of taking a walk.

Focus   To work on hitters covering as much of the plate as they can.

Setup   Set up a home plate at one end of the cage. Place a pitching screen about 15 feet in front of the plate. The coach can either sit or stand behind the screen. The screen should be placed so that the tall side is on the throwing-arm side.

Procedure   The hitter sets up in the batter's box in his customary position. The coach, from sitting or standing, tosses underhand pitches into the strike zone. There are two types of pitches: a firm toss on the inside corner or a soft toss on the outside corner. These are the two toughest balls for a batter to hit. The pitches are thrown at random so a batter cannot cheat, looking for one or the other. He must prepare to hit either.

Coaching Points   Very few hitters can protect the entire plate against good pitching. Working on this skill expands the area of the plate a hitter can use. The hitter learns to be short on the inside pitch, thus being less vulnerable to any given zone. This is a very challenging drill; consistent success is difficult. But the more comfortable the hitter becomes with this drill, the more confident he'll be in his ability to hit any pitch. A hitter will learn to wait and stay closed on a ball away and be quick and short on the ball inside. Once he has gained confidence in hitting these two pitch locations, all other pitches become easier to handle.

Focus   To teach hitters to look for pitches in different areas of the strike zone.

Setup   Set up home plate at one end of the cage. A coach stands and throws from 45 feet away, or closer, if necessary, to locate each pitch accordingly. He can sit in a chair 20 feet away and overhand toss or sit even closer and underhand toss—whatever works best.

Procedure   Instruct the hitter in which area of the zone he's looking for a pitch to drive. If he gets a pitch in another area, he'll let the ball go by. For example, if you say, "Inside," the hitter prepares the timing of his load and stride to drive an inside pitch. If he gets an outside pitch, he takes the pitch.

Coaching Points   A hitter should learn to choose his approach depending on the count and situation. He must learn which areas of the strike zone he handles best. It's nearly impossible for hitters to handle the entire strike zone in and out, up and down, but this drill helps them learn their best zones while significantly improving their discipline. There are all kinds of situations in which hitters look for location. If a hard-throwing pitcher likes to work inside, hitters can learn how to "sit on" a pitch in and drive it. Many pitchers prefer to stay away, so hitters should also learn to look for the outside pitch and drive it the other way. Hitters must develop the confidence to take a pitch they're not looking for, even if the pitch is a strike. This drill also helps hitters learn to study pitchers and determine their best plan for each at-bat.

Focus   To teach hitters to sit on certain pitches in certain situations.

Setup   A coach works with individual hitters. Set up home plate at one end of the cage, with a pitching screen 45 feet away. The coach prepares to throw a variety of fastballs, curveballs, change-ups, and other pitches.

Procedure   The coach tells the hitter which pitch he's looking to hit. If the coach calls out, "Fastball," the hitter swings only at fastballs thrown in the strike zone. The coach then randomly throws all type of pitches. The hitter should take any off-speed pitches, looking only for the fastball. When the coach calls out "Curveball," the hitter adjusts his timing and sights to hit a curveball. Now he takes any fastballs or change-ups.

Coaching Points   One reason experienced hitters are more consistent is that they know what to look for in each situation. This drill teaches discipline in choosing which pitches to swing on and which to lay off of. When facing pitching at the highest level, hitters must develop certain strategies. They learn that by taking away other pitches, the pitch they're sitting on becomes easier to hit. Adjusting timing to a given pitch allows for consistency and decreases the chances of being fooled. All pitchers fall into patterns. As a hitter gains confidence in identifying pitches, he'll learn to think along with the pitchers. If he gets a pitch he doesn't like, he'll take it with less than two strikes. Most great hitters take this approach. An example is a hitter who with less than two strikes swings only at fastballs. This drill allows hitters to work on that strategy.

Focus   To improve ability to hit breaking balls.

Setup   A coach works with individual hitters. This drill can be done in a batting cage or on the field. Throw pitches from at least 45 feet to make the hitter wait on the ball.

Procedure   The coach throws repeated curveballs and sliders to the batter. If a pitch can be driven, the hitter takes an aggressive swing. If the pitch is a ball, the hitter takes it. After each pitch taken, the hitter checks his hitting position.

Coaching Points   At high levels of baseball, all hitters can hit fastballs. If they couldn't, they wouldn't have advanced so far. Too many hitters neglect preparation to hit the off-speed pitch. As a result, their weakness is soon discovered by the pitcher and exploited. A hitter should strive to become complete so that no one area can be easily attacked by a pitcher. Taking the time to hit breaking balls improves many facets of a hitter. The hitter should feel that he can't come out of his hitting position until the ball is on top of him. This results in increased body control. Also, performing a number of reps at curveballs and sliders improves hand-eye coordination, which makes it seem easier to get good contact on fastballs. Hitters gain confidence that they can hit anything.

Focus   To help players recognize what the ball is doing, process the information, and correctly hit or take the pitch.

Setup   A coach works with individual hitters. Set up home plate at one end of the cage. The hitter is in his normal position in the box; the coach is at the opposite side of the plate.

Procedure   This drill is similar to the traditional soft-toss drill. We add a variation that forces the hitter to improve his ability to recognize the pitch. To challenge the hitter, the coach randomly changes the toss. The coach has three options:

1. Toss a ball with no spin.
2. Toss a ball with spin.
3. Hold the ball as a fake.

The hitter reacts to the coach's choices. At a ball with spin, the hitter takes an aggressive swing. Balls with no spin he lets pass. For a fake, the hitter completes a proper stride but takes no swing, holding the hitting position.

Coaching Points   Use this drill as a supplement to the traditional soft-toss drill to add a higher level of concentration. Both speed of recognition and body control are improved. Emphasize avoiding inefficient movements. Hitters should swing only at balls with spin.

75 STRIKE ZONE RECOGNITION DRILL

Focus   To work on recognizing each pitch as a ball or a strike.

Setup   A coach works with individual hitters. Set up home plate at one end of the cage. The coach throws from 45 to 60 feet away. This drill can also be done on the field.

Procedure   The coach throws any type of pitch he wants to the hitter. The hitter is in his stance preparing to load up and stride. No swings are taken. Once the pitch has been thrown, the hitter says yes if the pitch is a strike or no if the pitch is a ball. The hitter takes his stride in a normal sequence and holds his hitting position once the ball has passed.

Coaching Points   By removing the swing, this drill encourages a hitter to concentrate on seeing the ball and deciding whether it's a strike or a ball. Too many hitters take for granted that they know the strike zone. This drill reinforces and improves knowledge, leading to a more selective hitter. All good hitters can control the strike zone; this drill improves that ability.

This is a simple drill. Results are higher batting averages and increased walk totals. As hitters get adept at the drill, they should say yes or no with the ball farther and farther away. The sooner hitters can make the distinction between a strike and a ball, the longer they have to react with a swing. As hitters become advanced from 60 feet, slowly reduce the distance to make the drill more difficult. Constant challenges lead to constant improvement. Eventually the hitter develops a disciplined approach.

76 TENNIS BALL GAME

Focus   To put hitters in as many different situations as possible to improve their recognition and adjustments.

Setup   Ideally, you'll have two equal-sized teams with no more than four players per side, but you can use more or fewer as suits your situation. You'll need these materials: as many tennis balls as you can find, a plastic garbage can, a backstop, and bases. Set up home plate at a 45-degree angle about 180 feet from the left-field foul pole. Put bases 60 feet apart and the mound 45 feet from home plate. The outfield wall and foul territory fence serve as the home run fence. While this is one recommended setup, any location with an outfield will work fine.

Procedure   Do the drill with two teams of equal size. The rules of the game go this way:

1. Two outs per inning.

2. A ball over the fence is a home run, a ball in the air off the fence is a triple, one hop off the fence is a double, any ground ball that reaches the fence is a single, and anything else is an out.
3. There's no base running by the players, only ghost runners who advance the same number of bases as the batter.
4. The garbage can serves as the umpire; any ball not swung at that hits the can is a strike.
5. Normal counts apply.

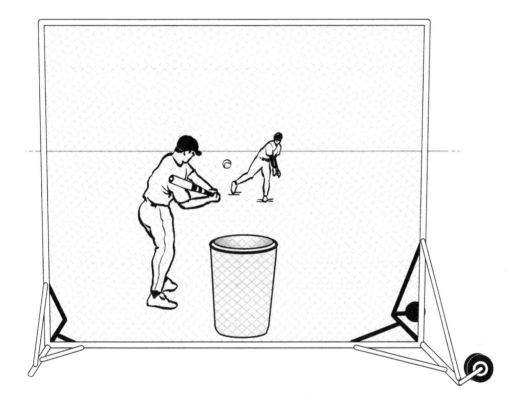

Coaching Points   This drill gives hitters several at-bats in a short time. Because of the high degree of difficulty of the drill, they get instant feedback on the quality of their swing. Tennis balls are used for several reasons. They're smaller than a baseball so improve hand-eye coordination. They are easier on the arm for the pitchers, which leads to many more reps. They can be used anywhere with no risk of injury or damage. The pitcher should throw his best array of fastballs, curveballs, change-ups, and other pitches. From this distance, the equivalent of 90 mile-per-hour fastballs can be thrown. This reaction time teaches the hitter to be short and gives him instant feedback when there is lunging, upper cutting, or other flaws in technique. You can incorporate many other drills into this one, including Look for Location (see page 128) and other drills from this chapter.

Focus To give hitters chances to visualize exactly where each located pitch should be hit.

Setup A coach works with individual hitters. You'll need three tees. Set up home plate at one end of the cage. Set up the first tee on the inside corner at the front of the plate. Set up the second tee in the middle of the plate. Set up the third tee on the outside corner at the back of the plate. All three tees should be level to allow a swing through a ball on any one of them.

Procedure The batter sets up his stance in relation to the plate. The coach is on the opposite side of the plate in position to place balls on a tee. Once the hitter is ready, he closes his eyes. The coach places a ball on the inside, middle, or outside tee. Once the ball is placed on a tee, the coach says, "Now." The hitter loads up his hands and body. As the front foot is about to hit the ground, he opens his eyes. He identifies which tee the ball is on and instantly drives the ball in the correct direction.

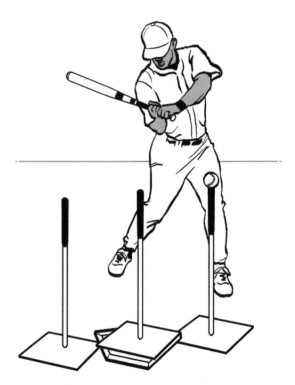

Coaching Points Many young hitters try to hit every ball at the same contact point. Many start their swing before they know what they want to do with the ball. This drill helps them learn to change their point of contact. Hitters learn contact for pitches thrown inside, down the middle, or outside. They learn to see and identify a pitch before taking a swing. Have hitters occasionally open their eyes with no ball on the tee. Check the result. No swing should be taken, and the hitter should remain in proper hitting position. Repetitions of this drill give hitters a feel for where to make contact on each pitch and reinforce the importance of pitch identification.

Chapter 10

Bunting Drills

Gordon Gillespie

A lot of baseball fans, players, and coaches ask how today's game compares to the game of the 1920s, '30s, and '40s. What did the old timers do differently? One of the major differences is today's lack of execution of the bunting game. In all of baseball, professional and amateur, management and players don't place enough importance on the bunting game; consequently, players today can't execute this phase of the game. Many players can't bunt for base hits or sacrifice at critical times to get runners into scoring position. In failing to develop a good bunting game, teams lose the other values of hitting that come from bunting concepts. The threat of the drag bunt keeps the flanks (third and first basemen) playing close to the hitter, which increases the chance of driving the ball past them. In sacrifice bunt situations, good bunters can slash hit from a bunting stance, another way of taking advantage of a drawn-in infield. The ability to drag bunt, sacrifice bunt, and slash hit from a bunting stance can increase a player's batting by 100 points. Yes, 100 points! If our teams can bunt, we have the weaponry to attack and score even on excellent defensive teams or in adverse weather conditions, with wind blowing in or when it's cold and wet.

Bunting in baseball is as important as blocking in football. In football, if you can't block, you won't move the football, you won't get your offense going, and you'll lose. In baseball, especially in Major League Baseball, there's a "ho-hum, don't ask me to bunt" attitude. In pro baseball you actually hear players say, "I don't get paid to bunt the ball." The manager—usually the lowest paid person on the team—has a hard time convincing the millionaires that they're getting paid to win games, be it by the home run or the squeeze play.

Here's a typical baseball scenario from pro or college ball: Runners are on first and second, with no outs in a close game. The batter looks to the third base coach for the sign, hoping it's not the bunt sign. But it is; he sees clearly that the bunt is on. From a bunter's stance, the batter takes the first pitch right down the middle, pulling the bat backward for strike one. He again looks at the third base coach and sees that the bunt is still on. On the next pitch, he makes a feeble attempt to bunt and tips a foul ball back to the screen. With two strikes, the bunt sign is off, so finally "mighty Casey" can swing away. The infield has moved back to normal depth. The batter hits a hard ground ball into a 6-4-3 double play. The next batter flies out. The team loses 3 to 2.

Does it really happen that way? Only all the time! In another scenario for the same situation, the batter wants to execute the sacrifice and knows how. He does so, and the runners advance to second and third. The infield draws in tight. The next hitter hits a hard ground ball through the drawn-in infield, scoring the two runners. Now the final score is 4 to 3 good guys. Simple execution of the sacrifice bunt made the following hitter's chances of getting a ground ball through the infield about 50 percent. Smart coaches and intelligent players like those odds.

Treat the bunting game as the foundation of your offensive weaponry.

Treat the bunting game as the foundation of your offensive weaponry. There are so many things you can do with a strong bunting game—the drag bunt, the threat of the drag to keep the flanks up, the sacrifice bunt, the slash hit from the bunt stance, the safety squeeze, the suicide squeeze play. Each of these places tremendous psychological pressure on the defense, which can totally upset the pitcher and cause errors by the opposing team. Bill Madlock, former Major League all-star, related that the year he won the National League batting championship by one percentage point, he was successful in 22 out of 23 drag bunt attempts over the year. Twenty-two hits adds quite a few points to your batting average. And I bet some other balls he hit passed by a drawn-in third baseman.

On the other side, think of the great power hitters at the plate and how the flank men play them two steps into the outfield grass. These hitters blister balls that get caught, and they're thrown out at first base. I'm reminded of Ted Williams and the Ted Williams' shift. Opposing teams played three infielders on the right side, all in the outfield grass. Williams would smash his hits, but the infielders flagged them down and threw him out. If Ted had been able to get the flanks up or considered bunting, he could have hit .500 instead of his measly .406. (What a hitter!)

Here are some key coaching expressions to use when teaching drag bunt concepts:

1. Bunt on the chalk. If you bunt foul, bunt again (that is, if you don't have two strikes when you attempt to drag).

2. Keep the flanks in tight with the bunt threat. Then drive the ball past them.

3. Bunt first, then run. Many bunt attempts are unsuccessful because the batter tries to run first and does not get the ball in good location. A great bunter, with speed, can bunt for a .300 average. There's no question that in every 10 at-bats, he can bunt successfully 3 times. If he gets 2 hits in his remaining 7 at-bats, that's a .500 batting average. When's the last time anyone hit .500?

4. What's your 30 time? Drag bunting is married to a stopwatch. Your 30 time is how long it takes you to run the 90 feet from home to first base. As soon as you start timing your players out of the box, I guarantee you'll see an improvement in their 30 time. In track, sprinters spend hours practicing getting out of the starting blocks. How much time do ball players spend? When I talk to my players about the importance of getting out of the box, I say, "You as quick as Cool Papa Bell." Cool Papa played way back when in the Negro League. He was probably baseball's fastest human ever. They say he could circle the bases in 12 seconds. That's not running, that's flying. Cool Papa must have hit .500 every season. Remember the name. I love it. Cool Papa Bell, the human jet.

5. Study the pitcher. Know his follow-through and pitch selection. When the opportunity arises, always drag or push bunt opposite his follow-through.

Look for a ball away from you to bunt so you can get out of the box quickly. Curve balls and sliders away are ideal pitches to drag bunt. The great bunters have great pitch anticipation. They know what to expect from pitchers and look for "a pitch to get the ball on the chalk."

6. Use visualization. This is extremely important in all phases of hitting. Good bunters visualize opposing pitchers and see themselves bunting successfully. They can see the spin on the ball, the location, the bat meeting the ball, the dash to first, the foot touching the front of the base. The more you visualize, the more successful you'll be.

7. Practice game awareness. Game awareness, game smarts—the great ones have it because they train their minds to concentrate every moment of every game. In the bunting game they know the strengths and weaknesses of the third baseman, the fielding ability of the pitcher and the first baseman. They watch how other players are being played, and when they step into the batter's box, they know where the third baseman is playing. They take full advantage of what the offense is giving them.

8. Learn from women's fast-pitch softball. I commend the softball coaches who have taught the drag bunt so well. Some women can "feather" the bat, almost throwing the bat at the ball. They get to first base as fast as Cool Papa. If you can train your hitters to get on top of those "fastball risers" and hit hard grounders, they'll hit a ton against a drawn-in infield. Just two infielders, the shortstop and the first baseman, are trying to cover the whole infield. Not easy.

9. Box running with the drag—work for "get-away speed." Shorten the bases and concentrate on bunt location and the first six strides to first base. Use each base as a home base and bunt and break to the next base. Four pitchers are needed (positioned players act as pitchers, each one pitching up close to their plate). Change positions every few minutes. In 10 minutes, each player gets 20 drags on the chalk and quick starts out of the box. Use Wiffle balls or rubber balls on gym floor practice sessions. Focus on location and speed out of the box.

10. Drag one, hit one (hit and run). This is a Wee Willie Keeler drill. "Hit them where they ain't," was Willie's motto. This is a two-person drill. We use Wiffle balls from close range. Bunt one on the chalk, then hit the next one on the ground behind the runner (hit and run). In 10 minutes, hitters get 25 of each.

Wee Willie and Ty Cobb played at the same time. Cobb had a great concept at the plate. He was a great bunter with superb speed, and he hit with his hands separated on the bat. His top hand was about 10 to 12 inches above his bottom hand. This gave Ty great bat control. A lefty, he slashed balls to left field at will. When he wanted to pull the ball, he slid his top hand down to the bottom hand and pulled it. It's no wonder he led the major leagues in hitting year after year. A great slash hitter with a lifetime average of .350+ over a 20-year career—what a ball player!

11. Bunting in the springtime. Teams taught to use the bunting game as a major weapon in their offensive arsenal are especially successful in springtime weather conditions. In most places spring is cold, windy, and wet; infield grass is soft, and the base path is a little slow along the third base side. These conditions aid the bunting attack. The wind and cold are other factors. Up north, a northwest wind is often blowing in at the batters—not conducive to playing long ball. The bunting game is a key factor in such conditions. In Chicago, Wrigley Field is supposedly a hitters' paradise, but the wind blows in 60 percent of the time from Lake Michigan. Former Cubs manager Jim Lefebvre was once upset with his team because they couldn't make things happen offensively when playing into the wind. The Cubs lost a lot of 2-1 and 1-0 games during Jim's tenure. He tried to get his players to change their tactics and was making progress when upper management decided to make a change. But we can all take heed of Jim's words about his team: "You must know how to attack and win, even when the weather and wind are against you."

12. Drag bunt to advance runners with one out. A fine offensive weapon is the drag bunt with one out to advance a runner or runners into scoring position with the possibility of being safe at first. A great drag bunt can give you the best of both worlds. Many times (especially in bad weather) the pitcher or third baseman will slip and make a poor throw down the right-field line. Such a play can really upset a pitcher, causing him to lose it and allow a big inning. Even if the defense gets the runner at first base, we have still advanced the runner into scoring position, so a base hit gets us back in the game or puts us ahead.

13. Drag bunting in the big games. Tournament games, conference championships, playoff times, the World Series—the bigger the game, the more tension for the players. You see this most easily on defense. The bunting game brings out the worst in pressure game defenses. Players are more apt to fumble bunts or throw them away. Many playoff games have been won by players bunting into a tense infield.

Sacrifice Bunting

Bunting starts in the mind. Each player must convince himself that bunting can be the foundation of his hitting game. Sacrifice bunting is the essence of team play. Each player must be taught that giving up his at-bat to advance runners into scoring position is truly being a team player. Isn't this supposed to be what it's all about? The team first rather than me all the time? The attitude starts with the top man. That's why coaches have team members acknowledge the sacrifice bunter with high fives when he returns to the dugout, just as though he'd hit a home run. With this kind of attitude, players go to home plate hoping for the bunt sign. Like offensive linemen in football who won't let their quarterback get sacked, bunters are low-glamour heroes.

Another part of the sacrifice bunt concept and its importance to team offense is the slash hit from a bunting stance. This is not nearly as difficult as it might appear. Think of Ty Cobb with the divided hands slashing or pulling the ball. It's exactly the same concept. Players must grasp the full meaning of what they're trying to accomplish. There's a tremendous advantage in being able to hit from the bunt stance. The advantage starts with the drawn-in infield. Every infielder has moved in shallow and is playing out of position, so to speak. Only two infielders are left to cover the entire infield, as both flank men are thinking and covering the bunt. Another advantage is that the batter can guess fastball. Pitchers are taught to throw high fastballs in bunt situations, so hitters usually know what's coming. They can get on top of the ball and slash it through the infield.

Another excellent offensive concept in bunt situations is to start the runner on first base. The shortstop must cover the attempted steal at second base, and with the third baseman up 45 feet from home plate, no one's left on the left side of the infield. The hitter can slash hit through that area. This is an excellent hit-and-run play from a sacrifice situation.

Best Method of Executing the Safety Squeeze

The runner at third is attacking home 100 percent of the time, and has been taught to get a great start with a walking lead-off. The batter in the box has received a drag bunt sign before the first pitch is delivered. The runner has seen the sign and is looking for the drag. The batter can drag any pitch he wants to. It doesn't have to be the next pitch. The walking lead with the drag is successful 95 percent of the time, even against a drawn-in infield. We spend a lot of time on this concept and much prefer it to the suicide squeeze.

Play Your Game, Coach

Much criticism has been aimed at coaches who bunt with a five run lead or better. The criticism might be warranted if the opposition is truly a poor team with virtually no chance of coming back in the game. A worthy opponent is always a threat to come back and beat you with a big inning. You never have enough runs against the good teams. Coaches, play your game! I hope that bunting is a big part of your offense and that you bunt whenever you wish. The idea on offense is to score runs, not worry about the other team's feelings. To avoid scoring runs is an insult to your opponents—you're telling them they're so bad they'll never catch up and might as well go home. Remember, coaches: Don't rest easy with your early leads of more than four or five runs. Continue to attack. The game ain't over 'til it's over.

Hitting Concepts

The hitter should be thinking these kinds of thoughts about his abilities and possibilities:

1. I must know my physical capabilities and hit accordingly. If I don't have power, then I'll hit line drives, spray the ball, walk, bunt, and get on base. I'll use all my assets. I won't try to hit for power and reduce my value to the team. On the other hand, if I *can* hit for power, why not increase my value even more by learning the bunting game? They're looking for a long ball, and I can lay down a bunt.
2. I have got to be a tough out at the plate. I need to be aggressive and mean. I'll wipe out all fear of getting hit by the ball. If fear affects my at-bat, I might as well steer clear of the batter's box.
3. I won't ever concede to the pitcher. I won't give him a psychological edge. If I think for a moment that he's especially fast or that his slider is great or that his curve is unhittable, I have lost the battle. He has won!
4. I must get psychologically up every time I go to the plate. When adrenaline is flowing, everything becomes clearer. I want to see the ball coming to home plate in slow motion. I want to see the seams and think that ball's a balloon I'm going to smash and pop.

78   DRAG ON THE CHALK

Focus   To bunt the ball about 20 to 25 feet, as close to the foul line as possible.

Setup   You'll need three players for this drill and at least six baseballs. A pitcher throws from 40 feet to the batter; the third player fields the bunts and tosses them back to the pitcher.

Procedure   The pitcher throws the ball hard to the batter and can mix in some breaking balls to make the drill gamelike. The pitcher should have six or more balls at his disposal to keep the drill moving. Each batter bunts 10 balls, then rotates. I suggest running this drill in the outfield along the warning track using the outfield fence as a backstop. Besides bunting the ball on the third-base line, alternating batters can work on the push bunt (right-handed hitter) or drag bunt (left-handed hitter) between the pitcher and first baseman.

Coaching Points   The drag bunter bunts the ball as close to the foul line as possible, about 20 to 25 feet down the line. This location and distance make it very difficult for the catcher and third baseman to throw the runner out.

The main teaching points are setting the bat at the proper angle for good location, sliding the top hand toward the trademark on the bat, keeping the barrel of the bat higher than the handle, having soft hands, and catching the ball on the barrel rather than pushing the barrel at the ball.

A major point of instruction, is to get the body low. Right-handed hitters, as they drop the right leg back, should almost have that knee on the ground. We use the term "genuflect," as if kneeling in church. Left-handed hitters also stay real low on that back knee. Two things to repeat to the bunters: "Bunt first, then run" and "bunt on the chalk" (of the third-base line). Emphasize low body position, which brings the batter's eyes level with the ball. As the batter drags the ball, he takes a few steps toward first base, always practicing his "30-yard dash."

Modifications   Players can compete in this drill by putting a glove on the line at the proper distance and seeing who can bunt the ball into the glove the most times. Each player bunts 10 balls and then rotates.

79   DRAG AND DASH

Focus   To practice bunting techniques, including getting out of the box efficiently and exploding down the baseline with proper running form.

Setup   Set up a four-base diamond with bases 45 feet apart. Four "bunters" are at the bases; four "pitchers" are in the center of the diamond, kneeling down. Each pitcher has several balls at his side. A third group of four are "catchers" and stand about 10 feet behind their base to retrieve balls that get away.

Procedure   In this drill, players drag bunt, explode out of the box, and sprint to the next base. I suggest having one group bunt around the bases twice and then switch roles with pitchers or catchers. Hitters will have done eight drags and eight dashes to first base. Emphasize proper tagging of first base. Tagging the front of the base with the head down and a good forward lean is the proper form.

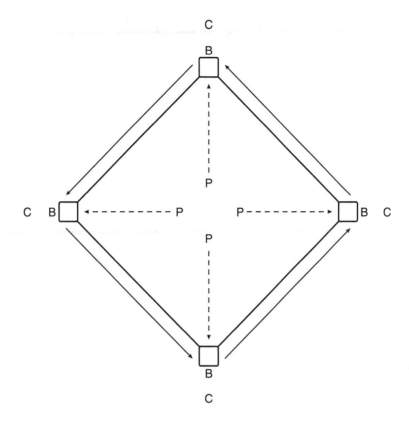

Coaching Points   Teach getting the body low with a great forward lean, pumping the arms, and relaxing the hands. With proper technique and repetition, players really improve their running time to first base.

Modifications   If you're working indoors in a gym, use Wiffle balls or pickle balls. Pickle balls have a heavier coat and smaller holes than the normal Wiffle ball. These balls won't damage the basketball floor or the lights in the gym.

80   DRAG, DASH, AND BEAT THE CLOCK

Focus   To determine the running time from home to first base for every player on the team.

Setup   Form a box with four bases 90 feet apart.

Procedure   Same as the Drag and Dash drill. Four bunters are at the bases; four pitchers are in the center of the diamond, kneeling down. Each pitcher has several balls at his side. A third group of four are catchers and stand about 10 feet behind their base to retrieve balls that get away. In this drill, players run 30 yards instead of 15 yards, as in the Drag and Dash. Use four stopwatches to time each bunter on his bunt and dash to first base. Emphasize good bunting form, a quick start out of the box, a glance at the location of the bunt, and tagging the front of first base with the head down. We use the expressions "nod the bag" (with the head) and "break the tape" (with the chest). After players are past first base, they quickly check foul territory to see if the ball got away from the first baseman; if so, the runner advances to second base.

Coaching Points   Football players are known for their 40-yard dash time. We want our players to know their 30-yard dash time, which of course is the distance from home to first. There are two ways a player can gain running speed. The first is to beat another player in a dash; the other is to beat the clock and improve running time. No baseball coach should be without his stopwatch. The stopwatch aids in all facets of the game, especially the short game of bunting and running. If you time your players frequently on the drag bunt and 30-yard dash, you'll see excellent improvement in speed.

81   DRAG AND THE WALKING LEAD FROM THIRD BASE

Focus   To practice the walking lead from third base.

Setup   Form a box with four bases 90 feet apart. Only two pitchers are needed for this drill; they should be alternated with other players.

Procedure   At two of the bases (first and third), two runners practice a walking lead from third base; at the other two bases (home and second), bunters execute drag bunts to score the runner from third base.

   This drill develops a valuable weapon in offensive baseball. The batter becomes the runner at the next base and leads off accordingly. Players go around a few times and then rotate with the pitchers or catchers. Stress proper footwork in the walking lead and proper drag technique for the batter. Use stopwatches to time the runner running from third and the batter running to first base.

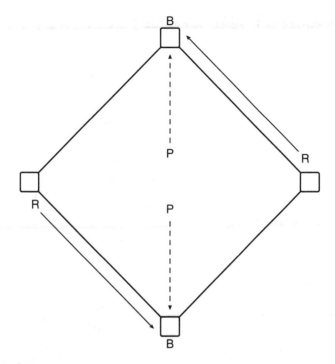

Coaching Points   Bunting and base running are certainly a marriage; you shouldn't teach bunting without a heavy emphasis on base running. We spend a lot of time practicing the walking lead from third base. The walking lead is meant to give a running start to the runner on third as he breaks on the hitter's contact with the ball. We use the drag bunt and create a kind of safety squeeze. The runner does not break for home until ball contact—a variation of the suicide squeeze, in which the runner breaks on the delivery of the ball from the pitcher.

Practice this drill often and you'll see significant technique improvement. We attack home plate 100 percent of the time on all contact. We find we're far more aggressive in our base running when we know we're "going home all the time."

Focus To bunt the ball into fair territory, 3 to 5 feet from the foul lines and 20 feet from home plate.

Setup This is a three-man drill. One player pitches to a bunter from 35 to 40 feet; the third player is fielding the bunts and returning balls to the pitcher.

Procedure Each player bunts 10 balls and then rotates. Emphasize the bunter running a few strides with each bunt attempt to get the feel of getting out of the box after bunting. All sacrifice rules apply.

Coaching Points The bunter wants to be skilled at bunting the ball on the left side or right side with equal efficiency. He should fully understand his role as a sacrifice bunter—this is most important. Once the batter appreciates his role, the bunt becomes a lot easier. The idea of sacrificing an at-bat for the good of the team should make all players want to bunt the ball. Unfortunately, it doesn't for some players.

The important mechanics of the sac bunt are to get in front of the batter's box, put your foot on the chalk in the front of the box, slide your top hand up to the trademark of the bat, and slide your bottom hand up the bat handle six to eight inches. The top hand should have a loose finger-tip grip so that the bat gives on contact and deadens the ball on contact. To make sure they bunt down on the ball, hitters keep the barrel of the bat 45 degrees higher than the handle. The back foot should be brought up almost parallel to the front foot. Some coaches (including me) prefer to bring the back foot only halfway up; the body is now at a 45-degree position rather than a complete 90-degree turn. The knees are bent, the hands are extended in front of the body as far as possible, the bat angle is set, and the eyes and head are almost at bat level. I like to have our bunters think they are making a pool shot ("eight ball in the side pocket"). Bunting is an art. Thinking they're Minnesota Fats up there might help them attain proper body position.

Remind your bunters, "Bunt first, then run—not vice versa." Tell them to get the bunt into a good location and then sprint to first base. A lot of bunters forget to apply good running techniques. We strive to make running a big part of our short game, which is obvious in these drills.

Focus   To bunt good bunts or pepper-like ground balls through the infield or to an infielder. Fielders practice good communication.

Setup   This is another three-man drill, with one batter and two fielders at pepper game depth (30 to 35 feet from the hitter). You'll need at least a dozen balls at each three-man station. Use the outfield fence as a backstop.

Procedure   One of the fielders acts as the pitcher and tells the bunter to bunt or slash left or right. He calls out, "Bunt-right," "Bunt-left," "Slash right," or "Slash left."

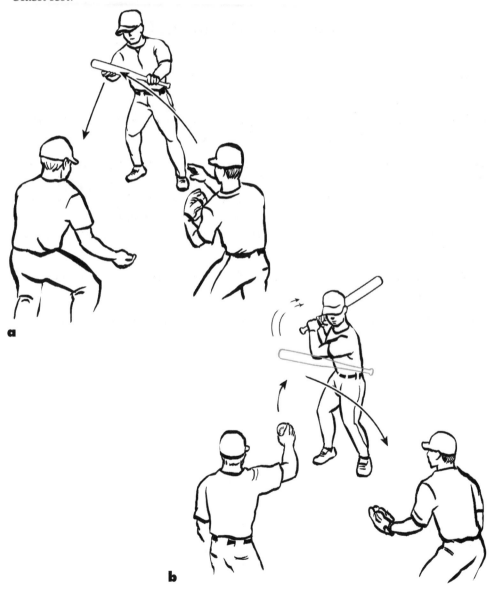

a

b

Coaching Points   Players bunt the ball on the chalk into fair territory, 3 to 5 feet from the foul lines and 20 feet from home plate. The slash hit is when the batter assumes a bunting stance and then slides his hands together, wheels into a hitting posture, and slashes a hard ground ball through the drawn-in infield. This is an effective short game weapon. Players who master this technique can produce a lot of base hits in bunt situations. Have young players start with hands apart on the bat and then slide their hands together for the slash hit, like Ty Cobb. Six bunts, six slashes, and out (rotate). When slashing, players try to hit one-hoppers to the open fielder, as in a pepper game. Pepper is one of baseball's best drills and shows the importance of the short game.

84   DRAG ONE HIT AND RUN

Focus   To drag bunt down one foul line, push bunt down the other, and follow with a hit and run.

Setup   One batter, two fielders at pepper game depth (30 to 35 feet from the hitter). Do this drill in the outfield, using the outfield fence as a backstop.

Procedure   The batter drags a bunt down on the foul line and pushes a bunt down the other line; then he hits a one-hopper to the opposite field. The sequence is drag one, push one, then hit and run. Players position so that the opposite-field hit and run is in the proper location. On the drag bunts and push bunts, emphasize the importance of getting out of the box quickly.

Coaching Points   Timing, contact, and bunting fundamentals are important in this drill, along with sound fielding fundamentals.

Modifications   If running the drill in a gym, use a Wiffle ball or pickle ball.

Focus   To cushion the ball with the bat or "catch" the ball with the barrel of the bat.

Setup   You'll need two or more pitchers and two or more bunters to do this drill.

Procedure   To emphasize the importance of feathering the ball onto the bat—sort of a "catching" action—tape a glove onto the barrel of the bat. This gives players a sense of the top hand actually giving a little when contact is made for the bunt. The proper technique is more like catching a baseball than hitting a baseball. Most young players have difficulty with this fundamental, and sometimes the difficulty carries over into high school and college ball. This drill is more of a demonstration tool than an activity; it teaches an important concept that players need to hear and see often.

Modifications   The glove on the bat helps players visualize what you're looking for. Some coaches have players put a glove on their "barrel hand" instead of using a bat. They then catch balls and roll them to a bunting location. This emphasizes the importance of the top hand giving on the bunt.

Focus   To make contact with the ball on the bunt; to break from third base as soon as the pitcher's stride foot hits the ground.

Setup   Two bunters and two runners are at the bases; two pitchers are in the center of the diamond, kneeling down. Each pitcher has several balls at his side. A third group of four players are catchers and stand about 10 feet behind each base to retrieve balls that get away.

Procedure   Two players are base runners ready to attack home off the pitcher's delivery. Two players are bunters who quickly assume a bunting stance as the ball is delivered. Bunters must get their bat on the ball and lay a bunt on the ground. Runners break for home when the practice pitchers' stride foot hits the ground. The mentality of the bunter is, "I must make contact; I must get the ball on the ground." As we know, the suicide squeeze has won many games and championships throughout baseball history.

Modification   You can run this drill with as few as three players (bunter, runner, pitcher).

Chapter 11

Base-Running Drills

Rich Alday

Base running can help win or lose more games than any other phase of the offense. Good base running can create and prolong rallies. Poor base running, when fundamentals are not followed doggedly, is often a rally killer.

Solid base running maximizes the efforts of the offensive team. Aggressive and smart base runners put intense pressure on the opposition, sometimes enough pressure to cause mistakes. Alert and energetic base runners are formidable foes. Sometimes the difference between safe and out is a 10th of a second, a turn, a lead, a reaction, or a plan of action. Each plays a part in the base-running game.

Players should work persistently on their base running. Even players without great speed can become very good base runners. An aggressive but smart base runner puts pressure on the pitcher, catcher, infielders, and outfielders. All defensive positions are challenged by good base runners.

When a player is on base, the pitcher's concentration can't be singular. He must be concerned about the base runner as well as the hitter. A smart and aggressive base runner demands a good deal of the pitcher's attention. Both pitch selection and location of pitchers are sometimes affected by the base runner. If the pitcher gets too involved with the base runner, the hitter gains an edge.

Often the catcher's pitch calling becomes more predictable with runners on base. If there's a speedy runner at first, the catcher will probably call more fastballs because of the potential steal. Or he might call a pitchout, which often gives the hitter an advantage.

A good base runner can cause infielders to move out of their position sooner or force them to adjust their positioning to cover a base. This creates holes for the hitter. Fast runners force infielders to play closer to home plate and hurry their throws.

Aggressive base running also affects outfielders. They rush to get to a ball and consequently misplay it. An aggressive base runner can even alter an outfielder's normal playing position.

We tell our players to try to gain and keep an advantage on the base paths. We teach them these tips and tactics:

1. Be aggressive but smart on the bases.
2. Learn to read the pitcher (not only on base but from the dugout as well).
3. Don't fear failing. Don't be reluctant or hesitant.
4. Always think one base ahead.
5. Match base running in practice to game situations.

87   COACH-BAG-COACH

Focus   To recognize the coach's signal at third base, round the bag, and return on the coach's verbal and hand signals.

Setup   All team members should practice this procedure. The drill is best done with four to eight base runners at second base. Other players can be involved in the defensive part of the drill if the ball is live. Form a line of four to eight runners near second base on the outfield grass. The player at the front quickly moves into the baseline and becomes the runner at second base.

You can run this drill with or without defensive players. Use the playing field. You'll need a third-base coach.

Procedure   The four to eight players in line near second base take turns as a base runner at second base. Each runner should repeat the drill as a base runner several times. You can time the drill or have each player do a set number of runs.

The coach signals each base runner to round third base. As the runner proceeds toward third and approaches the base, he looks at the third-base coach, looks at the base, and then looks at the coach again. The coach will then send the runner home or have him stop and return to third. During this process, the third-base coach might bring the runner down the line toward home plate or have the runner hold and then go either way. The player follows the coach's instruction.

Progress is measured by evaluating the runner's reactions to the hand signals and verbal commands of the third-base coach. Communication is a prerequisite to good base running. This is a bread-and-butter communication drill.

Coaching Points   Communication and reactions to both verbal and hand signals are the coaching points. At the same time, proper contact of the base and sound base-running techniques are repeated.

If a ball is hit in front of the runner, the runner decides whether to advance to third base. Our rule for the base runner and the third-base coach is to avoid making the first or third out of the inning at that base.

Modifications   You can run this drill during intrasquad games or in competitive live drills.

88   BALL IN THE DIRT

Focus   To study the pitcher's delivery, his release point, and the flight of the ball as it travels toward home plate; to react to a low pitch that bounces in the dirt.

Setup   All players should develop in this area of base running. Break the squad into offensive and partial defensive units. The defensive outfield and the third baseman become base runners and remain in that capacity throughout the drill. The offensive and defensive units alternate as base runners. A pitcher initiates the action by delivering a pitch to the plate.

Procedure   A group of four to eight players alternate as base runners for this drill at first base. The key to reading a ball in the dirt is to judge the ball in flight from the pitcher's hand. If the runner tries to get a jump based on the catcher dropping to his knees, the read comes too late.

Once the pitcher or coach throws the pitch, the runner shuffles off, reading the flight of the ball. If he thinks the ball is going to be in the dirt, he continues to shuffle and then sprints and slides into second base. If the runner hesitates, *he should not go!*

Coaching Points   Make sure each base runner learns to read the flight of the ball and reacts to each low pitch. Success or failure is easily measured by the runner's reaction to the pitch.

Modifications   More than one group of base runners can be involved. By adding the third baseman to the defensive unit, another group of base runners can perform this drill from second base at the same time the runners at first are executing their portion of the drill. This drill can also be modified to provide base-running practice at each base—all at the same time. Designate one group as the "hot" group while the other two work independently. Those two groups perform the proper fundamentals, but the defensive unit reacts only to the "hot" group of runners.

Focus To develop the skills needed to successfully execute the delay steal under game conditions.

Setup All team members participate. Small numbers of three to four players or large numbers including the entire team can be accommodated in this drill. If using large numbers, more than one runner at a time can participate. A practice area is needed to practice the skills. The base path from first to second base is the ideal setting. Base runners form a line on or near the outfield grass in line with the cut out (normally 13 feet) at first base. The player at the front of the line moves into the baseline and takes a normal lead. When the pitcher commits to home plate, the runner executes the play. Each player in line takes a turn and repeats the routine several times.

Procedure The delay steal is usually effective when middle infielders don't move toward second base after the ball gets by the batter or if the catcher is lazy getting the ball returned to the pitcher. Even below-average runners can steal a base on the delay steal in these scenarios.

Each runner in line takes his normal lead at first base; when the pitcher releases the ball to home plate, the runner takes three shuffle steps and then sprints to second base. Taking three full shuffle steps develops the proper timing. The runner has covered distance toward second but has not yet committed to that base. If the middle infielders remain in, or near, their position, the base runner has the edge.

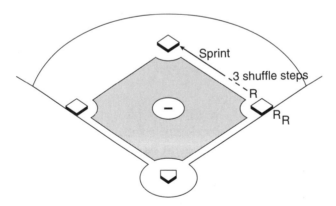

Coaching Points Observe the lead, the three-step shuffle, and the timing of each base runner. Success is measured in these areas. Timing is extremely important. The three shuffle steps create the proper timing. If the catcher is alert and the middle infielders move toward second base, the delay steal will probably not be strategically sound with average or below-average runners. Each runner should be ready at any time during the game or course of the season to take advantage of situations as they arise.

Modifications You can practice this drill with a pitcher simulating the throw to home plate, but it's more effective when the pitcher and the entire defensive infield is live during the drill. This drill can be practiced during intrasquad games.

90   LEAD AT THIRD BASE

Focus To practice taking proper leads at third base; to practice the method and direction of the lead and the return to the base.

Setup If working in stations, this drill accommodates four to eight players. Use the playing field. Form a line of players in foul territory between the dugout and third base. Defensively, the third baseman, catchers, and pitchers are the positions involved in the drill. If tag-ups are included, outfielders should take their respective positions.

Procedure The player at the front of the line moves to the base and takes a lead. If the pitcher is in the stretch position, the lead should be equal to the distance the third baseman stations himself from the base. That runner should lead off in foul territory and return to that base in fair territory. When the runner returns to the base in fair territory, the catcher has difficulty determining the distance between the runner and the base. Further, the runner's position increases the difficulty for the third baseman to make the catch because the catcher must throw over the runner or to one side.

    When the ball is delivered to home plate, the runner takes two steps, beginning with a crossover step, timing the pitch. His right foot lands as the ball is hit or missed. He then reacts according to what develops. On a short passed ball, he reacts in relation to the distance between the ball and the catcher. If the ball is caught, he returns to the base.

    Tagging up on fly balls should also be included in this drill. If the ball is in fair territory or in foul territory down the right-field foul line, tag the base with the left foot. If the ball is in foul territory down the left-field foul line, tag with the right foot.

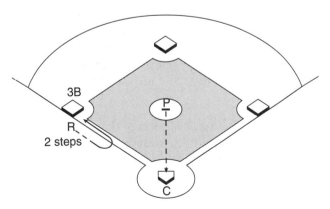

Coaching Points   The direction of the lead and return route to the base are important focal points. Coordinating the lead with the timing of the pitch to the plate is fundamental to the success of this base-running situation.

Modifications   The lead and two steps starting with a crossover can be practiced with more than one runner at a time.

91   REACTING TO THE COACH

Focus   To learn and understand when, how, and why the base runner must pick up the base coach when the ball is behind the runner.

Setup   You should do this drill on the infield. You'll need at least four runners at first base; this allows each runner to take a turn and have the chance to get back to the end of the line for more than one turn. Using four to eight runners is ideal. Have them form a line at first base. Each takes repeated turns at base running.

Procedure   The line should extend toward the first-base dugout. The player at the front of the line takes a lead at first base and reacts as though the pitcher is delivering the ball to the plate. The coach claps his hands to indicate that the ball is hit behind the runner into right field, which takes the ball out of the view of the base runner.

The base runner looks in and picks up the base coach about 13 feet before reaching second base. He gets the coach's information and looks as he steps on the inside corner of second base. As his foot contacts second base, he should once again pick up the base coach.

In this drill, the third-base coach beckons the runner to advance to third base or signals for the stop or the return to second base. As the base runner advances to third his eyes must stay in contact with the third-base coach, who directs him to advance to home, stop at third, round the base, or round the base and then return to it.

Coaching Points   All members of the team profit from this drill. The major points of concern are (1) looking in to pick up the base coach prior to reaching second base; (2) properly contacting second base; (3) picking up the third-base coach the moment the foot touches the base; (4) reacting to the information from the third-base coach by going back to second base or advancing to third; (5) properly contacting third base; and (6) properly reacting to the coach's signals at third base.

Modifications   A more advanced version of this drill is live action. Outfielders throw from right field to infielders in their respective positions. The ball is hit with a fungo bat by the coach.

Focus   To react properly to various ground balls when on base.

Procedure   All positions are involved in this drill. Place a defensive team on the field. A coach with a fungo bat is at home plate; a runner is at second base. The coach alternates hitting ground balls to the right and left sides of the infield. The base runner at second base reads the ball. Several valuable lessons can be learned in this drill: tuning in on every swing, reading the ball off the bat, and reacting properly to the direction and flight of the ball.

Good base-running strategy calls for the runner to freeze on a line drive and get back to the base, move to third base on a ground ball to the right side of the infield with less than two outs, and see the ball go through the infield on the left side before attempting to go to third. If, however, the ball is hit slowly to the left side of the infielder, the runner may advance.

Hit a variety of ground balls of all types, with a few line drives mixed in, to make this drill worthwhile. Learning the concepts and developing proper reactions to various types of ground balls and occasional line drives require many repetitions.

Coaching Points   Make sure each base runner knows the strategy. They should learn where to go, when to go, and when to stay.

Modifications   You can incorporate this drill into a controlled intrasquad game or use it as part of a base-running game drill.

Focus   To get out of the box quickly, maximize effort on the first three steps after contact, and check to see if the ball gets through the infield; to touch first base properly, slow down with control, find the ball, and react accordingly.

Setup   This drill accommodates all positions at once. Smaller groups can use the drill for introduction, correction, maintenance, or refinement. For best results, run this drill on the regular playing field. Have baselines marked and bases in place. Have players form a line between the on-deck circle and the right-handed batter box.

Procedure   Each player takes a turn executing the drill by simulating a gamelike swing, getting out of the box, exploding during the first three steps, and looking in to pick up the ball. These three phases make up the first part of the drill. Use the same procedure and add the last three phases of the drill: touching first base properly, breaking down, and picking up the ball again.

Each player should simulate his regular swing and get rid of the bat exactly as he would under game conditions. After finishing his swing, he disposes of the bat and practices exploding out of the box. He then checks to see if the ball gets through the infield. This might be difficult if the ball is hit to left field. When the ball is hit to right field, the ball is usually visible to the batter.

After picking up the ball, the runner takes full-speed strides, running in a straight line toward first base. He makes contact with the front part of first and then breaks to find the ball. If the ball gets by the first baseman, the runner takes off or chooses to return to first, depending on the ball location. If the ball is only a few feet from the first baseman, the runner stays put.

Coaching Points   A coach should watch each player and give encouragement or correction. Make sure each player takes a regular swing as he simulates. Watch for proper explosion out of the box for the first three steps and the check to find the ball. As the batter approaches first base, watch where he touches the base and check to see if he slows down to find the ball's location.

Modifications   This can be broken into two drills. In one drill, focus on the first three points of emphasis; in the second drill, focus on the last three points.

Focus   To practice the correct route and base-running procedure on a sure base hit to the outfield.

Setup   At least 4 players take turns at batting. As many as 12 players can efficiently function as a group of alternating batters. You'll need the home plate area, the first- and second-base lines, and perhaps a cone.

Procedure   The player at the front of the line at home plate is the batter. He simulates a swing that results in a sure base hit to the outfield; he sprints toward first base. The turn at first base starts at home plate, going directly to what we call the drive point. That point is approximately 20 feet from first base and 20 feet from the foul line. Touch the inside corner of the base with either foot, creating a straight path toward second base. This might be an aggressive turn, depending where the ball is hit. For example, if the ball is hit to left field, the runner advances a greater distance toward second base.

To create a good angle, put a cone between first and second base. Once the outfielder secures the catch, the runner should stop. He should not return to first base until the ball has been received by the relay man. The base runner's chest should face the ball at all times. Once the relay man receives the throw from the outfielder, the runner returns to the base, making sure he stays with the ball until it's in the center of the diamond.

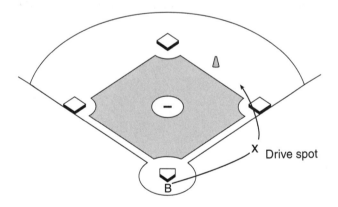

Coaching Points   Evaluate each base runner, focusing on proper routes, how the base is contacted, and the relation of the turn to the area in which the ball is hit. Stress the drive point, the tagging of the base, staying with the ball, the return to first base, and the distance and aggressiveness of the turn.

Modifications   You can incorporate this drill into intrasquad games or other controlled, competitive base-running situations.

Focus   To ingrain base-running rules and strategies.

Setup   You can do this drill in intrasquad games, controlled practices, or base-running games. In these cases, one player at a base activates the drill. You can also do the drill with a group of players alternating at a base or bases.

Procedure   Before taking a lead there are four things we expect of our base runners. These expectations apply to each and every lead throughout the game and also apply to the batter at the plate. We use the acronym BSBD to help players remember all four tasks. B = ball—never take your eye off the ball. Watch the ball at all times, making sure it's in the possession of the pitcher before taking a lead. S = sign—get the sign from the coach on the base. B = board (scoreboard)—know the outs, the score, and the situation. D = defense—read where the defense is playing. These four steps provide valuable information regarding taking another base.

Coaching Points   All players in our program work on this and other base-running drills that focus on base-running skills. Make sure each base runner carries out the BSBD rules.

Modifications   As we mentioned in the procedure, you can set up a special station at each base to practice these four tasks. Or players can practice them in all types of intrasquad or competitive base-running situations.

Focus   To read a pitcher and get a good jump off first base during a steal of second.

Setup   This drill is done on the playing field with a pitcher (or a coach acting as a pitcher) on the mound. A group of at least three and no more than eight base runners is needed at first base at one time. Several groups can rotate through the drill. The group of base runners forms a line outside the baseline and 8 to 10 feet toward home plate. The player at the front of the line takes a lead at first base, reads the move of the pitcher on the mound, and attempts to steal second base. Each player in line takes several turns.

Procedure   We want each base runner to take his normal lead and then adjust according to each pitcher and the game situation. His eyes should focus on the pitcher. To maximize this base runner's effort, he must learn to key on the various actions and movements of the pitcher. Keenly watching the subtle differences in the actions of the pitcher's body during his delivery is a key to getting a good jump.

When we work on stealing second base, we go full speed 45 feet, then relax. We stay on the pitched ball for about the first four steps. By that time the ball should be in the strike zone. Watching should not slow the runner's speed.

On pickoff attempts, we have our runners dive back with the head facing toward right field. This way if the ball is missed by the first baseman, it will hit the runner in the back of the helmet or else the runner can see the ball going toward the outfield or into foul territory.

Coaching Points   All offensive players benefit from this drill. These are the keys for each base runner:

1. Front elbow. If the elbow goes toward first, the pitcher is throwing to first base. If his elbow goes away from first base, he's throwing to the plate.
2. Front knee. If the pitcher's back knee bends, he must throw home. Be careful with this—some pitchers bend the knee and turn so quickly that the move goes undetected by both the runner and the umpires.
3. Back heel. If the back heel lifts, the pitcher is throwing to first. If the back heel stays on the ground, the pitcher will throw home.

Modifications   This drill can become a competition with live defensive players.

Focus   To work on base running against a gamelike defense.

Setup   Hitters, base runners, and all defensive players are active in this drill. Base coaches are needed at first and third base. Place a full nine-man defensive team on the field. Put a live base runner at each base and a batter at the plate.

Procedure   Pitchers want the batters to hit the ball, so everything is thrown soft and down the middle. The defensive team is instructed to play every batted ball as if there is one out and a runner on first base only. The defense should disregard the runners at the other bases. Runners at each base have assignments that are carried out as though there are no other runners aboard.

1. The runner on first base reacts to the batted ball. He runs independently from the other runners.
2. The runner at second base also reacts to the batted ball and is independent from the other runner.
3. The runner at third base reacts independently as well.

The base coaches control the base running. There may be times when the third-base coach will bring the runner at first to third base with a runner still at that base. (Remember that runners are running as if no other runners are on base.)

When each base runner circles the bases, he can continue on and join the line of batters at home plate or take a position on defense. If a batter hits an extra base hit, runners are again placed on each base after the play ends and the drill continues.

Coaching Points   Base-running discipline is the key element of this drill. There are several other important points of focus, such as reaction to the base coaches' verbal commands and hand signals.

Modifications   You can modify this drill in many ways. Here are some adaptations we use in our practice sessions.

1. Runners on first and second base
2. Runners on first and third
3. Bases loaded, infield in
4. Two outs and a full count
5. Runner on first stealing
6. Winning run on third base (last inning)
7. Top half of the inning with visitor at bat
8. Bottom half of the inning with home team at bat

Focus   To practice both offensive and defensive skills with runners on base.

Setup   A defensive unit (minus outfielders) works on stopping the running game. More than one defensive player at each defensive position is acceptable, or even desirable. All other players execute the first and third situation as base runners. Half of the offensive team rotates as runners at third base; the other half does the same at first base. The defense sets up in their defensive positions, looking at the coach to see what first and third defense will be run. The offense gets the play from another coach.

Procedure   We have two first and third offensives: the straight steal and the long lead.

1. Straight steal—the runner on first base tries to steal second base. The runner on third will run home when the catcher turns his back to the runner at third. What we're doing is guessing that the catcher will throw through to second base. If the catcher does throw through, the runner at third scores easily. If the catcher fakes the throw to second or throws back to the pitcher, the runner at third will be trapped before he reaches the plate. In this case, we want him to get into a rundown and stay long enough to advance the trailing runner to third base.
2. Long lead—in this scenario, we want the runner picked off at first. We extend our lead from about 12 inches to 15 inches, trying to draw a throw. If the pitcher throws to first base, the runner at first tries to steal second base. That runner should run inside the baseline and slide to the outside. The runner at third base extends his lead once the pitcher throws to first base. That runner will try to steal home when the first baseman throws the ball to the middle infielder that covers second base. If the pitcher does not take the bait and throws home, the runner at first steals second and the runner at third stays put.

With two outs, the runner at first won't run into a tag at second. He'll run hard, stop, and get into a rundown. He should try to stay in the rundown long enough to score the runner at third base.

Coaching Points   One coach gives the offensive signals while another coach operates the defense. Both units strive hard for proper timing and play execution.

Modifications   You can modify this drill to work in a single base-running situation. For example, the first base runner is live, and the third base runner is not. This adjustment might help younger players or aid in introducing the first and third base-running situation to the offense or defense.

Defensive Skills

Chapter 12

Infield Drills

Sonny Pittaro

Over the past 33 years as a Division I college baseball coach, it's become crystal clear to me that solid infield play is the key to successful team defense. As we all know, good defense wins baseball games.

In a perfect world, your infielders arrive at your first team practice equipped with good eye-hand coordination, quick feet, range, soft hands, strong throwing arms, and intelligence. The reality is that several lack some of these skills. I make it a point to spend practice time ensuring that my infielders are fundamentally sound when fielding ground balls. We accomplish this by teaching proper fielding techniques through meaningful, repetitive drills. The drills in this chapter have been developed through trial and error during my tenure at Rider. They are structured so that players learn the sequence of movements required to consistently make plays: the basics of the fielding stance, moving the feet into proper position, fielding the ball, and getting into throwing position to deliver a strong throw to the target. Coming from a cold weather area (Lawrenceville, New Jersey), my teams begin these drills indoors, but they can be easily adapted to the playing field outside.

The initial drills are designed for all infielders and important to developing proper fielding technique. These drills can be performed with an entire infield group or smaller groups of two or more players.

One final point I'd like to make before diving into these drills: My high school baseball coach, Carl "Kelly" Palumbo, was an outstanding teacher of the fundamentals, but he also stressed the importance of being mentally alert on the field. He taught his players to know the game situation at all times: the inning, score, number of outs, and count on the batter. This information often determines how an infielder approaches a batted ball and to what base he'll deliver his throw.

Finally, and this bears more importance than range or arm strength, Coach Palumbo taught me that all good infielders *want* the ball hit to them in tough situations. This impenetrable confidence is developed through repetitious training of the proper fundamentals of fielding. When this positive, competitive mindset is combined with solid fielding mechanics, a complete infielder is born.

Photo courtesy of Peter G. Borg, Rider University

When infielders learn correct mechanics of fielding, throwing, and footwork through drills, they gain the confidence to handle pressure situations in games.

Focus   (1) To put an infielder into a stance that allows him to move as quickly to the ball as possible; (2) to get into proper fielding position to catch the ball; (3) to move his feet correctly after receiving the ball and throw to the proper base.

Setup   This drill is executed with a group of infielders. No ball is used in this exercise, and it can be performed either indoors or outdoors. Make this drill as gamelike as possible with players reacting at game-speed to the commands.

Procedure   With his players facing him, the coach uses three verbal commands: "Set, Ready, Ball." On the first command, "Set," players assume a stance similar to a basketball player guarding his opponent. His feet are spread shoulder-width apart, his knees are slightly flexed, and his arms hang relaxed outside his body. (Middle infielders should be fairly upright in their stance, whereas corner infielders are slightly lower because there's less reaction time to a batted ball.)

On the second command, "Ready," players initiate some movement with their feet, using a creeping or swaying technique. This "keying up" or slight forward movement breaks inertia and allows the player to get a jump on the ball. Starting from a dead standstill reduces a player's reaction time and decreases his range.

On the third command, the coach holds up his index finger and says "Ball." As he voices the command, the coach points his index finger in the direction he wants the players to move—left, right, or straight ahead. At this point, the fielders should have their eyes up as if they're picking up the ball off the bat. They react to the command by breaking in the direction that the coach is pointing. The players field the imaginary ball using proper technique, quickly align their feet to the target, and make an imaginary throw to first base.

Coaching Points   Initially, I like to use a one-step-and-field approach, then a three-steps-and-field approach, followed by a five-steps-and-field approach. A point to remember is that the fielders must break hard to the ball whether it's to their left, right, or directly in front of them.

Modifications   You can enhance this drill by having a pitcher simulate his wind-up while the fielders react to his delivery. The fielders come "set" as the pitcher initiates his rocker step, get "ready" as he comes to his balance point, and read the "ball" at his point of release. I teach my players to carry their hands outside of their knees, holding their arms in a relaxed position. The fielder's thumbs should point up as if he's about to shake hands.

Focus   To teach infielders to properly catch a ground ball, that is, to "absorb" the ball into the glove.

Setup   The infielder sets up by kneeling with his glove-hand at his side (thumb held up in a handshake position) and his throwing hand behind his back. Holding the glove in the "shake hands" position helps eliminate tension from the glove-arm.

Procedure   A coach either rolls the ball or hits a short fungo (about 40 feet) to the fielder, who is resting on both knees. The ball needs to be rolled or fungoed directly at the fielder.

As the ball approaches the fielder, he slides his glove-hand forward to the ball and turns the glove so that the fingers point down. The arm is extended out in front of his body; the back of the glove rests on the ground. The ball should be fielded on the left side of the body for a right-handed thrower and on the right side of the body for a left-handed thrower. As the ball enters the glove, the fielder brings the ball into his belly in a funneling motion. The purpose for this is to have all balls caught out in front of the body, not off to the side.

a   b

Coaching Points   As fielders become proficient in catching (absorbing) the ball into the belly area with one hand, have them field with two hands. Again, the emphasis is on receiving the ball into the middle of the body. I teach "clamming" the ball—that is, the throwing hand covers the top of the ball as it enters the glove.

Modifications   Modify the drill by having the fielder assume his customary fielding stance but holding his throwing hand behind his back. It's essential that the fielder lower his rear end by bending from his knees rather than his waist. His feet should be spread slightly outside the width of his shoulders with his heels on the ground. Last, his weight should rest slightly forward on the balls of his feet. I do not teach a staggered stance; I prefer to have the feet parallel. The ball is then rolled or fungoed directly to the fielder. He catches the ball applying the same technique used when fielding on two knees. As the fielder becomes proficient catching the ball with one hand, the drill can progress to receiving the ball with two hands.

101   THE TURN DRILL

Focus   To improve an infielder's ability to react to ground balls; to emphasize quickness, agility, and proper fielding technique.

Setup   Like most drills, the Turn Drill can be done indoors or outdoors. It can be run with a coach and player or in two lines with infielders feeding each other. In either case, each group has a ball and stands about 15 feet apart.

Procedure   The drill is initiated by line 1 turning their backs to their partners and assuming the "set" or fielding position. Line 2 rolls a ball to their partner and says "Turn." On the command "Turn!" the fielder jumps (not spins) around, keeping his feet as low to the ground as possible. He quickly gets into proper

a

b

fielding position and fields the ball into the middle of his body. The coach or partner rolling the ball checks the fielding posture of the receiver to make sure his feet are parallel, heels down, knees flexed, and arms extended, and that his glove is on the ground as he fields the ball. This procedure is repeated until the fielder has successfully caught five ground balls. After five successful "turns" and catches, the partners change positions. Line 2 now fields the ground ball, and line 1 rolls it.

Coaching Points   Make the drill more challenging by reducing the distance between the lines or increasing the speed at which the ball is rolled. If you want to make the drill competitive, each group can keep their score.

Modifications   To modify the drill, you can have the partner throw the ball off a wall or "toss back" instead of rolling the ball. Immediately after throwing the ball he says, "Turn." His partner jump-turns and fields the ball as it comes off the wall or toss back. Instead of fielding a rolling ball, the fielder now must react to a ball that is bouncing or hopping.

You can make the drill extremely difficult by fungoing a ground ball or line drive from various distances—generally from 60 or 70 feet. When hitting the ball in this phase of the drill, say "Turn" before the ball is hit. Speeding up the velocity of each ball hit obviously increases the difficulty of the drill.

Focus   To teach and practice the best method to recover a bobbled ball.

Setup   Infielders line up behind third base, the line extending into left field. Each infielder has his glove on backward.

Procedure   From about 20 feet away, a coach rolls a ball to the first player in line. The player deliberately bobbles or boots the ball with his glove so that it rolls a few steps away from him. He then quickly reacts by picking the ball up with his bare hand and throwing it to first base.

After each fielder has had several attempts, the coach continues the drill by hitting ground balls from home plate. In this case, the players should wear their gloves properly and bobble the ball by pushing it with the back of the glove.

a   b

Coaching Points   This bobble drill is a simple exercise but valuable for all infielders to understand and practice. I can't count the number of times I've seen an infielder miss or bobble a ground ball and then instinctively reach for the ball with his glove. One of two things usually transpires when he does this. The ball drops out of his glove because he's unable to feel the ball or the runner is safe because of all the time it takes to transfer the ball to his throwing hand.

The purpose of this drill is to teach infielders how to react to a ball not fielded cleanly. Fielders are taught to pick up a bobbled ball with the bare hand rather than the glove hand; by doing so they give themselves the chance to throw the runner out. This drill is popular among infielders because it's effective and fun.

Modifications   To enhance the drill, have a base runner run to first base immediately after the ball is hit. The fielder deliberately bobbles the ball before picking it up with his bare hand to make the play. Multiple base runners can be used to force fielders to quickly decide where they can record an out.

When space or time is limited, you can run this drill in a line or partner setup where no throw is attempted. Players in two lines roll a ball to each other and practice picking up the ball with their bare hand after they bobble it.

103   THE SLOW ROLLER

Focus   To execute the proper movements involved in a play involving a slow roller; to get fielders in the habit of charging a ball that is slowly hit or bunted and to throw on the run.

Setup   This drill can be practiced indoors or outside using third basemen, shortstops, or second basemen. A first baseman is also needed to field throws.

Procedure   Begin by demonstrating the various fielding positions. Place a ball on the floor or ground and walk through the proper approach, fielding technique, and throw. I like my infielders to use one of three methods on slow rollers: inside the left foot using two hands, outside the left foot using the glove hand only, or barehanding the ball outside the right foot. A point to stress is that the glove is to be used at all times if the ball is moving. Fielding the ball barehanded only occurs when the ball has stopped rolling. It's also important to charge the ball as quickly as possible, keeping momentum through the ball as it's fielded. An accurate throw is made by getting the elbow up as high as possible.

After demonstrating each method, have players place the ball on the ground and walk through each technique. As they mimic fielding a slow roller on the run, make suggestions or corrections if their form is flawed.

Once you're satisfied the players have a good understanding (and feel) for the proper techniques, move forward by having them field a moving ball. The players in a straight line face the coach, about 30 feet away. A first baseman is needed to field throws. Roll balls (one at a time) and run the players through each method of fielding slow rollers.

When a player fields balls inside his left foot, he should quickly charge the ball, break down his steps as he approaches the ball, and glove the ball with two hands inside his left foot. As the right foot lands, the fielder should get his throwing elbow as high as possible and fire the ball to first base. Throwing off the right foot allows the quickest release on this play.

Next, have infielders field the ball to the outside of their left foot. Players charge the ball and field it with the glove only. They take a step with the right foot and throw off the left foot. This technique entails an additional step, but the fielder is able to maintain momentum through the ball (instead of break-ing down his steps) and throw to first with greater velocity. Also, the position or angle of the ball might not allow the fielder to take the ball on the inside of his left foot, so he's forced to improvise.

Fielding a ball that has stopped rolling is the final phase of the drill. Place a ball on the ground and have each player charge it one at a time. The fielder barehands the ball on the outside of his right foot and then throws the ball as his left foot lands. Emphasize that the bare hand needs to be open and the fingers extended underneath the ball, not on top.

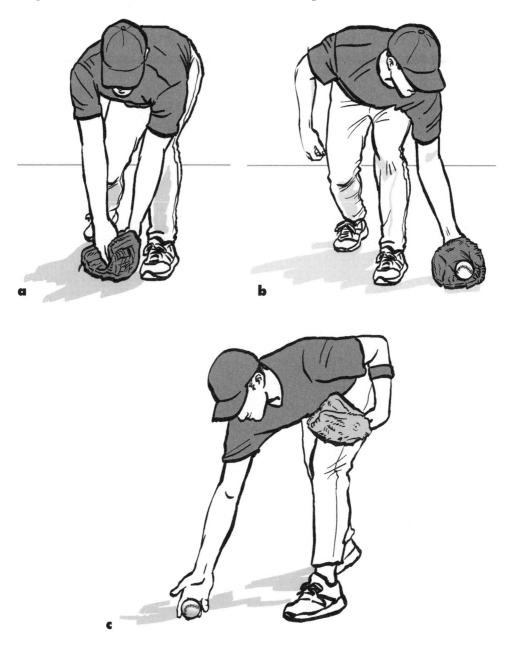

Coaching Points   The slow roller is a difficult play for infielders to execute because it entails precise footwork and throwing from a difficult arm angle. Ensure that infielders execute the proper movements involved in the play. Remind fielders to charge a ball that is slowly hit or bunted to them and to throw on the run.

Modifications   This drill can be practiced with all the infielders at each position (third base, shortstop, and second base) or simply at their primary positions. To make the drill more realistic, fungo slow rollers from home plate and include base runners. Remind fielders that they need to practice each method.

104   DIVING FOR GROUNDERS

Focus   To teach infielders when and how to dive for ground balls.

Setup   This drill is done primarily indoors but can be adapted for outdoor use. You *must* have one or two sliding mats for this drill. Place the mats to the diving side of the player. Regular baseballs, tennis balls, or Incrediballs can be used.

Procedure   The drill begins with a player kneeling on his throwing-side knee. The glove-arm is extended with the glove in shake-hands position. Using a "dry run" procedure, the player dives for an imaginary ball to his glove side. He then quickly scrambles to his feet and makes an imaginary throw to first base. After making several diving plays to the glove-hand side, players should practice some dry runs to the backhand side. Make sure the glove-hand and arm are extended in preparation before each dive.

Use tennis balls or Incrediballs for the second phase of the drill. The use of a softer ball allows players to focus on executing proper technique without fear of injury. Start by working on dives to the glove side. Stand about 15 feet away from the player and roll or bounce balls within his range. From his knee, the player dives to his glove side, catches the ball, quickly gets to his feet and fires a throw to first base. The next player then takes his place alongside the mat. Continue until each player has gone at least three times and then switch to the backhand side. Make sure players are reminded to dive onto the mat on every play.

Once players become comfortable with dives from one knee, start them from their normal fielding position. With the player set in the ready position, roll or throw balls toward the mat that force the fielder to dive. I start this phase using tennis balls or Incrediballs and gradually introduce hardballs as

the repetitions increase. Work players to both their glove-hand and backhand sides. After catching the ball or knocking it down, players must get to their feet quickly and make a throw. In the infield, a great play is only great if the fielder can throw the runner out.

The final step of the drill is to hit balls with a fungo from 30 or 40 feet using regular baseballs. How hard the balls are hit depends on the skill level of the players and accuracy of the fungo hitter.

Coaching Points   I use this drill in the preseason once or twice a week. The players enjoy it, and it creates competition as they see who can make the most spectacular play. Stress to your fielders that diving for balls should occur in only two instances: (1) when the fielder has a legitimate chance to catch the ball and throw the runner out and (2) when the game situation calls for the fielder to dive for every ball in his territory with runners in scoring position, thus preventing the ball from reaching the outfield and saving a run. In all other occurrences, infielders should stay on their feet when fielding batted balls.

Focus　To stress proper fielding technique for ground balls hit directly at the fielder, to his glove, and to his backhand side.

Setup　This drill can be done indoors or outdoors. All infielders participate.

Procedure　The drill begins with infielders standing in a straight line facing the coach, who is at a distance of about 25 feet. At the command of "Set," the first fielder "keys up" and comes to ready position. The coach then hits short fungoes directly at the fielder, who fields the ball and throws to first base.

While the player at the front of the line is fielding the ball, the next infielder in line is directly behind him, shadowing his movements. This accomplishes two things. It gives the players more repetitions and allows them to focus on their movements without worrying about fielding the ball.

Continue the drill by hitting balls to the glove and backhand sides. The goal of the players is to move their feet so they field the ball in *front* of their body. Don't allow them to field the ball off to the glove or backhand side. Again, rhythm is the primary focus. Fielding the ball and throwing to first should be achieved in a smooth, continuous motion.

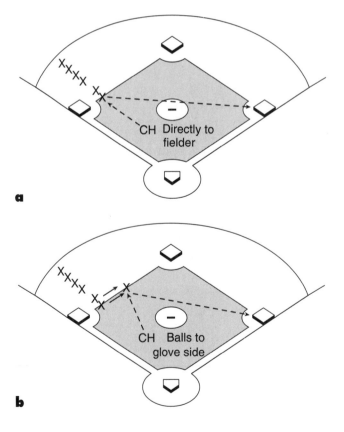

a

b

Repeat the process until all infielders have fielded five ground balls directly at them, to their glove side, and to their backhand side.

In the next phase, hit fungoes to the infielders from home plate. Start with balls hit directly at the infielders, then to the glove side, and finally to the backhand side. Continue having the fielder next in line shadow the person in front of him.

Coaching Points   While proper fielding techniques and footwork are essential, also focus on the fielder's rhythm. His movements should be fluid and pressure-free; he should maintain balance from start to finish.

106   SHORT HOP

Focus   To help infielders become proficient at fielding short hops hit directly at or to the side of them; to develop those much-coveted "good hands."

Setup   Infielders stand in a straight line and get set in the proper fielding position.

Procedure   This drill begins with an infielder short-hopping a ball to himself. At your command, players bounce a short hop into their glove. They should concentrate on "absorbing" the ball into the glove by giving in toward the body with the glove-hand. Another method of self-practice is to have infielders throw balls off a wall or "toss back." This is an excellent method of developing soft hands and good hand-eye coordination.

After bouncing short hops to themselves, fielders separate into two lines about 15 feet apart. Their partner throws short hops directly at them and to either side. One important note is that when fielding a short hop to the backhand side, players should take a short drop step (to the throwing-hand side) to create a slight angle from which he can better absorb the ball into his glove.

a   b

Once players have thrown 20 to 25 short hops to each other, hit fungoes to them from about 40 feet. Hit five consecutive balls directly at the fielder before moving onto the next player in line. After each infielder has completed the first set of five short hops, hit a second round of short hops to his glove side. Follow this with a third set of five to the backhand side. Make sure infielders employ a drop-step when fielding these.

The final phase of the drill is to fungo balls to all three areas at random. Have players throw to a designated base. Infielders must field the short hop cleanly but also use proper footwork to get the body into position to make a strong, accurate throw. After hitting the ball, call out, "First," "Second," "Third," or "Home" to alert the fielder where to throw the ball.

Coaching Points   Quality infielders are often described as having "good hands" or "soft hands." They are able to read and react to the many types of hops a ball can take. This drill helps infielders become proficient at fielding short hops hit directly at or to the side of them. Watch for players taking the short dropstep when fielding a short hop to the backhand side.

107   TEXAS LEAGUER

Focus   To teach infielders to catch short fly balls with their backs to the infield.

Setup   This drill can be run indoors or outdoors. If you're outside, line up all the fielders in the hole between shortstop and third base.

Procedure   Infielders stand on the edge of the infield grass with the first fielder facing you in the set position. Indicate that you'll throw the ball over the fielder's right shoulder. On your command of "Ball!" the fielder takes a dropstep with his left foot and sprints toward the outfield. (His back must be to the infield, which enables him to sprint.) Throw the ball over his right shoulder as if you're a quarterback throwing a pass to a receiver. The infielder should look for the ball over his right shoulder and catch the ball on the run. Continue until each player has caught four or five balls over his right shoulder.

Next, throw balls over their left shoulder. Now fielders take a dropstep with the right foot. Each infielder again catches four or five short fly balls over his left shoulder.

The final phase of the drill involves catching Texas Leaguers hit directly over the infielder's head. On the command of "Ball!" the infielder dropsteps either to his glove or throwing side, sprints straight back, and looks for the ball directly over his head. (Which side the infielder chooses to break to is a matter of personal preference.) Throw the ball so the fielder must catch it looking straight over his head.

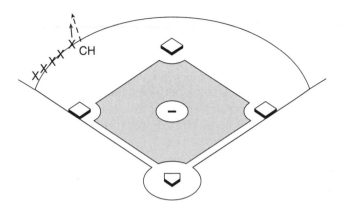

Coaching Points   From time to time during a game, short pop-ups are hit between the infielders and outfielders. These are often referred to as "Texas Leaguers." They are not hit high or hard enough for outfielders to catch, so it's usually up to the infielders to make a play.

Two points to stress to players when practicing this drill: (1) They must sprint as hard as they can to the ball, and (2) they must look for the ball as soon as they turn their back to the infield. An additional point to remember is that catches on balls over the right shoulder are made with the glove in the backhand position.

108 QUICK HANDS–QUICK FEET

Focus   To teach fielders to quickly catch and throw the ball, using their hands and feet properly.

Setup   Fielders pair off and stand about 20 to 25 feet apart. One player holds the ball preparing to throw while his partner stands with hands held chest high extended in front of his body. He must also be moving his feet by running in place or using short, choppy steps as he awaits the throw.

Procedure   Instruct the thrower to deliver a crisp throw to his partner's throwing-hand side, not the glove side. (Catching the ball on the throwing side allows the player to quickly transfer the ball from his glove to his throwing hand.)

The receiver catches the ball in the middle of his body and quickly squares his shoulders by using a crow hop or jump turn. He then transfers the ball from glove to hand and returns a throw to his partner, who uses the same technique. The two players continue throwing back and forth until the ball is dropped or missed. They should establish a rhythm and receive and release quickly and accurately.

Coaching Points   I use this drill after infielders complete their long-toss exercises so their arms are good and loose. Two coaching points are integral to this drill: (1) Accurate throws to the throwing-side arm are essential, and (2) the first two throws should be at medium speed. As the drill progresses, speed is increased, and the distance between the players is decreased. Stress that footwork is critical to a quick transfer and release. Players can challenge each other by seeing how close they can get to one another before someone drops the ball.

Modifications   To make this drill competitive, groups can be timed on how long they can go without making an error throwing or catching. A group is eliminated when they make an error, and the competition continues until one group remains. The competition can be held from 20, 15, or 10 feet.

Adding a third fielder to form a triangle or a fourth to create a box formation modifies the drill. Vary the distance from 25 to 15 feet. Various feeds for double plays can be practiced from the triangle formation. Players should practice underhand and backhand feeds with emphasis on quick hands and quick feet.

109   THE BACKHAND DRILL

Focus   To train infielders to catch a ball hit to their backhand side when they're unable to field it in front of them.

Setup   All infielders participate.

Procedure   I use a four-step progression when working on developing the backhand. In the first step, have all the infielders form a straight line facing you. Instruct them to take a crossover step (glove-side foot over the throwing-side foot), planting their foot with the knee bent. They should then place their glove (without a ball) on the ground in front of their lead foot. Clap your hands to signal the infielders to simulate catching the ball in the web of the glove, step with their back leg, plant the back foot, and make an imaginary throw to first base. (Right-handed fielders field the ball off their left foot and plant with their right foot.)

After the dry run phase, infielders pair off and roll balls to one another to the backhand side. They stand about 10 to 15 feet apart. Each fielder starts in the backhand position, as described in phase one. The first infielder catches the ball, plants on his back foot, and fires an imaginary throw to first base. He rolls the ball back to his partner, who repeats the procedure. Teammates roll four or five balls to each other.

In the third phase of this drill, balls are rolled by partners so that each fielder must take a few steps to the backhand side to field the ball. They should start with three steps and build to five or six steps. Each fielder receives four or five balls.

In the final phase of the drill, hit short fungoes to the infielders' backhand side. The fielders are positioned in a straight line about 45 feet away. Each fielder should field three balls while in the backhand-crossover position. After catching three balls in the stationary backhand position, hit balls to the backhand side so that the players must take four or five steps to field the ball.

Coaching Points   Stress that the ball on the backhand side should be fielded in the web of the glove, just in front of the lead foot with the knees flexed.

Focus   To practice the various feeds of the shortstop and second baseman.

Setup   This drill can obviously be done outside, but if you're indoors, three or four flat bases are necessary to allow infielders to work in groups of two.

Procedure   Each twosome starts at a base without a ball. Players simulate catching an imaginary ball, pivot over the base, and make an imaginary throw to first base. Begin with pivots and throws from the shortstop and then from the second baseman. As they are shadowing their pivots and throws, observe each group and make suggestions or corrections as necessary.

The second step of this drill is to give each player a ball. Each again simulates a catch and pivot, but this time each actually throws the ball to the first baseman. Have the first baseman stationed about 25 feet from second base. Each player should practice three pivots and throws as the shortstop and then three pivots and throws as the second baseman.

In the next phase of the drill, the shortstops and second basemen work together feeding or throwing each other balls from different areas. They should vary the types of pivots they execute. I like to set up a first baseman halfway between first and second base to force fielders to make a crisp throw.

In the last phase of the drill, gather all the infielders at one base. Roll the ball to the second baseman. He feeds the shortstop, who throws to first. After each feed and pivot, the two players rotate until all infielders have practiced five or six feeds, pivots, and throws from both positions. It's important to roll balls to different areas, thus forcing the feeder to use different throws—underhand, three-quarter, and long.

a

b

Coaching Points   This drill is designed for middle infielders, but I like my third basemen to participate as well. It helps improve agility and quickness. In addition, it provides your team with a backup in the event of an injury.

Modifications   Hitting short or long fungoes can modify this drill, depending on the time allotted and the space available. Also, you can make the drill gamelike by introducing a player sliding into the base and having the pivot man avoid the slide. Indoors, you can use a slide mat or blanket and have your outfielders be base runners. (Make sure they wear helmets.) Roll or hit short fungoes to the infielders. When the ball is thrown or hit, the runner (standing halfway between the bases) takes off and slides into the base. The pivot man makes his pivot and tries to avoid the runner.

Outdoors, you can work on the outfield grass. (Have runners take off their spikes.) If you don't want to use a slider, roll a basketball or barrel so that the pivot man feels some pressure at his feet when making the pivot and throw.

Timing the double play with a stopwatch is also a good way to determine which type of pivot is the fastest method of "turning two" for each infielder.

Focus   To give infielders opportunities to work on many of the plays they must make during the course of a game.

Setup   The infielders set up in their respective positions. Four fungo hitters are stationed at home plate with two hitters on the left side of home and two hitters on the right side. I use my pitchers to hit fungoes. If you don't have enough pitchers to hit, have outfielders or coaches fill in. The fungo hitters on the left side of home plate hit to the first basemen and the shortstops. The fungo hitters on the right side hit to the third basemen and second basemen.

Procedure   The drill begins with each fungo hitter hitting ground balls to his designated infielders. Time each segment to last two minutes. In the first segment, the third basemen field ground balls and throw to first base. The other infielders at short, second, and first field their ground balls and throw them back to their fungo hitters (figure a). In addition to ground balls right at the fielder, balls should be fungoed to the backhand and the glove side. (Make sure that a protective screen is placed in front of first to protect the player catching the throws from getting hit by ground balls being hit to the first basemen.) Repeat this process for two minutes. After the first two-minute segment, the shortstops field and throw to first, followed by the second basemen in the third two-minute segment (figure b). The first basemen don't throw in this segment. They work on fielding ground balls and receiving throws at first with emphasis on proper footwork. While infielders are taking ground balls, you can walk around the back of the infield to observe fielding techniques and offer suggestions or encouragement.

     When the third basemen, shortstops, and second basemen have completed their two-minute segments of throwing to first, the emphasis then shifts to working on double plays started by the third basemen and the first basemen, specifically turning 5-4-3 and 3-6-3 double plays. Only two fungo hitters are required for this part of the drill. The fungo hitter on the first-base side begins the segment by hitting a ground ball to the third baseman, who throws to second base. The second baseman catches the ball, pivots and makes the double-play throw to first. After this has been completed, the fungo hitter on the third-base side hits a ground ball to the first baseman, who catches and throws the ball to second base, where the shortstop works on his pivots and throws while making the 3-6-3 double play (figure c). Each fungo hitter alternates hitting until two minutes have elapsed. This requires a different angle of throw as well as a different pivot by the second basemen and shortstops.

     The emphasis on the next two-minute segment is on turning double plays on balls hit to the middle infielders, specifically 6-4-3 and 4-6-3 double plays. The fungo hitter on the third-base side hits to the shortstops; the fungo hitter on the first-base side hits to the second basemen (figure d). Each hitter again alternates hitting ground balls to the shortstops and the second basemen, who

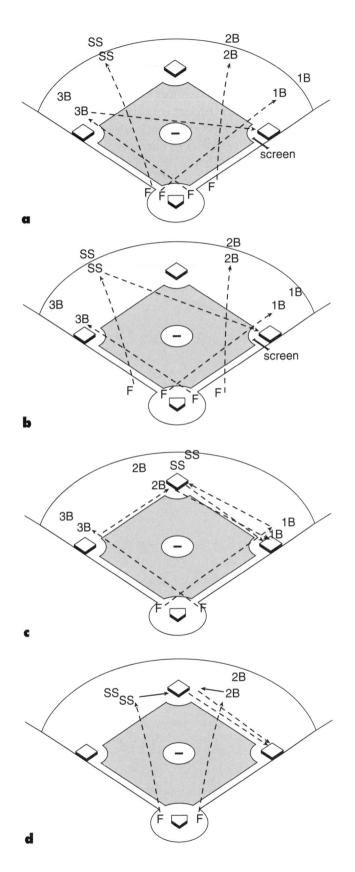

work with their partners on making the various double-play pivots and throws. I will often have my third basemen involved in this segment as well to keep them involved. You might also have infielders rotate after each ground ball so they practice feeds, pivots, and throws from both second and short.

The drill concludes with infielders practicing slow rollers for one minute. A coach rolls or fungoes a slow roller to each fielder one at a time. The fielder charges the ball and throws to first, making the play on the run. To make the play more gamelike, add a runner.

Coaching Points   The infield circus is one of my favorite drills. You can do it every day, and it takes only 15 minutes to run. I call it a circus drill because there are multiple ground balls being hit, fielded, and thrown at the same time, which makes it a popular drill with the players. Make sure that the third basemen and the first basemen field ground balls in front of their bases as well as in back.

Chapter 13

Outfield Drills

Jim Wells

Outfield play is many times among the most undercoached aspects of the game. Beginning with tee-ball, the outfielder is often the player not quite good enough to play in the infield. The youngster is relegated to watching the birds light on the power lines.

To play at a championship level, your team must be sound in all areas of the game, both offensively and defensively. If the old adage is true that pitching and defense wins ball games, then one third of the formula resides in the outfield.

Specific drills are the key to improvement. Another important ingredient in the majority of the drills is to be as close to gamelike action as possible. Having your outfielders go live in batting practice along with scrimmages gives your players the live action they require. But to improve on a daily basis we implement a series of drills in our first hour of practice just for our outfielders. Fundamentals are the key, from proper footwork to throwing action. In our drills we stress fundamentals and variety. In many of our drills, a coach works individually with players to improve a particular part of their game.

Our drills cover every facet of the game an outfielder must face. The drills are prioritized according to the percentages of the game. For example, we spend more time on fly balls than on cone drills. But they are all important and targeted at our particular team needs at the time.

Focus (1) To work on footwork in various paths to the ball (backward, forward, laterally, diagonally) in the air or ground; (2) to assess strengths and weaknesses in changing directions.

Setup One outfielder participates at a time. You'll need eight cones and a ball; a fungo bat is optional. It works better to toss or roll the ball. Set the cones up in a square 15 feet apart. The outfielder positions in the middle of the square and reacts to thrown balls. A coach positions 15 feet in front of the cones.

Procedure The fielder sets up in the middle of the cone square; the coach can call out any situation. For example, on a fly ball the player might have to take a dropstep, cross over, catch the ball, and stop at the middle back cone. From that position he can simulate a do or die by running straight ahead to the middle front cone. From this point, he might run diagonally to the right or left back corner cone to catch a fly ball overhead. A sinking line drive with a sliding catch can be simulated either straight ahead or diagonally. A line drive in the gap with a diving catch can be worked by simply running from one corner cone to the next.

In the second part of the drill the player reacts to balls being tossed or rolled while a coach or player uses a stopwatch to time his quickness from one cone to the other. Players have fun with this drill and can readily see where they are quicker.

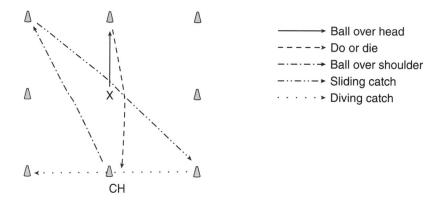

Coaching Points The outfielder is in constant motion and can cover most every outfield situation in a matter of 60 seconds. This is a great warm-up or indoor drill. Every aspect of outfield play from reverse pivots to diving catches with emphasis on proper technique is covered within a very small area.

Focus   To improve fielders' ability to break in or back on line drives hit directly at them.

Setup   You'll need a pitching machine (the type of machine with two rotating wheels or tires), a fungo bat, and baseballs. Outfielders position 140 to 200 feet from the pitching machine.

Procedure   Set the bottom wheel of the pitching machine at double the speed of the top wheel (this gives the baseball the backspin of a line drive) and aim the balls right at the outfielders. By making small adjustments in the trajectory of the machine, the ball might go directly to, over the head of, or land in front of the outfielder. Fielding these different types of line drives helps the outfielder get quicker reads and better jumps on balls.

Coaching Points   This is the hardest play for outfielders to master. One reason is that the play is very difficult to simulate and thus tough to practice. The good outfielder always takes the first step back when the ball is hit; this helps ensure that nothing gets over his head. The greatest outfielders in baseball history had one thing in common: They all had the ability to go back and catch the ball. Make sure outfielders are taking their first step back on every ball. It's equally important that they get good jumps on balls hit in front of them. Many outfielders lose valuable time by not reacting instantly to balls hit directly at them. This drill can help outfielders get better jumps on both kinds of balls.

Modifications   Alter the drill by hitting live fungos at the outfielders. You can make the drill competitive by dividing outfielders into two groups. The group that catches more balls and does a better job of reacting is the winner.

Focus   To give outfielders confidence as they approach (or think they're approaching) the wall or fence while chasing a fly ball.

Setup   All you need are baseballs. A fungo bat is optional, but it's better to throw the balls. All your outfielders can participate at once.

Procedure   Outfielders start by walking around the warning track (or fenced area of the outfield) to get familiar with the footing and depth of the track. Next, they begin at the fence and sprint forward 8 to 10 strides; then they return to the fence walking backward. Don't allow them to look back over their shoulders at the wall as they walk. Because they're walking, there's little chance of injury. They need to learn where the wall is without looking at it.

The next step is for outfielders to sprint back and forth from the wall. While they're sprinting back, hold up a baseball and have your players look back at it. Encourage them to hold out their throwing hand to feel the wall as they sense themselves getting closer. After safely reaching the wall, have them repeat the process until they feel comfortable. Have each outfielder look back over his left and right shoulder at least five times each.

When outfielders run into a wall (padded or not), they risk serious injury. If your fielders are still uncomfortable running toward the wall while looking the other direction, have them repeat these first steps as many times as necessary.

Once your fielders are comfortable running toward the wall, it's time to have them catch balls while running. Start with outfielders 20 to 30 feet in front of the wall and facing the infield. Next, throw fly balls over their heads, forcing them to chase down balls and make catches without taking their eyes off the ball. As your outfielders get better at feeling for the wall, gradually throw the fly balls closer to the wall.

The final phase of the drill is to move outfielders to their regular position in the field and fungo them fly balls over their head. It's a good idea to have one player stand at the wall and communicate to the outfielder chasing the fly ball down. If the fielder gets too close, the other player yells, "Fence!"

Coaching Points   By throwing rather than hitting the balls, you can make sure nobody gets too close to the wall before he's ready. Some players might need to do the drill a few times before they're ready to progress to fungoed balls.

You always want your players to play with aggressiveness, which can only occur when they are confident. When it comes to going back to the wall, the key for most outfielders is confidence. This comes with practice and repetition.

115   REVERSE PIVOT

Focus   To work on the ability to cut off a ball hit to the outfielder's glove side and make a strong, accurate throw to the infield.

Setup   You'll need a fungo batter and a relay man. While standing in the outfield, players should have at least 50 to 90 feet of room to run laterally; the fungo hitter should position far enough away to create at least a 45-degree angle between the fungo and the area in which the ball is to be caught (about 180 to 250 feet away from the outfielders). The cutoff man can stand beside the fungo hitter.

Procedure   During the drill, balls are hit to the outfielders on their glove side, forcing the fielder to pursue the ball by sprinting to one side. The outfielder is told to cut the ball off quickly. If the outfielder has to turn his back to the fungo hitter, then he has taken a bad angle. As a consequence, the fielder reaches the ball with his momentum going away from the cutoff man. To get a strong and accurate throw off quickly, the player will need to pivot to his glove side, turning his back to the target (instead of taking 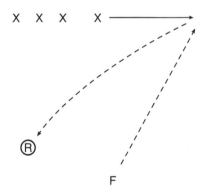 unnecessary extra steps needed to regain body control). To do this, the outfielder should catch the ball while fully extended, and then take one step and plant on the ball of the throwing-side foot without straightening up. It's important that the fielder keeps his center of gravity low; this ensures body control and a stronger throw. The fielder should not be allowed to throw while spinning out of control. Instead, he is now ready to step directly toward his target and make a strong, accurate throw to the cutoff man.

Coaching Points Remind your outfielders that a lack of arm strength can be overcome by getting accurate throws off quickly; good angles along with proper foot work and body control are the keys to achieving this.

Modifications You can modify this drill by eliminating the fungo hitter. By laying a ball on the ground at the place you want it cut off, you avoid wasting time with fungos hit at the wrong angle or the wrong speed.

116   DO OR DIE

Focus To charge a baseball, catch it, and make an accurate throw as quickly as possible with the game on the line.

Setup You'll need a base, a fungo batter, and someone to catch balls being thrown by the outfielder. Outfielders go to their positions or gather in one place in the outfield. The fungo hitter positions from 150 to 275 feet from the outfielders, depending on the strength and condition of their arm. You should have your outfielders throw to a target, so the person catching the ball should position next to a base to suggest the need for accuracy.

Procedure Tell your outfielders to charge the ball hard and catch it as close to the infield as they can. They should begin to regain body control by "chopping" their steps. Next, they should bend at the knees and waist to achieve balance. They should catch the ball with the glove-side foot out. As they transfer the ball to their throwing hand, they stride onto their throwing-side foot. If necessary, the outfielder can bounce on his throwing-side foot to get a little extra on the throw. This bounce should not be allowed to turn into a full crow hop because the time he spends in the air is wasted. By using body control and proper foot work, your outfielders should be able to catch the ball and release a throw in fewer than two steps.

Coaching Points Outfielders should get into the habit of making their throws take one skip before reaching the target, which makes catching the throw and making the tag much easier for the infielder. In this drill, the receiver is told to stay at the base as if to make such a tag.

Modifications You can modify this drill by hitting fly balls. You can also make the drill competitive for the outfielders by offering rewards for the perfect throw.

Focus   To increase the level of communication among outfielders, resulting in a safer and more efficient level of play.

Setup   You need a base, a fungo batter, a relay man, and a catcher. Outfielders should divide themselves into two lines at least 100 feet apart. The fungo hitter should position from 150 to 275 feet from the outfielders, depending on the strength and condition of their arms. The relay man should stand no farther than 150 feet from the outfielders. The catcher should stand beside the fungo hitter and in front of a base.

Procedure   Before getting started, assign one of the lines "centerfielder" status; the centerfielder always has the right of way over the other outfielders. During the drill, the fungo hitter should hit both fly balls and ground balls in between the two lines. As the two outfielders converge on the ball, they call, "I've got it! I've got it!" or "Take it! Take it!" depending on where the ball has been hit. As one player fields the ball, the other should take a back-up position. At the same time, the catcher should be lining up the cutoff man. After making an accurate throw to the cutoff man, the two outfielders switch lines and wait for the next ball to be hit. It's important that the players get experience in both lines for two reasons: (1) Because the ball is being hit between the two lines, they'll pursue balls to both their right and their left, and (2) outfielders should get experience at being the centerfielder.

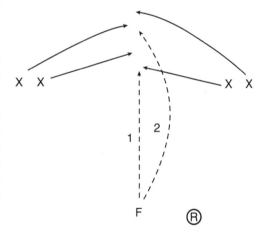

Coaching Points Communication is the key for any outfield. These three players should trust one another and function as a team. The communication skills developed in this drill will decrease the possibility of collisions and give players confidence to dive for balls because they know their teammate is backing them up. Stress accurate throws to the cutoff man.

Modifications You can instruct your outfielders to miss balls on purpose to ensure that the back-up outfielder is doing his job.

118 SUN IN THE EYES

Focus To improve your outfielders' ability to catch fly balls on a sunny day and avoid losing the ball in the sun.

Setup This drill requires a baseball, a fungo batter, sunglasses, and a sunny day. All outfielders should participate. The fungo hitter positions with his back to the sun. Outfielders are 180 to 250 feet from the fungo hitter and facing the sun. This drill might require an unusual setup (e.g., the fungo hitter might need to stand in the right-field corner and the outfielders on second base), but it should be easy to make the adjustment.

Procedure Begin the drill with a coach standing 10 to 15 feet away and tossing balls to the outfielders while they're on their knees. The risk of injury is reduced because the ball is tossed from such a short distance. In the beginning, outfielders wear sunglasses to ensure they don't get hit by the ball. When you feel your outfielders are ready, back up and begin hitting fly balls into the sun.

Coaching Points Do this drill on sunny days. The fielder's glove should be used to block the sun because it offers the largest amount of shade. Plus, having the glove up to the face helps the fielder catch a ball that comes out of the sun at the last second. Another thing to keep in mind when battling the sun is to move to the side of the ball. This changes the position of the ball in relation to the sun and might give the fielder an unobstructed view. Finally, outfielders should always have sunglasses accessible. Outfielders should never lose a ball in the sun and have to ask for his glasses afterward.

Focus   To teach outfielders to retrieve and throw with quickness and accuracy balls that hit the wall and stop next to it.

Setup   You'll need a fungo batter, baseballs, and a cutoff man. Outfielders should take their own position or all go to one position, whichever works better. If balls bounce differently off the wall in left, center, and right fields, players should take balls off all three.

     The fungo hitter stands at the pitcher's mound because the balls he hits need to travel all the way to the wall. The cutoff man stands on the outfield grass behind second base about 150 to 180 feet from the wall, depending on the strength and condition of the outfielders' arms.

Procedure   The fungo hitter should hit the ball hard enough to travel all the way to the wall, alternating between the outfielders' right side and left. This is important because when pursuing balls hit behind them, outfielders must adjust to balls hit to their right or left. As the outfielder gets to the ball, he breaks down directly over the ball (that by now is sitting still). A good rule is to have the outfielder put his chest directly over the ball. They should also have their bodies turned to the side, with their throwing side closest to the wall, putting them in position to make a throw. The outfielder should be sure to pick the ball up with his throwing hand. Many times a player who reaches down to pick up a stationary ball with his glove drops it, which allows runners extra time on the bases. Once he has the ball in his bare hand, the outfielder throws it to the cutoff man without taking any extra steps.

a   b

Coaching Points   Retrieving and throwing a ball without taking extra steps results in a slightly weaker throw in to the cutoff man, but the time saved by the outfielder can be made up by the cutoff man positioning himself as the throw travels toward him. Outfielders must know ahead of time where their cutoff man will be positioned during a game. Of course, this depends on the situation. Thus, you should practice this drill with the cutoff man at different positions, making sure the outfielders and the cutoff men are in agreement on where the ball will be thrown.

Modifications   Modify the drill by including base runners and fielders. This way the team can work on communication and relay throws.

120   CLOSING DRILL

Focus   To help outfielders develop the ability to "close" on a fly ball.

Setup   Each outfielder needs a ball. The outfielders and a coach go to the outfield, where there's plenty of open space for running. With the coach's back to home plate, one outfielder gets into "ready" position, facing the coach.

Procedure   This drill can be done in three separate directions. Outfielders can run to the left and away from the coach, to the right and away from the coach, or straight away from the coach. After tossing the ball to the coach, outfielders should take a crossover first step and begin running at full speed. The coach should throw the ball in the air, leading the outfielder like a quarterback leads a receiver in football. By tossing the ball just out of their reach, the coach chal-

lenges outfielders to expand their range. After going left and right, outfielders take a dropstep and run directly away from the coach. This time the coach waits until the outfielder looks back over his shoulder, and then throws the ball over the opposite shoulder. The outfielder must now make an adjustment with his head and not slow down. It's important that the outfielder turn his head over the other shoulder without turning around because turning takes the outfielder off stride.

a

b

Coaching Points   When outfielders are pursuing fly balls that appear to be out of their range, the best fielders seem to consistently catch up to balls that others can't. Improvement in this skill can be taught. Make sure your outfielders aren't chasing the ball with their glove. They should run after the ball as if they didn't have a glove on and then extend the glove only to catch the ball. Also, when chasing a fly ball to their throwing-arm side, the outfielder should reach across his body and catch the ball with his thumb down. This allows him to extend his arm and glove farther. An outfielder's range isn't determined by running speed alone. Getting good jumps and taking proper angles of pursuit are just as important as speed. The ability to close on a ball is an aspect of outfield play that can be improved on; this drill can help.

Modifications   Stand farther away from the outfielders and throw the ball when they're already in ready position. The added distance provides the outfielders a better setting for practicing getting a good jump.

121   INTO THE CORNER

Focus   To improve your outfielders' ability to play a fly ball or ground ball in the right-field or left-field corner.

Setup   Outfielders align 30 feet from the foul line with a coach hitting fungos from the first- or third-base coaching box.

Procedure   We start our drill by hitting fungo fly balls 10 to 15 feet from the side fence (figure a). This way the outfield can work on the proper method of playing just one wall. We follow this with fly balls near the side fence to allow outfielders to become accustomed to playing a side wall or tarp (figure b). Then we hit ground balls and line drives that kick off the side fence (figure c). This part of the drill is useful because the outfielder must negotiate different kinds of caroms off the chain link fence, wall, or pad and learn to stay chest up to the ball. We then hit fly balls into the very far reaches of the corner (which takes a little practice) so outfielders can work on making this difficult catch.

Even if the ball is not perfectly hit into the corner, the outfielder has the opportunity to work on several facets of his game, such as playing the fly ball or ground ball off the wall, doing reverse pivots, or making a sliding catch.

a

b

c

Coaching Points   The corner drill is a fun drill that we do at least once a week. It incorporates many of the individual drills we do into one. The outfielders love it and turn it into a game. A great feature of this drill is that outfielders become very aware of how much room they have to operate in. Many times you see an outfielder pull up because he's unsure of where the fences are located. This drill should help your players avoid doing that. One warning: If your side fence does not have pads, an extra player or coach should stand in the corner area to protect your outfielders.

122   ANTIDRIFT DRILL

Focus   To get behind and through a fly ball and not to lazily drift.

Setup   All you need are baseballs, a fungo batter, and your outfielders.

Procedure   Outfielders align 200 feet from the fungo batter. The batter hits fly balls directly over the outfielders' heads to where they must dropstep, cross over, and cover at least 15 feet. They then follow the proper technique of coming through the ball. Instead of the catch being made over the throwing shoulder at eye level, we add a little twist. We ask our outfielders to catch the ball between their legs. Obviously they can't drift and still make this play.

a   b

Coaching Points   We want our outfielders to always use proper technique, even when a throw is not necessary. The reason for not drifting is so the outfield can be in a position to make an accurate throw in the quickest fashion while retaining complete control.

Although the outfielder is not able to come through the baseball, he is forced to position himself correctly underneath. This can be accomplished only by properly going back on the ball.

Focus   To help younger players get over the fear of catching fly balls directly over their heads.

Setup   You'll need tennis balls and a tennis racket. You can substitute Wiffle balls or Incrediballs if you have them. Outfielders position themselves 60 to 100 feet from the coach and are divided into two or three groups or lines. Because the balls are hit into the air, the outfielders can take the opportunity to work on communication skills, yelling, "I've got it! I've got it!"

Procedure   Start by tossing the tennis balls into the air no higher than 10 to 15 feet. Have your outfielders let the balls hit them on top of the head. This should convince them that the ball won't hurt them if it hits them in the head. Next, outfielders back up to the full distance, and you start hitting fly balls with the tennis racket. Hit the fly balls progressively higher as players improve and gain confidence. While the ball is in the air, your outfielders decide who has it and one of them calls for the ball; the other outfielder has back-up duty. Arriving early at the spot where the ball will come down, the first outfielder lets the ball hit the top of his head, making it bounce high into the air. The second outfielder then catches the ball before it hits the ground. By turning this drill into a competition, players have so much fun that they're hardly aware of the good habits they're learning.

a

b

Coaching Points   A lot of young outfielders try to catch fly balls basket style because they're afraid of being hit in the head by a baseball. This drill should help them overcome this fear. The drill can also help older players practice getting under balls early (and not drifting) and work on their communication skills. Never try this drill with a baseball!

Chapter 14

Catcher Drills

Pete Dunn

An old baseball adage says that pitching is 75 percent of the game. If that's true, then catching has to rank right up there in degree of importance. In fact, very few teams have won a championship without a catcher with leadership skills and defensive prowess.

Catcher is not the most glamorous of positions. It's hot, dirty, and mentally and physically demanding. A catcher's offense often suffers because of the fatigue from playing defense. But if a young man enjoys the challenge of being involved in every pitch, having the entire field in front of him, and running the show as the quarterback of his team, then he has the mental makeup to be a catcher. Unfortunately, this alone guarantees little. He must also be very skilled in all aspects of the catching position. To excel, the young man must practice and drill long hours, day in and day out, to be the best he can be.

This chapter on catching drills is designed to give the catcher and coach some tools with which they can improve catcher fundamentals and overall ability. Most of the drills can be done inside or outside and within limited space.

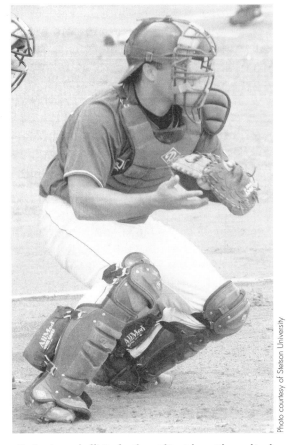

Photo courtesy of Stetson University

Motivation and affinity for the catching job must be combined with a good amount of practical skill drills for the catcher to be successful in his position.

All of them can be done with few participants, but some can be expanded to include other positions in gamelike situations. Keep in mind that repetition and proper technique are the keys to any drill.

Catching can be the most important and rewarding position on the field. And remember another old baseball adage—the quickest way to the big leagues is behind the plate!

124 BUNT ME ONE

Focus To develop proper approach, footwork, and fielding of bunts and blocked third strikes.

Setup This drill is best done with a first baseman, a catcher, and a coach. The catcher is in full gear and gets into ready position behind the plate with the coach standing behind him and facing the infield. The first baseman takes throws at first base.

Procedure From behind the catcher, the coach rolls out bunts at various angles in front of the plate. Depending on the location, the catcher takes the quickest and most efficient route to the ball and puts his head and shoulders over the ball as he "rakes" it into his glove. A ball that has stopped may be barehanded, but the glove still should be placed on the ground in front of the ball to keep the shoulders closed and head down. After cleanly grasping the ball, the catcher squares his shoulders up to first base, keeps rhythm by shuffling his feet, and makes a chest-high throw to the first baseman. The next catcher quickly moves to his ready position, and the sequence is repeated. All catchers involved should get work in all areas in front of the plate.

Coaching Points Balls bunted from the pitcher's mound over to the first-base line can be rounded off slightly as the catcher approaches the ball. This keeps the body squared and the front shoulder closed. A ball bunted to the left of the mound should be approached in a direct line, fielding the ball off the left of the body and the right foot planting just beyond the ball. The body turns in a reverse spin, and the throw is made. On balls near the first-base line, the catcher should shuffle his feet more aggressively to the inside or outside of the baseline to clear the runner. The catcher should always have knowledge of the runner's speed as he goes after the bunted ball. The catcher can use his preference as to whether to keep the mask on or discard it. The catcher should always aggressively call for the ball ("Mine! Mine!") so the pitcher and infielders move out of the way.

Modifications The first baseman can replicate game conditions by charging as the coach rolls out the bunt. As he reads the catcher's ball, he quickly stops, gets back to the bag, and sets up for the throw.

Focus　To develop and reinforce the catcher's positioning and footwork on home-to-first double plays; to teach catchers to recognize which throws to turn and which throws to take the force-out.

Setup　This drill can be done with three catchers only, but is best performed when integrated with infielders fielding fungo from a drawn-in position. If using only catchers, one is on the infield grass 40 to 50 feet away with ball in hand. The second catcher is at first base receiving throws. The third catcher is in full gear behind the plate. If infielders participate, they play in a drawn-in position. Pitchers too can take part in this drill.

Procedure　The drill is initiated either by throwing the ball from the catcher in the infield or by the coach hitting fungo to the infielder. The catcher sets up in an athletic position, facing the throw and straddling the back half of the plate. In this position he always has a feel as to where the plate is. He should give the thrower a good target by showing the mitt. When the ball is released, he'll receive the throw in front of the body, using the throwing hand to cover the ball as it enters his mitt. At the same time, he steps with his left foot toward the throw as he drags his right foot across the plate. His upper body quickly turns to first base so that his left shoulder is facing the bag and the ball is delivered to first base. You can run many repetitions in a short time, rotating catchers in and out.

a　　　　　　　　　　　　　　　　b

Coaching Points   The catcher should "find a seam" as his bare hand covers the ball and the transition to the throw begins. He should drag his foot over the plate, much like a shortstop does on a double play at second base. If the throw is off line, the catcher places a foot on the plate and stretches to the ball to ensure the force out. Because of the quickness of this play, the mask is usually kept on.

126   QUICK HANDS

Focus   To isolate upper-body throwing mechanics by eliminating footwork.

Setup   Use two catchers. If the drill is done indoors or on an artificial surface, no shin guards are required. If done on a dirt or grass surface, shin guards are recommended. The drill can be performed barehanded using a tennis ball, with a flat training glove and baseball, or using a standard catcher's mitt and baseball.

Procedure   Catchers kneel on one or both knees as they face one another 15 to 18 feet apart. The catcher receiving the throw gets into ready position with the glove-hand extended and his bare hand positioned behind the glove-hand or against the chest in a relaxed manner.

His partner initiates the drill by tossing a tennis ball (or baseball) to him so that the catch is made in front of the body. As the ball contacts the hand (glove), the throwing hand covers the ball while the fingers find a seam.

Using "short" arm action, the ball is brought back under the chin while the front shoulder closes. Hands break, and the ball is brought straight back to the throwing position. Without hesitating, the catcher tosses the ball back to his partner, who has assumed a ready position. Each catcher should do at least 15 to 20 repetitions.

Coaching Points   The catcher concentrates on proper form and quickness from the catch, through the transition phase, to the throw and release. Hand quickness and short, efficient arm action are major components of this drill. Because the drill simulates steal and pickoff throws, the catcher should not receive the "pitch" too far out in front of his body but rather let the ball "travel" to catch it close to his body. Emphasize that the ball is *not* caught one-handed and brought back to the throwing hand. The throwing hand covers the ball as it enters the bare hand (mitt), and at least one seam is grasped by the middle and index fingers to ensure proper 12 to 6 spin. The glove hand goes back with the ball and the throwing hand until they break under the chin. This ensures that the front shoulder closes properly. Proper arm action takes the throwing hand straight back under the chin to extension behind the head and eliminates the downward "loop."

Modifications   This drill can be done barehanded using a tennis ball, with a flat training glove and baseball, or using a catcher's mitt and baseball. Try a progression sequence using all three combinations.

Focus To enhance both correct technique and quickness in blocking balls in front of and at the side of the body.

Setup Two catchers are in full gear. They assume a ready position, facing each other six to eight feet apart. Each pair has three baseballs about two feet apart spread in front. This drill can be performed on grass, the dirt area, or artificial turf.

Procedure One catcher is designated to lead the drill. Both catchers set up in ready position facing the middle baseball. The lead catcher drives down into a blocking position to one of the three balls he chooses. His partner then shadows his movement. Both players again quickly assume their ready position, and the lead catcher repeats a block to one of the three balls; his partner again shadows. I recommend 8 to 12 repetitions.

Coaching Points The glove should always lead the body into blocking position. The catcher should gain ground toward the block from ready position (cut the distance to the ball). His body should be relaxed and cupped toward the plate on balls either in front of or to the side of the plate. The chin tucks against the chest protector.

Focus   To develop the feeling of receiving pitches with soft hands while reinforcing proper framing techniques.

Setup   Use two catchers or one catcher and a coach. No mitt or catching equipment is needed, but a throw-down plate is recommended. The catcher assumes a receiving stance with his bare left hand extended and his throwing hand behind his back or right heel. His partner or a coach faces him 10 to 12 feet away with 12 to 15 tennis balls close at hand. Any available area or surface can be used.

Procedure   The coach or part-ner uses a short overhand toss to position the tennis ball in the location where he wants the catcher to receive the "pitch." The catcher receives the pitch with a relaxed hand so that the tennis ball doesn't pop out. The catcher drops the balls in front of him after each repetition. The coach or partner works the strike zone and also four to six inches outside the perimeter of the zone to develop framing skills.

Coaching Points   Remind catchers to think of "receiving" the ball, not catching it. Relax the left hand by dropping the fingers toward the pitcher at the release point (quarter turn). Track the ball

into the hand with the head as well as the eyes. Use slight body sway without moving the feet on pitches that are either on the corners or outside the strike zone but frameable. When framing a pitch, the palm of the hand should face inward toward the plate. Don't show up the umpires by trying to frame pitches that are not strikes and outside the framing area.

Focus   To emphasize blocking techniques using a relaxed body and not trying to "pick" the ball cleanly with the mitt.

Setup   Use two catchers or one catcher and a coach. The catcher is in full gear. He assumes a ready position with his body but puts both arms behind his back. His partner or coach faces him 15 to 20 feet away with 10 to 12 baseballs close at hand. A grass or dirt area is recommended.

Procedure   The coach or partner tosses each ball in front of the catcher, replicating a pitch in the dirt. The catcher should react by keeping both arms behind his back and driving his body down into a blocking position. The body should be "cupped" and relaxed. The coach can work balls in front of and to each side of the catcher.

a

b

Coaching Points   The body should be "cupped" and relaxed with butt between heels. Knees remain wide. Chin on chest protector. Catcher should develop the feeling of smothering the pitch with a relaxed body and not picking it cleanly like an infielder. Catcher and coach should not be concerned with balls that skip under his rear end that would normally be blocked with the mitt.

Modifications   You can substitute tennis balls or Incrediballs for baseballs.

Focus   To develop the proper framing technique by receiving both inside and outside pitches with the palm facing inward.

Setup   One catcher works with two partners or two coaches. The catcher performing the drill should be in full gear. A plate is recommended. The catcher sets up behind the plate in a receiving position. Two "feeders" set up in a triangle position to his right and left, facing the catcher 12 to 15 feet away. Each has 10 to 12 baseballs close at hand.

Procedure   As the catcher gives a simulated target to his pitcher, the feeder to his left (glove side) uses a short overhand toss across the plate to a framing position on the catcher's throwing side. After framing the pitch, the catcher quickly drops the ball in front and returns to his receiving and target position. The process is repeated to the other side of the plate by the feeder on the catcher's right. This is done in rapid-fire fashion until all balls have been used.

Coaching Points   Catchers relax the glove hand by dropping the fingers toward the pitcher at the release point. Track the ball into the mitt with the head as well as the eyes. Use slight body sway without moving the feet while framing inside and outside pitches. When framing, the palm of the hand should face inward toward the plate. When receiving the inside pitch on a right-handed batter (glove side), don't chase the pitch with a high elbow. This "hardens" the hands and carries a borderline pitch out of the strike zone!

Focus   To develop proper catcher mechanics and confidence in catching pop-ups in foul and fair territory.

Setup   This drill can be run with one, two, three, or more catchers. It's most easily performed with an ATEC machine but is most realistic with the coach hitting pop-ups with a fungo bat. Catchers must be in full gear. If a machine is used, it's preferable to run the drill in the home plate area. If hitting fungos, use the outfield area.

Procedure   Fungo hitter (or ATEC machine) is in front of home plate. The catcher squats in receiving stance in the catcher's box with his head down. When he hears the machine or bat meet the ball, he quickly turns and looks upward to the area he reads the ball to be. At the same time he removes his mask with his right hand. After gauging the flight of the ball, he moves quickly but under control to the spot where the catch can be made. He tosses the mask away from the catch area so he won't trip over it should the ball drift. He catches the ball with two hands above the head and in front of the chin.

a   b

Coaching Points   A general rule in game situations: For balls fouled off on the inside half of the plate (right-handed hitter), catchers look first over the left shoulder; for balls fouled off on the outside half of the plate, they look over the right shoulder. Watch for the catchers overrunning the ball when they first locate it off the bat. Foul balls above or behind home plate have reverse spin and will move back toward the infield area (infield drift). Many catchers now use the hockey-style mask that does not require being removed for bunts, plays at the plate, or pop-ups. During the setup under the ball before the catch, watch the catcher's feet—they should be at a slight angle on the balls of the feet so he doesn't get back on his heels should the ball drift. On balls directly over the plate or in fair territory, the catcher moves quickly out onto the infield grass so that the ball drifts to him and the catch is made with his back to infield. Tell your catchers to be aggressive on balls to the first-base and third-base side and balls in fair territory. They should plan to make the catch until they are called off by an infielder.

132   30-SECOND QUICKNESS DRILL

Focus   To develop quickness and proper mechanics in all aspects of the receiving and throwing phases.

Setup   Use at least two catchers, but you can make the drill competitive by using up to six pairs of participants. The drill is best performed in the outfield or an enclosed area with adequate throwing room. Each pair of catchers is about 60 feet apart and at least 10 to 12 feet from the player next to them. It's helpful if the catcher or line of catchers begins on the outfield foul line. A coach stands off to the side with a stopwatch. It's desirable but not necessary for catchers to be in full gear. Each pair of participants has one baseball. If more than one pair of catchers (or middle infielders) are participating, the drill begins with all the baseballs on the same line.

Procedure   On the coach's command to "Go!" the catcher with the baseball throws with accuracy and velocity to his drill partner. With quick footwork, the partner positions himself to catch the baseball in front of his body. As the ball is received and the transition to the throw begins, the partner loudly calls out "One!" Using quick and efficient footwork and mechanics, he then returns the ball to his partner, who calls out "Two!" and the process is repeated until, after 30 seconds, the coach yells "Stop!"

Coaching Points   The drill emphasizes receiving the throw in front of the body, the transition phase, proper arm extension, quick feet with proper footwork, and making accurate throws with good velocity. This drill is made more enjoyable through competition with other catchers or middle infielders. All throws should be aimed at the partner's chest and should be made using the same footwork that the catcher uses in game situations. The receiving partner should use "quick feet" to position in front of the throw. The throw should be received with two hands, "finding a seam" as the mitt and ball are taken back to the chin. "Short" arm action is used, eliminating a downward loop with the throwing hand. A pair (or pairs) of participants attempt to make as many throws as they can during the 30-second time period. Competition with other catchers or middle infielders makes the drill more enjoyable.

133   WILD PITCH

Focus   To practice techniques of retrieving a wild pitch and getting the ball to the pitcher covering home plate.

Setup   This drill can be run with catchers and a coach only but works best when catchers and pitchers do it together. It's best done at home plate using your field's backstop or wall. Catchers are in full gear. The catcher sets up ready position behind the plate; the coach (or another catcher) faces him about 45 to 50 feet away.

Procedure   If pitchers are incorporated into the drill they simulate a delivery to the plate. The coach skips a ball to either side past the catcher and to the backstop. The catcher turns to the side of the wild pitch and quickly moves

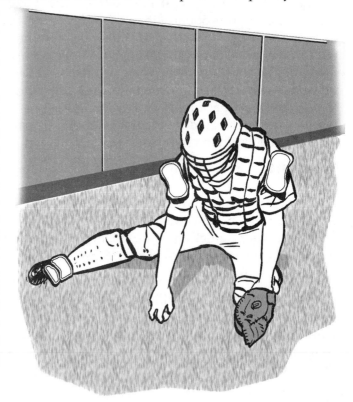

to a location where he anticipates the ball to be or rebound to. At the same time, the pitcher (or the other catcher) sprints to the plate and prepares for the throw. As the catcher approaches the ball, he goes into a controlled slide to the right of the baseball with his left knee on the ground and his right leg extended toward the backstop. The ball is barehanded and, staying in same the position, a snap throw is delivered to the pitcher covering the plate.

Coaching Points   This is usually a "do or die" situation so the catcher cannot be too deliberate in his approach and mechanics. The mask can be kept on or discarded on the approach to the ball, as the catcher prefers. If the ball is stopped or is moving slowly, it should be barehanded. If it's rolling fast, it should be raked into the mitt with the throwing hand. The catcher should not try to pick up the plate area too quickly. He should keep his head and eyes down on the ball during retrieval.

Modifications   This drill can be rough on the grass area behind home plate. Another area such as a softball field with a clay surface in front of a backstop might work better.

134   BLOCK AND RECOVER

Focus   To reinforce correct blocking techniques and develop quickness in retrieving blocked balls and throwing to bases.

Setup   You need one or more catchers, in full gear, and a "feeder" to throw balls into the dirt. This drill is best done using infielders covering bases and making tags. The catcher assumes the ready position behind the plate. If other catchers are involved in the drill, they stand off to the side, ready to replace the catcher after his block and throw. The feeder stands facing the catcher about 15 to 30 feet away with a bucket of baseballs. If infielders participate, they hold their normal positioning until after the block.

Procedure   Using adequate velocity to make the ball skip (not bounce), the feeder throws the ball into the dirt. The catcher drives his hands and knees downward into the correct blocking position. His body is cupped and relaxed. Immediately after the block, he locates the ball as he quickly scrambles to his feet, getting his body into position to barehand the baseball and make an accurate throw. His head stays over the baseball, with his shoulders closed as he picks the baseball up. Using quick feet and short arm action, he makes the throw to his target base. The next catcher rotates in, and the drill is repeated for 8 to 10 repetitions each.

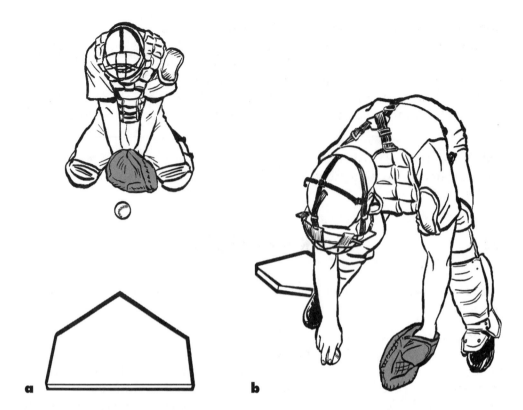

a   b

Coaching Points   After the block, catchers *never* glance at the runner to see if he's attempting to advance before they first initiate the retrieval of the ball. The catcher should always assume the runner is running. Teammates will communicate what he needs to know. If the body is relaxed during the block, the ball will be cushioned and will not carom far from the catcher. The feeder should work the catcher with balls in front of him as well as to his left and right. Catchers should always try to hit the infielder in the chest with his throw.

Modifications   You can use other position players as base runners in this drill to work on recognition and reaction. This is a good base-running drill.

Focus To develop technique and quickness on the snap throw behind the runner at first base, the throw to second base on a steal, and the throw to third base on a pickoff or steal attempt.

Setup Along with catcher(s), you need a feeder to throw pitches and players at first base, second base, and third base to receive throws. This drill is best performed with infielders working on holding their positions until the ball passes the hitter and then breaking to the bag and applying the tag. Another catcher should stand in the batter's box and swing "through" the pitch to keep the catcher back. The catcher assumes his ready position behind the plate, with the feeder 30 to 40 feet in front (with three baseballs in hand). Another catcher stands in the right-handed batter's box during the first round of the drill.

Procedure As the catcher receives the first pitch, he drives his left knee downward and toward first base as he rotates his upper body to first base. Using a short snap throw, he delivers the ball to the first baseman breaking behind the imaginary runner. As quickly as possible, he recovers and returns to ready position. The next pitch is delivered, and he throws through to second base, defending a steal of that base. The jump pivot, jab step, or rock and fire method is used according to the catcher's preference and abilities. Again, he returns to his ready position and this time makes the throw to third base, replicating a steal or pickoff attempt to that base. With the exception of a pitchout, the catcher should dropstep with his right foot behind the right-handed hitter to create a clear throw to the bag. All three throws are done in rapid fire fashion. The next catcher jumps in and repeats the drill.

Coaching Points The pickoff at first base is most successful with quickness and surprise, not with great velocity. Depending on his arm strength and quickness, the catcher, along with his coach, should identify and perfect the footwork that is most efficient and successful for him in throwing to second base. The catcher standing in the batter's box should rotate from one side to the other, giving each catcher a different look each time they perform the drill. All throws, regardless to which base, should be thrown to the infielder's chest.

Chapter 15

Pitcher Drills

Steve Smith

A pitcher practicing his skills on a daily basis is fundamental to his development. He can't rely only on throwing off a mound for his practice. The use of drills (1) allows us to isolate phases of the delivery, (2) allows us to work daily, minimizing risk of overuse injuries, and (3) allows us to construct a systematic program of pitcher delivery development. Once the pitcher learns to perform the drills correctly and incorporates them into his daily practice routine, significant improvement in performance occurs. In this way, a coach can allow the drills to be the teacher. The player improves his physical skills as well as his understanding of what constitutes a sound delivery. Ultimately, what coaches want is a pitcher who knows his delivery well enough to make corrections himself during the course of a practice or game.

The following pitching drills can be grouped into two categories: (1) delivery drills, which focus on different phases of the pitching delivery, and (2) specialty drills, which supplement the delivery drill sequence and address specific mechanical problems.

The delivery drill sequence includes the following drills:

1. Second Balance No Break
2. Second Balance and Break
3. Low First Balance
4. High First Balance
5. High to Low
6. Rhythm Drill

The specialty drill sequence includes these drills:

1. Long-Toss Cap Drill
2. Lead-Leg Maneuvers
3. Uphill Throwing
4. Towel Drill
5. One-Knee Finish
6. Lateral Screen

7. Two-Knee Chest to Glove
8. Upright Extension
9. Rope Drill

Three important principles of a sound delivery are addressed in some or all of the drills. These principles are balance, direction, and timing. Regardless of the particular nuances of any pitcher's delivery, the ability to achieve and maintain balance—that is, body control—throughout his delivery is important. Maintaining direction to the target and the overall timing of the delivery as it relates to the separation of the hands and the movement forward to the target play huge roles as well

136   SECOND BALANCE NO BREAK

Focus   To teach the proper position of the upper and lower body before the release of the pitch.

Setup   This drill is done with no ball, individually or with a partner.

Procedure   The pitcher begins by setting his feet as far apart as comfortable, attempting to simulate a sound landing position in the delivery. The back foot remains perpendicular to a line to the target. The front foot is pointed almost completely to the target. Weight should be evenly distributed, and the front knee should be "inside the foot." Shoulders are level with the glove-side shoulder pointing to the target. Head and eyes are level, looking at the target. Elbows are both at shoulder height and inside the shoulders. Palms are down; the throwing hand is on top of the ball.

From this position, the pitcher on command pivots on his back foot and completes the throwing motion until his elbows are at shoulder height. Once at shoulder height, the pitcher visually checks to ensure that (1) the front side is closed, (2) the throwing hand is on top of the ball, and (3) the ball is facing toward second base. If not, the pitcher should make corrections and repeat the drill.

Coaching Points   The drill should be introduced without the use of a ball. Repeat the drill as necessary to allow the pitcher to get the feel of a proper throwing position. This drill allows pitchers to feel what it's like to have the elbows up and the upper body in the correct posture with good lower body balance and direction as he completes his rotation and delivery of the ball. On completion of the throwing motion, the pitcher should be at full extension off his back side with his glove pulled to and fixed in front of his upper body. The back foot remains in contact with the ground.

Modifications   You can easily modify this drill by adding a baseball, allowing pitchers to execute a throw to a partner or net.

137   SECOND BALANCE AND BREAK

Focus   To isolate the upper-body mechanics during the pitching delivery, allowing for the instruction of proper separation of hands, proper glove-side action, and proper arm action.

Setup   This drill can be done individually or with a partner; no ball.

Procedure   The pitcher begins by setting his feet as far apart as comfortable, attempting to simulate a sound landing position in the delivery. The back foot remains perpendicular to a line to the target. The front foot is pointed almost completely to the target. Weight should be evenly distributed, and the front knee should be "inside the foot." Shoulders are level, with the glove-side shoulder pointed to the target. Head and eyes are level, looking at the target. Hands are together at the chest near the midline of the body.

From this position, the pitcher on command separates his hands with his palms down, continuing the movement until his elbows are at shoulder height. Once at shoulder height, the pitcher visually checks to ensure that (1) the front side is closed, (2) the throwing hand is on top of the ball, and (3) the ball is facing toward second base. If not, the pitcher should make corrections and repeat the drill.

Coaching Points   Begin the drill without using a ball. Repeat the drill as necessary to allow the pitcher to get the feel of a proper break and separation of the hands.

The important keys are that the elbows are shoulder height and that the front side is closed, the throwing hand is on top of the baseball and not underneath, and the path of the break allows the pitcher to show the ball to the imaginary second-base bag.

Modifications   Modify this drill by adding a baseball, allowing the pitcher to throw either to a partner or to a net once his elbows have reached shoulder height.

138   LOW FIRST BALANCE

Focus   To teach the proper timing of separation of the hands and direction of the front side during delivery.

Setup   This drill can be done individually or with a partner, on flat ground or off the mound.

Procedure   The pitcher positions with his pivot foot parallel to the pitching rubber with his glove-shoulder pointed at the target. Hands are at the midline near chest with hands separated four to five inches apart. Head and eyes are level and on the target. Lead leg is one to two inches off the ground, slightly bent with the stride foot directly in front of the pivot foot. From this position, the pitcher on command continues the break of the hands and "reaches" to the target with his front side remaining on line to the target, completing the delivery with a throw to the target.

Coaching Points   Before executing this drill with a ball to a partner, allow the pitcher to practice without a ball. Keys to the success of this drill are the ability of the pitcher to (1) reach with the glove side and the lead leg simultaneously, (2) keep the front side on line to the target, (3) keep the front side closed until landing and (4) keep the head over the rubber as long as possible as the front side moves forward to the target.

Modifications   Modify the drill by allowing the pitcher to complete it in front of a mirror, which enables him to "see" the timing of the break and the direction of his front side. You could also have the pitcher perform the drill on a balance beam five to six inches wide, four to six inches high, and at least six feet long.

Focus To improve the initial point of balance in the delivery.

Setup This drill can be done individually or with a partner, with or without a ball, on any level surface.

Procedure This drill begins by assuming a postpivot position on the mound or on flat ground. In the postpivot position the pivot foot is parallel to the pitching rubber, and the glove shoulder is pointed toward the target. From this position, the pitcher lifts his lead leg as high as he can while maintaining balance on his back leg. The pitcher's hands are together at his midline; his head and eyes are level and on the target. On reaching and maintaining this position for a count of three, the pitcher then completes his delivery and throws to his target.

a   b

Coaching Points The ability for a pitcher to reach and maintain this first balance position is imperative to his development of a sound delivery. Emphasize to the pitcher that the raising of his lead leg to this balance position is a lift, not a kick. His foot should remain as much underneath his lift knee as possible. He remains "tall" on his back leg; his upper body should be relaxed with hands together at the midline of his body. From this position, he breaks his hands and reaches to his target with his front side as he completes his delivery to the target. Encourage him to keep his stride foot on line to his target as opposed to swinging his lead leg down to his landing.

Modifications   The drill can be done without a ball using a towel.

140   HIGH TO LOW

Focus   To improve balance, front-side control, and direction during delivery.

Setup   This drill can be done individually or with a partner, on flat ground or on the mound.

Procedure   The pitcher assumes the first balance position in the delivery. In this position the pitcher simulates the point he reaches in his delivery after the pivot of the back foot and the lift of his lead leg to its highest point. From this position, the pitcher, on command, lowers his lead leg down to a point just before the foot strikes the ground and then lifts the leg back up to the starting point. He then lowers the leg again, completing the delivery by breaking the hands and reaching on line with the front side to the target.

a   b

Coaching Points Proper execution of this drill helps the pitcher improve his overall balance on the mound and his control of the front side of his body. It also allows him to improve the timing and rhythm of his delivery as it relates to the simultaneous separation of the hands and reaching forward to the plate of the lower half of the body.

Modifications Modify the drill by increasing the number of pumps of the lead leg and by reversing the direction of pumps, starting in a low first balance position.

141 RHYTHM DRILL

Focus To improve proper timing and rhythm of delivery.

Setup The drill can be done individually or with a partner, on flat ground or on the mound.

Procedure The pitcher takes a postpivot position with his lead shoulder pointed at his target. He has his feet together, and his hands are straight down by his side. On command, he simultaneously lifts his lead leg and both hands in such a manner that his hands are brought together at the same time as his lead leg reaches its peak in the lift. From this point, the pitcher continues his delivery to the target. This drill is a continuous movement drill designed to add flow to the delivery and improve its overall timing and rhythm.

a   b

Coaching Points   The pitcher should be able to move his feet and hands simultaneously without "leaking" forward to the plate before his hands and the lift reach their peak.

Modifications   This is the type of drill that can be enhanced by using a mirror. This can be especially helpful if the pitcher is having difficulty "feeling" that his hands and feet are not moving at the same time. The mirror allows him to see the timing of his movement as opposed to only feeling it.

142   LONG-TOSS CAP DRILL

Focus   To improve the overall conditioning and strength of the throwing arm at longer distances without sacrificing sound arm action and delivery mechanics.

Setup   Two pitchers do the drill together; ideally, they'll have similar arm strength. This drill is typically done in the outfield, but any open area that allows for throws up to 150 to 200 feet will work fine. You'll need one baseball and a cap for each pitcher to use as a target.

Procedure   The two pitchers play catch, gradually moving apart as they get warmed up. They continue moving apart until they're at the maximum distance they can throw the ball on a line to each other. At this point, they each take their cap off and place it on the ground. They then back up an additional 15 to 20 feet directly behind the hat and continue throwing. The objective now is to throw the ball as much on a line as possible and to hit the cap with the throw. On completing a set number of throws, each partner picks up his cap, and they move closer as they continue to play catch.

Coaching Points   Pitchers should use proper footwork; when they reach a distance that it becomes necessary to keep the throw on a line, they should use a crow hop, simulating the initial balance position on the mound. Make sure they have done a good job closing their front side. Encourage this by having them use a "step-behind" approach to the crow hop. Pitchers should finish their throw with full extension, allowing their arm to decelerate appropriately.

Modifications   Mark your outfield so that pitchers can chart their progress as their arm strength improves and their distances increase. Draw with chalk or paint a circumference around the area in which the hat will be placed.

143   LEAD-LEG MANEUVERS

Focus   To improve balance and control of the lower body front side.

Setup   Pitchers can do this drill alone or with a partner. The drill is done without a ball and on any level surface.

Procedure   The pitcher assumes the first balance position (also called "post position") in the delivery. In this position the pitcher simulates the point he reaches in his delivery after the pivot of the back leg and the lift of his lead leg to its highest point. From this position, the pitcher, on command, maneuvers his lead leg through three different positions (back, forward, ahead) while maintaining his balance on his back leg, keeping his hands together at the midline and his head and eyes on his target.

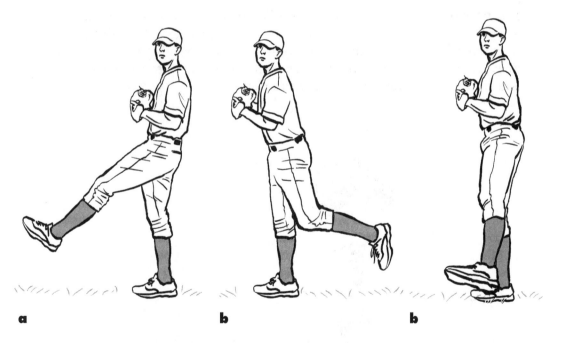

a   b   b

Coaching Points   Proper execution of this drill is essential to the overall development of your pitchers' delivery. They must be able to reach this balance point easily while maintaining eye contact with their target. Once pitchers have demonstrated the ability to reach the first balance position, you can begin to require them to make movements with their lead leg while maintaining balance on the back leg. Give verbal commands using a number system to indicate the direction (back, forward, ahead) you want a pitcher to move his leg. The pitcher should make the moves under control and return to the original post position before responding to the next command.

Modifications   Make the drill more difficult by having pitchers make movements with their eyes closed. They can also compete against each other and against the clock to determine who can maintain balance the longest.

144   UPHILL THROWING

Focus   To teach the feel of throwing after the stride foot lands; to stress the necessity of a good finish in the delivery.

Setup   This drill can be done individually or with a partner. It's most easily performed from the back side of the pitcher's mound, allowing the partner to move forward, thus making the throwing distance comfortable for the ability level of the pitcher.

Procedure   The pitcher assumes the first balance position in the delivery. In this position the pitcher simulates the point he reaches in his delivery after the pivot of the back leg and the lift of his lead leg to its highest point in the delivery. From this position, the pitcher, on command, throws to his partner and completes his delivery to follow through.

a

b

Coaching Points   At first do the drill without a ball, allowing the pitcher to get the feel of his stride foot landing earlier than he's accustomed to. Once he's oriented to the mechanics of the drill, allow the pitcher to incorporate the ball and complete a throw to his partner. This drill is excellent for teaching the pitcher the feel of rotating and throwing after landing. He should land with a bend in his lead leg and take his chest to his glove to get over his front side on the finish.

Modifications   Modify the drill by requiring the pitcher to execute uphill from the stretch or windup; this can be especially helpful when used to practice throwing change-ups.

Focus   To isolate throwing arm acceleration and deceleration action and teach proper throwing arm extension.

Setup   A pitcher works with a partner. All that's needed is a towel.

Procedure   The pitcher holds a small towel in his throwing hand. He then spreads his feet as far apart as comfortable, attempting to simulate a sound landing position in the delivery. The back foot remains perpendicular to a line to the target. The front foot is pointed almost completely to the target. Weight should be evenly distributed, and the front knee should be "inside the foot." Shoulders are level, with the glove-side shoulder pointed to the target. Head and eyes are level, looking at the target. Elbows are raised to shoulder height and inside the shoulders. From this position, the pitcher, on command, pivots on his back foot and completes his throwing motion, using the towel to make contact with his partner's hand. The partner is on one knee with his palm up at such a distance away from the thrower that the thrower must fully extend to hit the palm with the towel.

a

b

Coaching Points   The key teaching point in the drill is to help pitchers learn how proper arm action improves hand speed. In performing the drill, pitchers must keep their head still; the throwing arm should remain relaxed, not stiff. The towel aids in helping the pitcher feel and actually hear the "whipping" action that accompanies good hand speed. He won't be able to achieve this whiplike action with his arm if the arm is stiff.

Modifications   Modify the drill by having pitchers perform it in front of a mirror or on a low balance beam. You can also allow the pitcher to release his back side and finish balanced out over his front leg.

Focus   To teach proper balance and positioning of the upper body over the lead leg following release.

Setup   This drill can be done individually or with a partner, with or without a ball.

Procedure   The pitcher assumes a position with his throwing-side knee on the ground and his hands together at his chest. He turns his upper body, breaks his hands, and executes the throwing motion with good upper-body mechanics. As he reaches the release point, he presses his glove-side foot into the ground. This allows him to lift himself into a finish position with his chest and glove over his knee.

Coaching Points   This drill is excellent for helping pitchers who need to firm up their front side at release. As the pitcher presses his glove-side foot into the ground, he'll be forced to firm up his front leg to provide support and balance on release. Failure to firm up the lead leg at release reduces a pitcher's power and his ability to get full extension to his target. The pitcher should keep his head and eyes level and on his target. If he can do this, he has good balance as well as good direction to the target.

Modifications   Modify this drill by having the pitcher execute the throwing motion with a towel, reaching forward to a target, such as a chair. This adds an additional degree of difficulty that serves to improve extension as well as balance at the finish.

Focus   To improve arm action by indicating to the pitcher if the path of his arm deviates too far offline after separation from the glove.

Setup   Pitchers can do this drill alone or with a partner, on flat ground or on the mound. The drill requires a protective screen or other solid surface.

Procedure   The pitcher assumes a postpivot position with his lead shoulder pointed at his target and his hands together at his midline. Place a protective screen parallel to the pitcher's line to the target about one or two inches away from the pitcher's back. On command, the pitcher separates his hands and executes a throw to his target without allowing his throwing arm to contact the screen.

a

b

Coaching Points   Arm action is one of the most difficult aspects of a pitcher's delivery to correct. Significant improvement in arm action is more likely to occur in younger pitchers than in older pitchers, whose arm action has become a much stronger habit. Proper execution of this lateral screen drill might help the pitcher improve his arm action, allowing him to self-correct for arm action that results in "digging" or "hooking" behind his body, thus making contact with the screen. Although the emphasis of this drill is on the action of the throwing arm, also stress the action of the glove-arm. It might help to have the pitcher focus more on lifting his elbows at the separation of his hands, rather than focusing on the path of his throwing arm.

Modifications   Doing the drill in front of a mirror can give the pitcher useful information. He can see his arm action as opposed to just feeling it. Alternating sets of throws with and without the screen is also helpful.

148   TWO-KNEE CHEST TO GLOVE

Focus   To develop a feel for the chest going to the glove as opposed to a pulling of the glove; to feel the torque created when the upper body is rotated closed while the hips are open.

Setup   Pitchers do this drill on flat ground with a partner who catches the ball for the pitcher.

Procedure   Players face each other about 15 feet apart on their knees. The pitcher has a ball; he rotates his upper body into a closed position, keeping his eyes level and fixed on a target. As he rotates his upper body, he breaks his hands, assuming a power position. His glove extends toward his partner with his throwing arm up. After pausing with the upper body in a good throwing position, he then takes his chest to his glove and completes the throw. He should fall forward with his chest toward his glove; his throwing hand braces his upper body.

a   b

Coaching Points   As the pitcher rotates (closes his upper body), his knees should remain fixed and his lower body should face the target as much as possible. This is important in helping the pitcher understand and feel the torque involved in his delivery. As he rotates his upper body to throw, he should not spin or overrotate but rather take his chest toward his extended glove. In so doing, he'll learn the feel and understand the importance of staying on line with his target. The partner catching the ball should always give a target.

Modifications   Instead of pausing in the power position, the pitcher can continue his motion to complete the throw. This drill can also be done using a towel, with or without a partner.

149   UPRIGHT EXTENSION

Focus   To isolate the upper-body delivery mechanics just before the release of the ball; to emphasize proper alignment and direction at the finish of the delivery.

Setup   This drill is done with a towel, not a ball. It can be done alone or with a partner.

Procedure   The pitcher begins by setting his feet as far apart as comfortable, attempting to simulate a sound landing position in the delivery. He then rotates his back foot so that his shoestrings are pointed to his target (either a partner or a stationary object). His upper body is rotated so that his chest is open to his target. His throwing arm is in a power L position, his palm facing his target. The lead leg needs to be firm, not soft but also not rigid. His glove-hand extends toward his target; the glove should be on line with the target. He then places the towel comfortably between his throwing-hand fingers. The target should be waist high so that he can keep his head and eyes level on the target. The target should be far enough in front of him to require full extension of the throwing arm in order to contact the target. From this position, he completes the delivery so that he hits his partner's glove (or stationary target) with the towel. He should strive to take his chest to his glove rather than pull the glove toward his body. He should keep his back foot on the ground.

Coaching Points   Make sure the pitcher is on line with his target and that he keeps his head and eyes level throughout the drill. Encourage him to get full extension of his throwing arm. This requires him to fully extend his back side so that his back foot remains on the ground. Remind him not to allow his glove to pull off his target.

Modifications   You can modify this drill by allowing the pitcher to release his backside foot.

Focus To teach pitchers to "reach" to the target with their front side while keeping the back side over the rubber.

Setup Pitchers do this drill with a partner. They'll need a rope about six to eight feet long to loop around the pitcher's waist; the partner holds the ends of the rope a safe distance away.

Procedure Loop the rope around the pitcher's waist. He then gets into a postpivot balance position in which his pivot foot is parallel to the rubber and his lead leg is lifted to the top of its lift. His thigh should be at least parallel to the ground; his hands should be together at his midline. His head and eyes should be level and on his target. On reaching this balanced position, he holds the position for three seconds before completing his delivery to his target. The partner positions directly behind the pitcher, holding the rope firmly. If the pitcher is falling or leaking to the plate as he completes his delivery, he'll feel the rope pulling at his waist. If he is reaching appropriately to the plate with his lower body, he won't feel the initial pressure from the rope; in this case, the partner lets go of the rope and allows him to complete his delivery.

Coaching Points   This drill is excellent for teaching pitchers the difficult transition from the balance position to the landing. Emphasize the following: (1) the pitcher's stride foot should lead the delivery to the plate, not the front hip, (2) his lead leg should stay on line to the target and not swing in an arc to the plate, and (3) his back knee should break toward the target and not out over his pivot foot. It's also very important that the movement of the lead foot to the plate and the separation of the hands occur simultaneously. Encourage your pitcher to separate his hands at his midline and not to carry them toward his back hip as he reaches to the plate.

Modifications   This drill can be done off the mound with the pitcher throwing to a catcher or other partner.

Team Tactics

Chapter 16

Offensive Team Drills

Gene Stephenson and Jim Dimick

Aggressive base running and the ability to manufacture runs are vital parts of baseball success at all levels of the game. An effective bunting game that includes bunting for base hits as well as sacrificing to advance runners, coupled with aggressiveness on the base paths, is often the difference between winning and losing close games. Players enjoy an aggressive approach to the game, so building aggressiveness into your offensive philosophy can result in an inherent advantage, especially early in the season.

Applying pressure to the defense by way of taking the extra base, executing the bunting game, and exploiting hit and run and double steal situations has positive results in closely contested games. Too often, teams that rely on the big inning run into trouble when facing an outstanding pitcher. On such days the ability to manufacture runs becomes critical. Short game situations and aggressive base running must be included in daily practice plans and practiced diligently. The attitude that "we've been there before" promotes proper execution on game days.

Some baseball tacticians believe that such tactics as effective execution of double steals, squeeze bunts, and scoring from third base on ground balls through aggressive running give teams a built-in advantage equivalent to a one- or two-run lead at the outset of a game over opponents that lack an aggressive philosophy in their approach to the game.

Game-situation batting practice is another tool in building an offensive philosophy. Hitting with a purpose and adjusting to the situation at hand involve a team approach and should be incorporated into regular batting practice. Hitting with two strikes, for example, is a different challenge than hitting while ahead in the count. You should emphasize both during hitting drills. With two strikes, players should expand the strike zone, shorten the swing slightly, and try to hit the ball up the middle or straight back at the pitcher. Concentration on hitting up the middle forces the hitter to watch the ball more closely and reduces the risk of striking out. Of course, expanding the strike zone also greatly decreases the chance of being called out on strikes by the umpire.

Hitting while ahead in the count enables hitters to look for a pitch in their "zone"—the area over home plate where they most often get the best contact. This is called "zone hitting" and should be practiced periodically.

The many aggressive strategies, such as the hit and run, the fake bunt and slash, the down-angle approach with a runner at third base, and the squeeze bunt should be part of a hitter's practice routine. Players who execute well on the little things should be praised for their efforts. Rewarding players with extra swings or positive reinforcement adds luster to a well-organized practice and can lead to more quality at-bats on game day.

Game-situation drills often spice up a practice, usually at the end of the session. Emphasizing an aggressive offensive approach during practice sessions also better prepares your team for playing opponents who have a similar approach to the game. Taking the extra base, laying down a successful sacrifice bunt, fighting for a good lead, advancing on a pitch in the dirt, taking a pitcher deep in the count during a quality at-bat—all of this leads to good things happening for your team. By emphasizing the little things in practice and praising players who execute them in games, you create better team chemistry as well as the thrill that comes from shaking the hand of a losing coach.

When running base-running drills, look for proper angles, body lean, and stepping on the inside corner of the base—all critical fundamentals of aggressive base running.

Focus   To react to the situation on the down angle (contact play) and apply pressure to the defense.

Setup   Set up a complete defensive team; put a runner at third base. Tell your players there's one out. Flash the "down angle" sign.

Procedure   On the pitch, the runner attempts to read the angle of the ball off the bat. If the angle is down (ground ball), he reacts instantly and attempts to advance. If the ball is hit directly at an infielder and the throw is to home plate, the runner stops, gets into a rundown, and tries to delay the out until the hitter has reached second base.

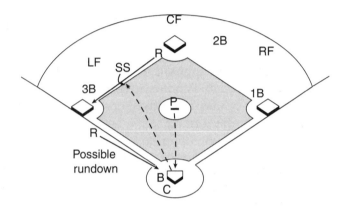

Coaching Points   By introducing this aggressive concept to high school coaches in the upper Midwest some years ago, the offensive phase of baseball was revolutionized in certain areas. By reacting quickly to the down angle of the ball, runners will score in most every situation except for the sharp ground ball hit directly at an infielder. When this occurs, forcing a rundown is usually the best the runner can do. Once in the rundown, he tries to prolong the play long enough for the batter to reach second base. Defensive teams expecting the down-angle play with a runner on third base often move the infield in for a play at home plate. Drawing the infielders in creates holes for a sharp ground ball to go through for a base hit. Even if the ball doesn't go through a hole, any ball hit with force against a drawn-in infield usually forces a fielder to move laterally, which almost always results in the runner at third scoring. The mere thought of the down-angle play poses a threat to the defense, and the ensuing pressure on the defense provides an advantage to the offensive team. Through practicing this play in game situations, runners learn to react quickly and become adept in executing the play.

Modifications   You can start this drill with runners at second and third.

Focus　To advance runners and put pressure on the defense.

Setup　A full defensive team is in place, including a pitcher on the mound. Coaches are in the coaching boxes. A few batters form a batting order.

Procedure　Place runners on various bases, call out the situation, and flash signs for each of them. Many situations can be worked into this drill, such as the following:

- Sacrifice bunt with runners at first and second
- Going for the chalk—quick players drop the ball down the third-base line for a base hit.
- Squeeze bunt with runners at third or at third and second, emphasizing keeping the bunt on the grass.
- Bunt and run
  1. With a runner at first moving with the pitch, bunt the ball on the left side, looking to advance the runner to third base.
  2. Runner at second attempts to steal third base; bunt down the third-base line, looking to score the runner.
- Fake bunt and slash in a bunt situation

This drill lets you decide which players can effectively be worked into a short-game offense, which might be necessary to manufacture runs when facing an overpowering pitcher.

Coaching Points　When executed successfully, short-game plays can have a huge psychological effect on the opponent.

1. On the squeeze bunt, emphasize bunting the ball in the original direction of the shortstop or second baseman. This reduces the chance of bunting foul or hitting a bunt that's easily handled by the pitcher.
2. On the bunt and run, the third-base coach reads the bunt and directs the advancing runner. A long throw from first base to a moving infielder retreating to third base often results in an overthrow, leading to a cheap run being scored.
3. On the fake bunt and slash, the hitter pivots at the hips, shows bunt, draws the bat back, and swings down at the pitch in an attempt to slap the ball through a moving defense intent on stopping the sacrifice bunt play.

153 MULTIPLE BASE RUNNING—LIVE SITUATION

Focus   To practice basic base-running skills, especially in early season practices.

Setup   Your entire squad participates, with multiple base runners. If outdoors, use a complete defensive team. If indoors, use infielders with a pitcher and catcher. Base runners line up in foul territory between the dugout and home plate. If space allows, you can run this drill simultaneously with batting practice, pitching workouts, or additional station work.

Procedure   Position base runners at various bases and have them react to the basic base-running situations that occur in a game. Base runners replace each other as they work their way around the bases. The drill begins with a pitched ball and runners reacting accordingly. A fungo hitter may be used rather than a live hitter to create more situations. All runners practice primary and secondary leads and read the ball off the bat. Coaches call out the situation (outs, score, pitch, and count).

Coaching Points   Give special emphasis to quick reactions to the ball angle:

- Freezing on line drives
- Tags and advancing on fly balls
- Reading the down angle of the ball quickly
- Reading the angle and reacting to the pitch in the dirt

Have pitchers occasionally throw breaking pitches into the dirt to elicit quick reactions from base runners. Hitters should react quickly to balls in the dirt and signal the runner on third base.

Modifications   In indoor situations, use semisoft balls, and players can react to the angle of the ball off the bat. This involves concentration on the part of the runner but leads to quick reactions once players move to outdoor conditions. If outdoors, coaches can modify the drill by fungoing balls instead of having hitters swing. This might make for more base-running situations. You can also run the drill using a tee, asking hitters to hit balls to all fields.

Focus   To practice situational hitting with competition between hitting groups.

Setup   Players are in groups of four or five, as follows:

Group 1—hitting from home plate

Groups 2 and 3—in defensive positions

Group 4—toss hitting or playing pepper prior to hitting

Group 5—with coach, who is throwing from normal batting practice distance

Procedure   The drill is timed and competitive; the winning group is determined by a stopwatch. Each hitting group begins with a runner at first base (this runner will be the last hitter in his group). The stopwatch begins with the initial pitch to home plate in a batting practice situation. Each hitter must successfully execute the following:

1. Sacrifice bunt—advance runner at first base to second base successfully. On an unsuccessful bunt attempt, the runner returns to first base.
2. With the advancing runner now on second base, the hitter must advance him to third base with a ground ball to the right side or a fly ball to the right field. The runner remains on second base until the hitter successfully moves him to third.
3. Once on third base, the hitter must execute a successful squeeze bunt, either a suicide or safety squeeze (predetermined by the coach and the same for each group).
4. Once the runner scores, the hitter must get a legitimate base hit, and then he becomes the runner at first base, and the cycle is repeated. The coach decides whether a hit is a base hit or not; the hitter remains at home plate until he gets a hit.
5. Once the last hitter completes his routine with a base hit, the runners line up at home plate and circle the bases, one after the other, just as they would on an inside-the-park home run. When the last runner touches home plate, the stopwatch records that group's time.
6. Announce each group's time.

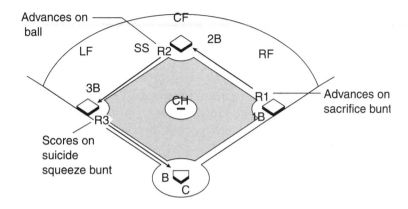

Coaching Points   This is an excellent drill to run near the end of practice. One of our assistant coaches saw a similar drill while observing the Houston Astros a few years ago, and we modified it to fit our situation. The enthusiasm runs high in this drill, and players enjoy the friendly competition. The drill is especially effective while on the road near the end of the season. Hitters focus on advancing runners in a game situation. Defensive players attempt to make each play while in the field, although sometimes they might be playing out of position. The coach always rules on whether the bunt or hit would have advanced the runner in a game situation.

Modifications   Limiting the hitting groups to small numbers makes for more fun and enthusiasm. Modifications to fit your players' skill level are a good idea.

- For younger players—with a runner on second base, a sacrifice bunt might be more appropriate than hitting to the right side.
- Substituting the down-angle contact play for the squeeze bunt might be an innovative change with the runner on third base.
- On squads where pitchers don't hit, try dividing them evenly and allowing them to hit after the last hitter completes the cycle. Pitchers take part in only the successful base hit part of the drill, with pitchers attempting to showcase their hitting prowess amid cheers and jeers. This adds to the fun at the end of a practice day.

Focus   To bunt and hit with a specific purpose.

Setup   Hitting groups of four are at home plate while coaches fungo between pitches to players in the field. Hitting groups are posted before practice and rotate quickly after each set. Use a regular batting practice situation—a coach throws behind an L screen, and other protective screens are in place to accommodate station work. Coaches fungo between pitches, and infielders throw to first base or work on double plays. Only three outfielders play the ball from home plate. This additional practice can be regulated by conditions of the day, available equipment, and the skill level of your players.

Procedure   Other station work can accompany the drill for practice efficiency, but we'll focus on the situational batting practice here. Hitters attempt to successfully execute the following:

- Six bunts—two sacrifice bunts, two suicide squeeze bunts, and two "going for the chalk" bunts

For each set of bunts executed properly, the hitter gets an extra swing in the ensuing part of the routine (for example, proper execution in all six bunts increases the round of five swings to eight). Players move in and out of the cage after each set of swings. The number of swings is as follows:

- Five routine
- Four with two strikes
- Three with a runner on third base
- Two hit and run
- One happy zone—3-0 count and the green light is on!

Coaching Points   Players react positively to situational hitting and concentrate on the task at hand. A batting practice pitcher with excellent control is an asset to this routine. Here are points for the various scenarios in the drill:

- With two strikes—the batting practice pitcher attempts to establish a bigger hitting zone, forcing hitters to protect the plate. Encourage hitters to hit any pitch that's even close to the plate and to drive the ball back up the middle.
- With a runner on third base—hitters attempt to hit the ball hard on the ground.
- On the hit and run—hitters try to make contact on any hittable pitch, driving it the opposite way, if possible.
- Happy zone—pitcher pitches into the heart of the strike zone.

Modifications   Hitting groups rotate through the drill as many times as practice allows. Award players extra swings for good execution (such as fouling off or making good contact on two-strike pitches or hitting sharp line drives or ground balls with a runner at third base.) Runners can proceed to first base and react to balls off the bat through the first two or three parts of the drill.

156 MULTIPLE BASE RUNNING—MOCK SITUATION II

Focus   To practice basic base-running skills and reactions to base coach instructions.

Setup   Use multiple base runners and a complete infield. Players are placed at various bases and replace each other as they make their way through the drill. This drill can be run effectively indoors or outdoors.

Procedure   Place runners in any desired situation and run the squad rapidly through the drill. Each repetition begins with a mock throw by a pitcher. Here are examples of what could occur:

1. Hitter takes a good swing, gets out of the batter's box with the rear foot, and runs straight through first base.
2. Runner at first base works for a good lead and breaks for second base.
3. Runners at second and third fight for a good primary lead and secondary lead and react quickly to an imaginary fly ball. Coaches can vary tag and part-way situations for runners. Players replace the runner ahead of them, and the drill is repeated as quickly as possible.

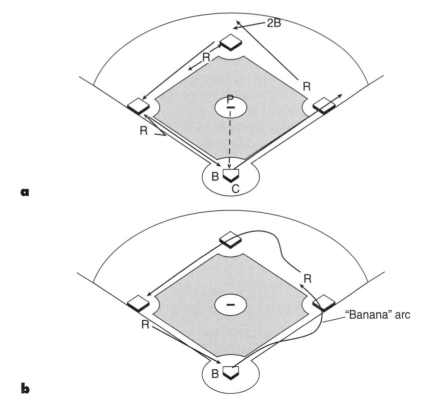

Coaching Points   This is a good early-season drill to improve reaction time and condition your players. You can present multiple base-running situations, emphasizing detailed coaching points. The value of this drill is directly related to how well you convince your players of the importance of base-running details in a mock situation. Each player works his way through the cycle as many times as you determine.

For the batters:

1. Takes a good swing and gets out of the batter's box, leading with the rear foot.
2. "Takes a peek" over his left shoulder on an imaginary ground ball to the left side of the infield.
3. Runs hard through first base, stepping on the front part of the base (never leap or slide, but run through the base) unless attempting to avoid a tag on an errant throw to the first baseman.
4. Stops quickly after tagging first base and turns to locate the imaginary ball. (First-base coach can verbally create situations.)

For the runners:

1. The runner at first base fights for a good lead and reacts quickly with a crossover step and runs behind second base on a steal situation.
2. Runners at second and third react quickly to either a tag or part-way situation.

Modifications   Set up various base-running situations. Here are some examples:

1. The batter takes a good swing, peeks, and reacts to a ball that goes through the infield. He makes a "banana arc," hitting the inside corner of first base and either stopping or continuing on to second base.
2. The runner at first base works on a good primary and secondary lead and reacts to a ball through the hole to right field. He instantly turns for help from the third-base coach and reacts to his signal, either holding at second base or continuing to third base.
3. The runner at third base (on an imaginary ground ball) shifts his weight to his front foot after the secondary lead, breaks quickly for home, and reacts to the on-deck hitter's instruction to stand or slide.

Focus To emphasize offensive situations that can occur off pop flies.

Setup Use a complete defensive team; put base runners at assigned positions.

Procedure Position runner or runners on bases. A coach hits fungo pop flies in attempts to create these offensive situations:

1. Runner at third base—pop fly behind first base; second baseman or first baseman catches the ball with his back to home plate (figure a). The runner tags up and attempts to score.
2. Runners at first and third—pop fly near first base dugout with one out (figure b). Both runners tag. The runner on first base breaks for second if no cutoff man positions properly. If it's a long throw to second base, the third-base runner scores.

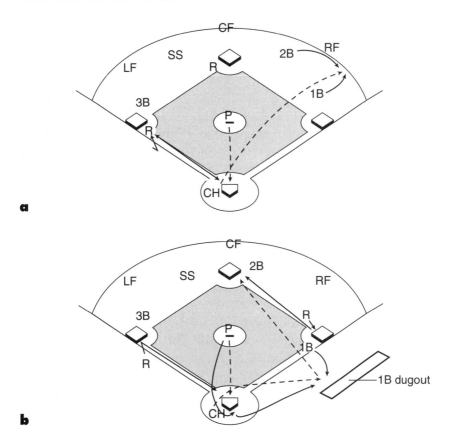

a

b

Coaching Points Offensive plays originating off pop flies can be very effective, especially in early season play or on windy days in which several players will converge on fly balls creating possible gaps in the defense.

Focus To practice first-and-third steal situations as an offensive threat.

Setup Use a full defensive team and part of the batting order. After detailed explanation and demonstrations, players practice various first-and-third plays in a scrimmage situation.

Procedure Players take turns in various first-and-third steal situations. With the defensive infield in place, a coach flashes signals and, with various combinations at first and third base, the team attempts all double-steal possibilities. Here are the possible variations:

1. Straight steal. With a quick runner at first, the goal is to steal second. The runner at third bluffs hard toward home, hoping to cause the middle infielder to cut the throw in an attempt to throw home. The runner at third reacts to the throw and breaks to score on a high or low throw, while being very alert to avoid being picked off at third base. The score, inning, number of outs, strengths of the hitter, and batting order play a part in dictating the gambling odds on this play and all first-and-third steals.

2. Early break or forced balk-steal. There are various ways to execute this play, but the most common occurs with the first-base runner breaking for second just as the pitcher comes to the set position. This could lead to a balk, which is one of the desired goals. If the pitcher steps off the rubber and a rundown occurs, the goal is to score the runner from third. This play occurs most often with two outs and a weak hitter at the plate or when a hitter is behind in the count with two strikes. Here are the points to focus on:

   a. The runner at first attempts to sprint hard, in an effort to prevent the pitcher from throwing to the second baseman, forcing a throw to the shortstop. Forcing a throw to the shortstop makes the play more difficult to defend because it could be a relatively long throw to home plate. The runner at first stays alive as long as possible in the rundown.

   b. The runner at third extends his lead with the pitcher's throw and breaks hard, forcing a throw home. The best time to break may be a calculated guess, depending on the quickness of the runner at first, the arm strength of the infielders, how hard the shortstop is running, and wind conditions. With the shortstop running hard, a runner at third can often score while the shortstop shifts his feet in attempt to throw to the catcher. Also, if the runner at third breaks hard just as the shortstop throws to the first baseman, the odds of scoring might increase if the runner at first can prolong the rundown.

A variation of this play occurs with a runner at third base and a three-ball count on a good base runner. If ball four is called, the runner runs at three quarter speed to first base. The first-base coach checks the position of the middle infielders. If one of the middle infielders is not on second base, he yells "Go!" and the runner who has just walked sprints hard to second base. A variety of things could happen now, including a throw into centerfield. This might be a good play to try with two outs and the bottom of the order due up.

3. Long-lead steal. This steal is similar to the early-break steal—the major difference is that by forcing a pickoff, the ball ends up in the first baseman's possession, and many first basemen do not throw as well as most shortstops. Here are the points to focus on:

   a. The runner at first extends his lead slightly beyond his normal distance (about one extra step). The lead should not be so obvious as to alert the entire defense.

   b. With the pickoff move to first base, the runner breaks hard for second base, and the runner at third extends his lead to a maximum distance off third base.

   c. The runner at third breaks for home as the first baseman sets to throw to second. He must be sure not to move on a bluffed throw. With a quick runner at third base, it takes two excellent throws to get him out at the plate.

Variations of the long-lead steal can be effective also. Here are some examples:

- The runner at first bluffs a break for second base and pretends to slip and fall. With the pickoff move from the pitcher, he quickly rights himself and gets into the rundown.

- The runner at first takes an exaggerated secondary lead, drawing a throw from the catcher and forcing a rundown play.

- If the runner at first base has good foot speed and no pickoff attempt occurs, he should steal second base in what becomes a straight double steal.

4. Delayed double steal. There are variations of this steal, but one very effective one goes this way: With the pitcher's move home, the runner at first takes three exaggerated bounding hops toward second base and then breaks hard on an attempted steal. If executed properly, the middle infielder and catcher might not be alerted to the steal because the first baseman might not differentiate the three hops from a normal secondary lead. At times, the catcher might throw to an empty base or to a late-arriving middle infielder; better yet, he might hold the ball.

5. Backdoor double steal. This steal involves a one-out situation in which the offensive team attempts to sacrifice an out for a run. The runner at first takes a slightly longer lead than normal, leading off one stride deeper than a straight line to second base. He is now three or four feet toward right field. On the pickoff move, he dives straight for the foul line and

scrambles to the backside of first base. On the tag attempt of the first baseman, he'll often step toward right field with his left foot and end up in an awkward position to throw home. The runner at third lengthens his lead with the pickoff move and breaks hard for home the instant the ball is caught by the first baseman.

Coaching Points   Defending against the double steal is difficult, especially for younger players. Exploiting defensive weaknesses can lead to an extra run or two and also gain a psychological advantage. By practicing first-and-third situations diligently from an offensive angle, a team learns to defend the various situations as well.

This is an excellent drill for both offense and defense. It also gives coaches an idea which players might be the most effective in double-steal situations. It's best to run this drill with your regular batting order because this way the same first-and-third runners are more likely to follow in ensuing game situations. This drill can also be mixed with bunt and hit-and-run situations.

159   MODIFIED SCRIMMAGE

Focus   To expose players to game situations in a modified scrimmage.

Setup   All players take their positions.

Procedure   Pitchers work two innings straight, with teams staying on the field until six outs occur. Runners leave the field after three outs. At this point, coaches can add runners at various bases to create desired situations. Teams switch quickly after six outs.

Coaching Points   This drills works well for creating a variety of game situations in a limited amount of time.

Modifications
- Hitters start with a 2-1 count to speed up play.
- Runners must steal within three pitches.
- All balls in live ball territory must be played as fair balls. This modification makes for a wide-open offensive game, forcing the defense to set up relay situations.

Focus   To practice base-running techniques and react effectively to various base-running situations.

Setup   All team members participate. These base-running situations are practiced on the field, some in daily practice and some during pregame batting practice.

1. Practice setting. Divide the squad into three groups to practice base running. The regular infielders, catchers, and pitchers make up two groups; the outfielders and extra players make up the third group.
2. During pregame batting practice. After completing his swings, each batter routinely works on various base-running situations at each base.

Procedure   One drill is done on the practice field and provides an opportunity for outfielders and extra players to practice their base-running skill while giving the defense gamelike competition. The two defensive teams alternate on defense. The two situations confronting the defense are the bunt situation with runners on first and second and the steal situation with runners on first and third. In this controlled intrasquad game setting, these two game situations can be practiced repeatedly.

In pregame batting practice, each batter works his way around the bases, reacting to designated and various base-running situations. The number of outs at each base is designated by the coaching staff before the pregame practice. All kinds of base-running situations can be covered during the course of the season. Players get multiple repetitions on particular base-running situations during each drill session. In both practice settings, encourage players to attend to hustle and proper execution.

Coaching Points   Monitor your players as they refine their defensive skills and base-running techniques. Consistently repeating these situations under vigilant supervision produces good results.

Modifications   The first-and-third situation and the situation with runners on first and second base can be set up to work repeatedly on one part of the drill at a time. The base-running during pregame batting practice can be adjusted to emphasize almost any base-running situation.

161 CONCENTRATION AND HAND-EYE DRILL

Focus   To practice and develop concentration and hand-eye coordination.

Setup   A coach or a partner ball tosses to a hitter. You need a screen or a net and several baseballs.

Procedure   We refer to this as a two-ball, soft-toss drill, but it's different than the drill commonly associated with that name. The feeder (coach or player) assumes a normal soft-toss position. He stacks two balls in one hand, one on top of the other. He swings the hand back and then forward, releasing the balls so that they arrive over the hitting zone 6 to 10 inches apart, one over the other. When his hand starts forward, the feeder calls out "Top!" or "Bottom!" to the hitter to let him know which ball to locate and hit.

Coaching Points   This drill works concentration and hand-eye coordination skills. If the hitter commits too quickly, he'll have difficulty making good contact.

Modifications   With a ball in each hand, the feeder starts a circular motion with both hands. He then varies the time and hand from which he releases the ball.

162 EACH SWING QUICKER THAN THE LAST

Focus   To develop an explosive, quick swing.

Setup   It's best to run this drill in small groups, but it works fine with a single player. It can also be done in pairs or accommodate as many players as space allows. Each player in the drill needs enough room to take complete swings, free from distractions and danger.

Procedure   You can run this drill within any practice setting by designating a station and allowing a block of time between 10 and 15 minutes. To get the most out of hitting, hitters should develop a fundamentally sound swing; develop strength and quickness; and practice their swing with an emphasis on proper mechanics while attempting to make each swing quicker than the last. The results of this drill can be easily seen in both batting practice and game situations. A quicker swing allows the hitter to see the ball longer before needing to make a decision to swing at a pitcher.

Coaching Points   If done with the proper technique and focus, this simple activity can be among your most valuable hitting drills. Watch the speed and execution of each swing; tell players to make each swing quicker than the last—not harder, but quicker! For success, the practice swings must maximize bat speed and be fundamentally sound, and each player must be able to visualize pitches being thrown to him.

Modifications   This is a versatile drill that you can do with all of your players or just one or a few at a time. Use it in short sessions or spend a block of practice time giving players up to 200 swings a day to increase bat speed and consistency. There is *no* substitute for swinging the bat.

163   GAME-SITUATION BUNT

Focus   To execute bunts that match the game situation.

Setup   Both offensive and defensive players take the playing field to execute this drill. A pitching machine (or batting practice pitcher) throws all the pitches for the activity. Divide the squad into two groups, offense and defense. The offense will be challenged with several game situations. The defense uses all its weapons to stop the offensive team.

Procedure   In a game simulation, the hitter steps into the batter's box with a 2-1 count. To reach base, the hitter must bunt for a hit or draw a walk. With runners on base, the hit-and-run, bunting for a hit, the squeeze, or a fake squeeze can be attempted. Keep score; the winning team has no field duties after practice that day.

Coaching Points   Using the bunt at the right time in a game is a powerful offensive tool. The drill allows you to measure each player's bunting ability.

Modifications   During the course of this drill, you can interject as many game situations as you'd like.

164   GAME VELOCITY BUNT

Focus   To practice the skill of cushioning the ball with the bat to accomplish a successful bunt at high speed.

Setup   Each offensive player takes his turn executing all types of bunts. This drill is operated in the same manner as batting practice on the field. Instead of taking batting practice swings, each offensive player practices bunting.

Procedure   To simulate game velocity, we place a pitching machine 55 feet from home plate and set it at a good speed. Instead of taking swings in the live group on the field, we work to execute all types of bunts for 10 to 12 minutes. The increased velocity makes each hitter work on deadening the ball. If a player can deaden the ball, the angle of the bunted ball is less critical.

Coaching Points   It's important for bunters to get accustomed to game speeds so they learn to control the bat as it contacts the ball.

165   FIRST, THIRD, SQUEEZE, AND DRAG

Focus   To properly execute four kinds of bunts according to the situation.

Setup   All hitters participate on the playing field; a coach pitches.

Procedure   Before live batting practice on the field, we have our hitters execute a sacrifice to first base, then to third base, followed by a squeeze bunt, and finally a push or drag bunt. If a hitter fails to execute the bunts, he loses swings at regular batting practice. The hitter bunts until he has done all four bunts successfully.

Coaching Points   Successful execution of these four bunts is a priority. Bunting techniques have been emphasized previously, so now we're looking for successful results.

Modifications   If players have trouble with any of the four bunts, you might devote a drill to work on that bunt alone.

Focus   To complete the swing and develop power through resistance.

Setup   One to two hitters work at a tire station. A tire station is a piece of equipment the coaching staff can build or have built. Here's how it's done: Fill an old tire with cement and attach and extend a heavy pole through the center, resembling the base of a tether ball pole. Cut holes at the top and bottom of the second tire so that it can be placed on the pole (standing up) and spin freely. Make an adjustable platform for the second tire to rest on. The tire filled with cement lays flat, with the pole extending skyward. The second tire rests on its adjustable base and can rotate freely around the pole.

Procedure   The hitter works on making the tire spin by driving the bat into and through the side of the tire. This promotes lower body rotation and drive. Keeping the hands inside the ball is also enhanced. The hitter should power through the resistance and should not let the tire disrupt his swing. Repetitions develop a quick and powerful stroke as well as good hip rotation, correct thrust, and pivot with the back leg.

Coaching Points   Hitters work on the proper pivot and follow-through. The tire adds resistance. Make sure the hitter continues on through the tire with his swing.

Modifications   There are other types of resistance tools, such as blocking dummies or hanging tires. This particular tire drill, however, adds resistance while forcing the hitter to power through and finish his swing.

Focus   To work on proper hand extension and getting the hands "inside the ball."

Setup   For the first part of the drill, one player (or more) assumes a stance with his back foot six inches from a wall and a bat in his hand. To execute the second part of the drill, players assume a batting stance with feet parallel to the wall at a distance of a bat's length.

Procedure   There are two phases to this drill. In phase one, the hitter places his back foot within six inches from a wall. He should take free swings and avoid hitting the wall on his approach. This keeps him from dropping the barrel and casting the bat. It also takes the hands to the contact point efficiently. In phase two, the hitter faces the wall and places the knob end of the bat over his belly button; he extends the bat until the barrel end touches the wall. He takes his stance and takes free swings without hitting the wall.

Coaching Points   This exercise helps the hitter get his lead arm extended first and keeps him from casting the head of the bat. The hitter's hands will work inside the ball. We want our hitters' hands to get to the hitting zone quickly. Casting the bat drops the head of the bat and makes for a longer swing. This drill also helps the lead arm extend properly.

Modifications   If the drill is done outside, you can use a batting screen, net, or standing pad instead of a wall. Each phase of this drill could become a drill of its own.

Chapter 17

Defensive Team Drills

Ray Tanner

No defense likes to be scored on, and it's even worse when the runs are cheap. Our defensive teams pride themselves on making the other team earn their runs. The drills in this chapter will help your defense do the same. Your defensive players, even those who are offensive stars first and foremost, must strive to play great defense, both physically and mentally.

It's rare for an offense to bunch up enough hits to take the other team out of the game. This being the case, the defense needs to stay sharp and focused until the last out is recorded. It doesn't take that much for a three-run inning to become a six-run inning. A couple of missed opportunities, an ill-advised throw, and the next thing you know your offense's hard-earned lead has dwindled to nothing. It's going to happen sometimes; how often it happens depends on how committed your players are to working on defense fundamentals. All of the drills in this chapter share a common characteristic—they allow minimal to zero offensive output. They can help turn your team into a fine-tuned defensive machine.

In 2002, the University of Texas beat my team in the national championship game. But the University of South Carolina finished first in the country in team defense. You have to have some good offense and stellar pitching to play in the last game of the college season, but I'm convinced that our team defense is what catapulted us into the company of the country's elite teams. We generally handled our routine outs (.975 fielding percentage), and we kept the game in control by throwing to the right bases. We worked hard not to allow extra bases.

If your team practices these drills effectively with regularity, they'll have a much easier time executing in live games. Don't give the offensive team anything. Make them earn every run.

Focus   (1) To consistently catch balls hit into the air; (2) to communicate effectively with teammates.

Setup   All nine position players play their positions. Two coaches are in the batters' boxes (one in the right-hand box, one in the left-hand box), each with a fungo bat and a baseball. Do this drill on a regulation field.

Procedure   Once you have all nine defensive positions covered, you're ready for your coaches to begin the drill. The coaches rotate hitting balls high into the air in different areas of the field. The players converge on the ball, communicating as necessary. If more than one player can easily catch the ball, verbal communication decides who goes for it, based on priority of position. Coaches take turns hitting in the air for 20 to 30 minutes, using all areas of the field.

Figure a demonstrates a pop-up hit into shallow centerfield. Although the shortstop, centerfielder, and second baseman can make the catch, the out should be recorded by the centerfielder because he's the priority person in this triangle. If the centerfielder calls for the baseball, he's the one to make the catch.

Figure b illustrates a fly ball hit into the area behind third base that drifts into shallow left field. This catch becomes difficult for the third baseman, so the catch should be made by the shortstop or the left fielder. In this scenario, the shortstop makes the play because he called for the ball, and the left fielder didn't. If the left fielder had called for the ball, the shortstop would have cleared out of the way, allowing the left fielder to make the catch.

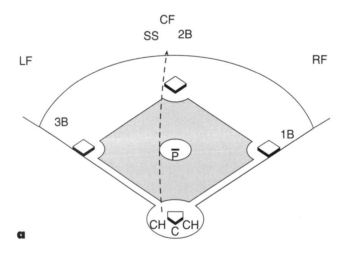

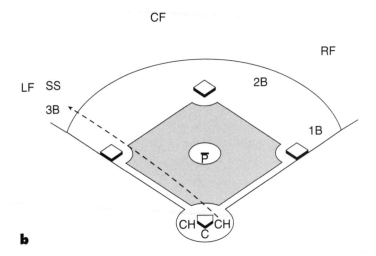

b

Coaching Points   Your centerfielder has ultimate priority over the field. Any time your centerfielder calls for the ball, all of the other players should clear the area so that he can make the catch. The left fielder and right fielder are next in the chain of command. There should never be a problem between the left fielder and right fielder because they should never converge on the same baseball. The third priority position is the shortstop. The shortstop should catch any ball that he is comfortable with unless one of the outfielders calls him off. The shortstop rules the infield. The next priority order is the second baseman, followed by the third baseman. The first baseman is next in order, followed by the catcher. The pitcher has the lowest priority in catching pop-ups. The verbal terminology used to call for the ball varies from team to team. The priority system beginning with the centerfielder should never vary unless the coach is more confident with one position over another.

Modifications   Once a coach hits the ball into the air and it's caught, have the player who made the catch throw the ball to a particular base or to home plate. I like for our players to throw the ball to home on at least one bounce. Our catchers are required to catch the throw and make a tag play as if a runner is trying to score. The importance of catching a fly ball is what's crucial in this drill, so I don't modify it often.

Focus   To prevent the runner at third base from scoring once the pitcher delivers to the plate or throws to first base.

Setup   You can do this drill with a defensive player in every position, but I recommend not using the outfielders. The outfielders can serve as base runners to make the practice more realistic. Run this drill on a regulation infield. You don't need to use the outfield. Infielders take their positions, including a pitcher on the mound. If your outfielders are base runners, put three at first base and three at third.

Procedure   This defensive team drill is used when the offensive team has runners at first base and third base. The pitcher operates from the stretch position, paying attention to the base runners at first and third. The base runner at first has options as to when he breaks for second. He can early steal, straight steal, or delay. The base runner at first wants to help the runner at third score by causing confusion or a bad throw. The defensive team's focus is to keep the runner on third from scoring.

If the pitcher delivers to the plate, the runner at first attempts to steal second. Our catcher receives the baseball, checks the runner at third to make sure he hasn't wandered too far off the bag, and throws to second. If the runner at third doesn't break for home, the infielder (shortstop or second baseman) takes the throw and tags the runner out. If the runner at third breaks for the plate once the catcher throws to second, the infielder (shortstop or second baseman) taking the throw leaves second base and catches the throw as he moves toward home. He then makes the throw back to the catcher to allow the catcher time to tag the runner out. This action is shown in the diagram, with the shortstop taking the throw.

If the runner at first base attempts an early steal to disrupt the pitcher, the pitcher should follow these easy steps: step off the rubber, check the runner at third, and throw the ball to the middle infielder with second-base coverage. The pitcher then runs behind the first baseman, getting into position to assist

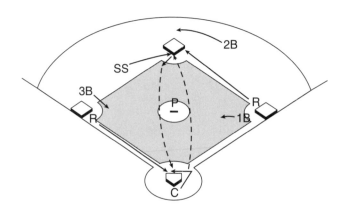

if a rundown should occur. The middle infielder taking the throw must be prepared to fire the ball home if the runner at third breaks toward the plate. If the runner at third plays "cat and mouse," then the middle infielder begins chasing the runner from first base back toward the first-base bag. Once that runner from third takes off for home, the defensive middle infielder pivots and throws to the catcher in time to record the out.

Coaching Points   We must prevent the runner from third scoring. Good defensive teams are eager to have offensive teams force base-running issues because outs are recorded without the pitcher adding to his pitch count.

Modifications   You can run this drill in a gym if a regular baseball infield isn't available. As long as you have enough space to lay the bases out 90 feet apart, you can do the drill effectively.

170   DEFENDING FIRST AND THIRD II

Focus   To get the runner at first base out if he tries to steal second or if he breaks early to assist the runner at third.

Setup   As mentioned in the previous drill, you can put a defensive player in every position, but I don't think that's necessary to execute the drill. Having your outfielders run the bases works better. Run this drill on a regulation infield. Infielders take their positions, along with the catcher and pitcher. If your outfielders are base runners, split them up between first base and third base. In this drill, the team in the field is leading the game 6-1 (having 5 or more runs, especially late in the game, strategically calls for giving up a run for an out).

Procedure   This defensive team drill is used when the offensive team has runners at first base and third base. In part I, our primary focus was the runner at third base. Now, because we're leading the game by five runs, we concentrate on getting the runner at first. We need three outs to end the game.

The pitcher prepares to deliver a pitch to the plate while the runners at first base and third base take their lead. When the pitch goes toward the plate, the runner at first breaks toward second to steal. Your focus is to get this runner out. The runner from third is of no concern because of the five-run lead. He can't beat you, so the important thing is to record the out, which is easier. The middle infielder who takes the throw from the catcher can tag the runner out. If the runner from first stops to get in a rundown (to help his runner at third get home), you disregard the third-base runner and go after the player on first. You should be able to record an easy out because the runner from first usually assumes that your defensive players will go after the runner from third if he breaks toward home. Wrong. This time your priority is to get the easiest out.

With the runners at first and third, the runner at first may break toward second even before the pitcher delivers to the plate. In this case, the pitcher steps off the rubber, ignores the runner at third, and attempts to get an out on the runner from first. If the base runner from first stops between first and second, the pitcher should run toward the base runner at an angle that forces the runner back to first. If the runner begins to run, the pitcher should immediately give the ball to the middle infielder and go behind the first baseman and be ready for a rundown. The middle infielder should chase the runner back to first, giving the ball to the first baseman at the point where he can step up, take the throw, and tag the base runner.

The diagram illustrates the runner from first breaking toward second before the pitcher delivers to the plate. The pitcher steps off the rubber (ignoring the runner at third) and goes toward the first-base runner, who has stopped between first and second. The pitcher realizes that he might not get the angle to push the ball to the second baseman. The second baseman will now begin the rundown back to first, where an out will be recorded on the base runner.

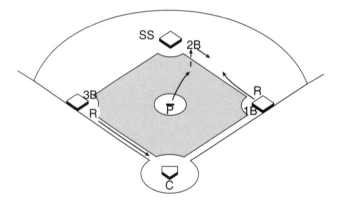

Coaching Points   In this situation, recording an out is the primary concern. You're gambling that letting the runner from third score won't come back to haunt you. Before your pitcher delivers the ball to the plate, your catcher signals to your infielders the play number designed to record the out on the runner at first if he attempts to move toward second. The signal indicates that the runner at third is of no concern. You are trying to shorten the game.

Modifications   As in part I, you can practice this drill anywhere you can lay out an infield.

Focus To prevent the runner at third from scoring.

Setup As in the previous two drills, you can choose to use a defensive player at every position, but the outfielders are more useful as base runners. Run the drill on a regulation infield. Your infielders take their positions, including a pitcher and catcher. If your outfielders are base runners, split them between first and third.

Procedure With runners at first and third, the pitcher goes into a set position (checking the base runners) and delivers the pitch home. The base runner at first can steal, delay, or break early to try to distract the pitcher. His goal is trying to score the runner from third.

If the runner at first takes an early break, the pitcher can either step off and allow him to go to second or continue his delivery to the plate. The pitcher is not distracted by the runner at first because the priority is the runner at third. Basically, the runner at first is ignored.

If the pitcher delivers to the plate, the catcher will do a full-arm fake to second if the runner at first attempts to steal second. After the full-arm fake, the catcher immediately sets his sights on the base runner at third. If the runner at third has leaned or drifted away from the bag, the catcher might make a throw to third. If the runner at third breaks toward the plate on the catcher's full-arm fake, the catcher pursues him with a rundown play, as shown in the diagram.

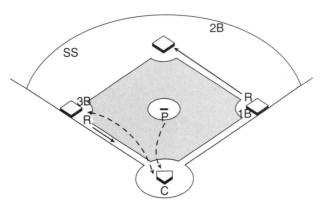

Coaching Points The game situation dictates that you cannot let the runner from third base score. This is why you ignore the runner at first. You can't afford to make a bad throw or bad decision that enables an easy score from third. The runner at third is to be treated as if he's the winning run.

Modifications As in parts I and II, you can practice this drill anywhere you can lay out an infield.

Focus   To attempt to get a runner at third out after the pitcher delivers to the plate.

Setup   Do this drill on a regulation infield. Infielders take position, including pitcher and catcher. Outfielders serve as base runners. Put half of them at first base and the other half at third.

Procedure   The pitcher goes into a set position while checking the runners at first and third. When the pitcher delivers to the plate, the runner at first attempts to steal second or get hung up between first and second. The runner at first does everything he can to be a distraction so that the runner at third can score.

Once the catcher receives the pitch, he's going to ignore the runner at first and throw directly to the third baseman. The third baseman will try to tag out the runner at third before he can return to the bag. This is simply the catcher trying to pick off the runner at third. The base runner at first base is not a factor.

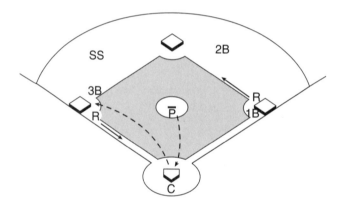

Coaching Points   This is the fourth and final part in defending first and third. You might want to establish four different signals to indicate to your team which part of this defensive drill is in effect.

If the base runner at third is not off the bag far enough to merit a throw, the catcher should hold the ball rather than risk an errant throw or misplay. A good time to use this defensive play is when there is an inexperienced base runner at third or a runner who appears to be overly aggressive.

The base runner at first attempts to be a distraction, but he is ignored in this drill. It doesn't matter if he goes to second. Our priority is the base runner at third.

Using verbal directions, move the third baseman off the line so that the base runner at third hears the direction. This verbal may lead the third-base runner to drift farther from the base.

Modifications   This drill can be practiced anywhere you can lay out an infield but is most realistic when you practice it on a regular infield so base runners can simulate at full speed.

Focus To put our defensive players in a position to field a bunted ball and get an out at either second base or first base.

Setup Players align themselves in their normal positions before the bunt play is put on by the catcher. You don't have to use base runners, but they give the drill a more gamelike feel.

Procedure Because there's a runner on first base and the offense has the bunt on, we want a defensive coverage that allows our corner infielders (first and third base), our pitcher, and our catcher to field the baseball and throw to either first or second base to get an out. Our shortstop will cover second base, and our second baseman will cover first base. If possible, we want to get the lead runner at second base out (because an offense will usually only bunt with no outs). This will give us one out with a runner on first base and keep a double play possibility alive. If this situation takes place, and we're successful in getting the lead runner out, we see this as a major plus. However, we feel the coverage has been successful if we get the out at first base, which happens more often than getting the lead runner. The key is to read the bunter's hands and body as he gets into the bunting position and to quickly move into our defensive coverage. Again, our focus is to get an out in any bunt situation.

The pitcher's responsibility is to throw a high strike, which is a difficult pitch for the bunter to bunt on the ground consistently. Once he delivers the pitch, he has responsibility for bunted balls in front of the mound and slightly toward the first-base side of the mound. He has priority over the first baseman on balls bunted in this area.

The catcher puts the bunt play on by verbally communicating with all infielders. Once the play has been put on, he calls for a high strike. He has responsibility for all balls bunted within close proximity of home plate. He has priority over the pitcher and first baseman on bunted balls. It's the catcher's responsibility to call what base the ball is being thrown to and to cover third base if the third baseman vacates his position to field the bunted ball.

The first baseman holds the runner at first base until the pitch is released. Once the pitch has been released and the batter squares to bunt, the first baseman charges quickly toward the batter. He has right-side responsibility and priority over the pitcher on bunted balls. If the third baseman fields the bunted ball, he must go back to the bag and peel off if the second baseman is already in position. Once the pitcher starts his delivery, the second baseman comes straight in to defend a possible push bunt. Once you see the batter is in a sacrifice position, go straight toward first base and cover the bag. Communicate with the first baseman to let him know the base is covered.

The shortstop plays at standard depth and waits to see the batter square into a bunting position, then breaks hard for second base and anticipates a throw.

The third baseman starts on infield grass 15 to 20 feet from third base. He has priority over everyone on a bunted ball. If someone else fields the ball, he'll cover third base to keep the runner from second base from advancing.

The left fielder backs up third base. The centerfielder backs up second base, and the right fielder backs up first base.

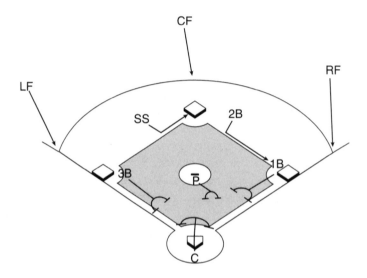

Coaching Points   Vary the placement of the bunts down the third-base line, between the third-base line and the pitcher's mound, down the first-base line, and between the first-base line and the mound. Make sure infielders know their priorities on bunted balls; check to ensure that your players not involved in fielding a bunt (shortstop, second base, outfielders) go to the base or back up the positions they're supposed to. Also check to see if your catcher, corner infielders, and pitcher are communicating on who will field the ball. If the third baseman fields the ball, make sure the catcher sprints to third to cover the bag and the pitcher covers the plate to hold the runner at second base.

Modifications   You can practice the fundamentals on a baseball diamond, in the outfield, or inside a gym. All you need are bases and your infielders, outfielders, and pitchers. You can use your outfielders as base runners to make the drill more realistic and competitive or have them practice backing up the bases.

Focus   To get an out by putting our defensive players in a position to field the bunted ball and make the play.

Setup   You'll need all of your infielders at their positions and a pitcher on the mound. You can use outfielders as base runners to give the drill a more gamelike feel.

Procedure   The pitcher has responsibility for bunted balls toward the mound and to the left of the mound. He will focus on throwing a high strike to the catcher, which is difficult to bunt on the ground.

The catcher puts the bunt play on by a verbal signal or going through a series of hand signals. He's responsible for a bunted ball in front of the plate.

The first baseman holds the runner at first base until the pitch is released. Once the pitch is released and the batter is squared to bunt, the first baseman charges quickly toward the batter. He has right-side responsibility on all bunts. If he fields the bunt, he listens to the catcher's instruction on where to throw the ball. If the ball is bunted right back to the pitcher or hard toward third base, then he must go back to first base and peel off if the second baseman is already in position.

Once the pitcher starts his delivery, the second baseman comes straight toward the batter to defend against a possible push bunt. Once the ball is bunted, he goes straight to first base to cover the bag because the first baseman has vacated his position.

The shortstop holds the runner at second base close to keep his lead minimal so that the runner has a greater distance to run to third base once the ball is bunted. When the batter bunts the ball, the shortstop goes to second base and anticipates a throw.

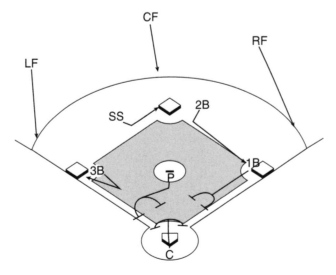

The third baseman starts on the infield grass about 10 feet in front of the bag. He will open up slightly toward second base to make sure the runner at second doesn't break early behind him. Once the batter squares, the third baseman charges hard on a ball bunted back down the line that the pitcher can't get to. If the pitcher, first baseman, or catcher can field the bunted ball, he will retreat back to the third-base bag and await a possible throw.

The left fielder backs up third base. The centerfielder backs up second base, and the right fielder backs up first base.

Coaching Points   In the standard bunt defense our priority is not necessarily to get the lead out at third base. However, if the bunted ball gets in the hands of our catcher, pitcher, or first baseman quickly, we might have a play at third. If the ball is bunted very hard into our coverage, we might be able to get the runner at third or second base, which keeps the double play possibility alive. Generally, with runners on first and second base, the batter will try to bunt down the third-base line, hoping to draw the third baseman in enough so that he must make the play. If this occurs, we can probably get the out only at first base. It's crucial to know what types of base runners we have and to hold these runners close to the base so that we can possibly get an out at third or second base. Our catcher plays a vital role in telling our corner infielders and pitchers which base to throw to.

Vary the placement of the bunts from the third-base line to the first-base line and all areas in between. Make sure infielders communicate with each other on who is fielding the bunt to ensure they're where they're supposed to be.

Modification   You can do this drill on a baseball diamond, in the outfield, or inside a gym. All you need are infielders, a catcher, and a pitcher to execute this coverage.

DEFENDING THE BUNT:
RUNNER ON FIRST (EARLY BREAK)

Focus   To move our corner infielders into their coverage early to be in position to get the lead runner.

Setup   All infielders, the catcher, and the pitcher take their positions. We also use base runners, which are generally outfielders, to make the drill more gamelike. We rotate all of our pitchers, infielders, and catchers into the drill in practice to make sure everyone can execute the coverage. You can run this drill on a regulation infield.

Procedure   The pitcher checks the runner at first and throws a high strike to the plate. He has coverage from the mound to the first-base line. The catcher puts the coverage on by signaling and then calls for a high strike. He has coverage of bunts in front of the plate. He communicates with the defense on where to throw the bunted ball. When the pitcher's hands reach the top of the stretch position, the first baseman breaks hard toward the plate and covers the bunt down the first-base line. The second baseman comes in toward the batter to defend a possible push bunt, then breaks for first base. The shortstop covers second base and waits for a possible throw from the pitcher, catcher, or corner infielders. The third baseman starts 15 feet in front of the bag and charges in if the ball is bunted anywhere from the third-base line to the mound. If the ball is bunted on the first-base side or toward the pitcher, he retreats quickly back to third base so the runner can't advance. The left fielder backs up third base. The centerfielder backs up second base, and the right fielder backs up first base.

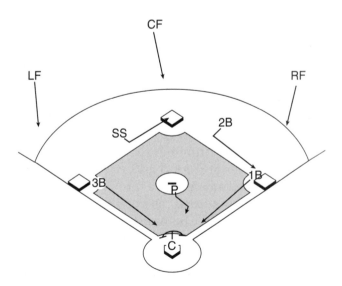

Coaching Points   We use this coverage in a late-inning situation when the runner on first represents the tying or winning run. Our priority is to get the lead runner out, but we *must* get the out even if that means going to first base. We emphasize not trying to force the throw to second base to get the lead out because we don't want a situation where we possibly have runners on first and second base due to a rushed throw to first. However, if our guys are in position to get the lead out, this is a big play for our defense because it leaves us with a runner on first base and one out and the double play possibility still alive.

During the course of this drill, vary the direction of the rolled bunts. This will get all four infielders involved in making plays. Also check to make sure your corner infielders are coming in when the pitcher comes to the top of the stretch so that by the time the ball has been bunted they are in position to get the lead out.

Modifications   To make the drill more gamelike, have your outfielders run the bases and even be the bunters. This gives them practice on their sacrifice skills and in base running.

176   DEFENDING THE BUNT: RUNNER ON FIRST AND SECOND (EARLY BREAK)

Focus   To get the lead out at third base.

Setup   All infielders, the catcher, and the pitcher take their positions. You can use outfielders as base runners.

Procedures   Once the pitcher receives the sign from the catcher, he throws a high strike to the catcher. He has coverage of bunts in front of the mound. Catchers give the sign. They have coverage on bunts in front of the plate. The first baseman starts in front of the runner at first base on the grass. When the pitcher reaches the top of the stretch, the first baseman breaks in toward the plate. He has coverage on bunts to the right of the mound and to the foul line. The second baseman cheats over toward first base. Once the pitcher starts his delivery, the second baseman comes in toward the plate to defend against the push bunt, then goes straight toward first base and anticipates a throw. The shortstop holds the runner at second base close to the bag. After the pitcher checks the runner at second and starts his leg lift, the shortstop breaks hard for third base and anticipates a throw. The third baseman starts 10 to 15 feet in front of the bag and turns his body toward the runner at second so he doesn't break for third base behind him. Once the pitcher starts his delivery, the third baseman breaks in hard toward the batter and covers the left side of the mound to the line for the bunted ball. The left fielder backs up third base. The center fielder backs up second base, and the right fielder backs up first base.

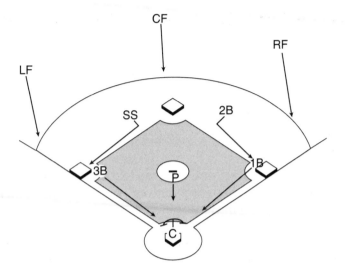

Coaching Points   We try to send our corner infielders in early to get in position to field the bunted ball and throw to the shortstop, who is covering third base. As with any bunt coverage, our catcher has to determine where the throw will go based on where and how hard the ball is bunted. We have two options for bases to throw to here, third base or first base. No one will be at second base in this coverage. We will use this coverage in a late-inning situation when the runner at second base represents the tying or winning run.

Hit bunts all over the infield to make sure your corners, infielders, pitchers, and catchers use proper footwork and make accurate throws to the bases. Check to make sure your players go where they're supposed to go on the coverage.

Modifications   You can run your pickoff plays with this coverage. Have your second baseman break for the bag after your shortstop breaks for third base.

177 EXTRA-BASE HIT DOUBLE DOWN THE LINE

Focus To get the ball to third base as quickly as possible to hold the runner at second base.

Setup All position players take their places on the field, including a pitcher. No runners are on base at the start of the drill. A coach hits doubles to left field with a fungo bat.

Procedure On sure doubles hit down the left-field line, our primary focus is to keep the runner from advancing to third. We want our outfielders to get to the ball quickly and get it into the hands of our middle fielder (cutoff man) as quickly as they can. This way we can relay the ball to the third baseman and keep the runner from advancing to third. We want to do this as quickly as possible and make two accurate throws, one from the outfielder to the cutoff man and one from the middle infielder to the third baseman.

After the ball has been hit down the line, the pitcher goes from the mound to back up the third baseman in a direct line from the cutoff man to third base. The catcher communicates with the cutoff man on where to throw the ball. The first baseman trails the runner to second base. The second baseman goes out 15 feet behind the shortstop in a direct line between the left fielder and third base near the left-field line. He backs up the shortstop and is ready to catch an overthrown or underthrown ball. The shortstop goes out almost halfway between the left fielder at the wall and third base. He opens up glove-side with his hands up and is ready to receive the throw, turn glove-side, and make an accurate throw to third base. The third baseman goes to the bag and awaits the throw from the shortstop or second baseman in the outfield. The center-fielder goes toward the left fielder and tells him where to throw the ball. The right fielder backs up the second baseman in a straight line from the shortstop

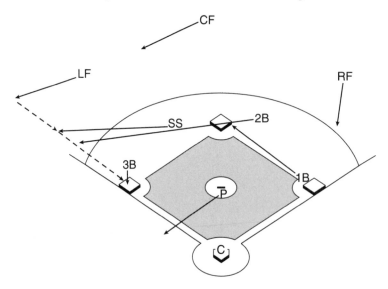

through the bag at second base. The left fielder picks the ball up with his bare hand, brings it to his glove, and in one step throws accurately to the cutoff man (shortstop).

Coaching Points   Preach to your outfielders about throwing accuracy. Stress the importance of hitting the cutoff man.

Modifications   You can hit balls down the line with a fungo bat or instead lay a few balls near the left-field wall. Have your left fielders alternate charging quickly into position, picking the ball up in a hand-to-glove manner, and making an accurate throw to the shortstop.

178   DOUBLE TO LEFT CENTERFIELD

Focus   To hold the hitter to only two bases on a ball hit into the gap.

Setup   All position players take their places on the field, including a pitcher. No runners are on base at the start of the drill. A coach hits doubles to left centerfield with a fungo bat.

Procedure   The pitcher backs up third base, staying in a direct line with the cutoff man through the third baseman. The catcher stays at the plate and communicates with the cutoff man on where to throw the ball. The first baseman trails the hitter to second base. The second baseman goes out with the shortstop into shallow leftfield and lines up between the outfielder with the ball and third base, 15 feet behind the shortstop. He catches any overthrown or underthrown ball that the shortstop has trouble with. The shortstop goes out into shallow left field and lines up between the ball and third base. He has his hands up with his body open slightly toward his glove-side to make a quick

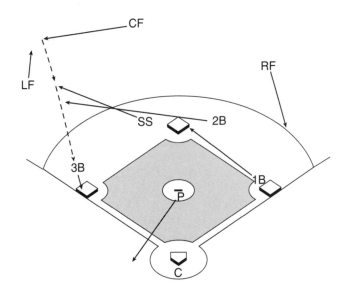

glove-to-hand exchange and make an accurate throw to third base. The third baseman goes to the bag and awaits the throw from the cutoff man in left field. He directs the cutoff man on whether he needs to move to the left or right to be in a straight line for the double relay. The left fielder and centerfielder go after the ball and communicate on who will make the throw. The right fielder backs up second base in case the runner at second gets into a rundown or a possible throw goes into second base.

Coaching Points   When you hit balls into the gap, tell your outfielders to let the ball get as close to the wall as possible before picking it up and throwing it. This makes the drill more gamelike.

Modifications   You can hit balls into the gap with a fungo bat or instead lay a few balls in the gap near the wall. Have your centerfielders and left fielders alternate charging quickly into position, picking the ball up in a hand-to-glove manner, and making an accurate throw to the shortstop.

179   EXTRA-BASE HIT TO RIGHT-CENTER

Focus   To get to the ball as quickly as possible and have our middle infielders in a position where they can make an accurate relay throw to third base to hold the runner at second base.

Setup   All position players take their places on the field, including a pitcher. No runners are on base at the start of the drill. A coach hits extra-base hits to right-center with a fungo bat.

Procedure   After the ball is hit to the right-center field gap, the pitcher backs up third base in a direct line with the cutoff man in the outfield. The catcher stays at the plate and communicates with everyone on where the throw is going. The first baseman trails the runner to second base. The second baseman leads the double relay by lining up in shallow right field with the ball in right-center field and third base. The shortstop is 15 feet behind him with his hands up and open slightly toward his glove-side to make a quick glove-to-hand exchange and an accurate throw to third base. The third baseman directs the cutoff man to right field to line up a straight line with him. He receives the throw from the second baseman or shortstop on the relay. The left fielder backs up third base. The centerfielder and right fielder go to the ball and communicate on who will throw to the relay man.

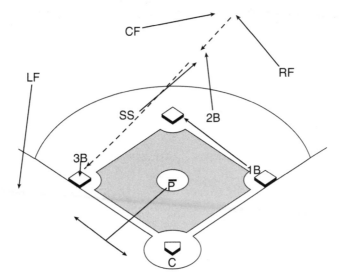

Coaching Points   We emphasize that our outfielders get the ball to our cutoff men quickly because generally this is a longer throw for our outfielders and the greatest distance to third base for our cutoff men to throw to.

Make it a point that your outfielders get to the ball quickly and that your left fielder and pitcher are backing up third base. Check to make sure your relay guys (second base and shortstop) are out in the outfield far enough so outfielders can make a strong throw on the line to their chest.

Modifications   You can hit balls into right-center with a fungo bat or instead lay a few balls in right-center near the wall. Have your centerfielders and right fielders alternate charging quickly into position, picking the ball up in a hand-to-glove manner, and making an accurate throw to the cutoff man.

180 EXTRA-BASE HIT DOWN THE RIGHT-FIELD LINE

Focus   To hold the runner to a double on balls hit down the right-field line.

Setup   All position players take their places on the field, including a pitcher. No runners are on base at the start of the drill. A coach hits long balls down the right-field line with a fungo bat.

Procedure   The second baseman and first baseman go out on the double relay into right field with the first baseman 15 feet directly behind the second baseman. The shortstop covers second base. The pitcher and left fielder back up the third baseman. The right fielder throws the ball to the second baseman, who relays the throw to third base.

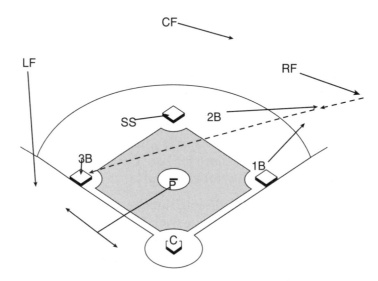

Coaching Points   We want our right fielder to get to the ball quickly and make an accurate throw to our cutoff man; we want our cutoff man to make an accurate throw to third base. Throws should be chest high and accurate. Our calls should be loud enough for everyone on the field to know where the throw is going.

Only on a sure double down the right-field line will the double relay involve the first baseman going into the outfield. Make sure your infielders remember this point on balls hit down the right-field line with no one on base.

Modifications   Have your right fielder pause when he gets to the ball so that you can make sure everyone is in their right positions.

181 EXTRA-BASE HIT DOWN THE LEFT-FIELD LINE WITH A RUNNER ON FIRST

Focus To keep a runner at first base from scoring on an extra-base hit down the left-field line.

Setup All position players take their places on the field, including a pitcher. A runner is on first base. A coach hits long balls down the left-field line with a fungo bat.

Procedure Once the ball has been hit, the left fielder goes to the ball as quickly as he can. The centerfielder goes to second base. The right fielder positions near the right-field line in a straight line with second base. The third baseman stays near the bag and anticipates a possible off-line throw or overthrow from the left fielder. He also communicates with the relay man to line him up with the plate. The shortstop goes into left field near the line; the second baseman sets up 15 feet behind him. The first baseman goes on the third-base side of the mound. The catcher positions in front of the plate and awaits the relay throw from the shortstop. The pitcher backs up home plate.

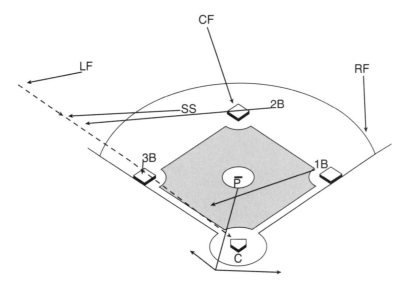

Coaching Points Emphasize quick, accurate throws from your left fielder and shortstop. Also make sure the second baseman and shortstop know that throws that are too low or too high need to be handled by the second baseman on the double relay.

Modifications Slow the play down to check that everyone is where they should be to execute the double relay.

182 EXTRA-BASE HIT TO LEFT-CENTER FIELD
WITH A RUNNER ON FIRST

Focus To keep a runner at first base from scoring on an extra-base hit to left-center.

Setup All position players take their places on the field, including a pitcher. A runner is on first base. A coach hits long balls to left-center with a fungo bat.

Procedure The coach hits the ball to the wall in left-center field to simulate a sure double. The left fielder and centerfielder sprint to the ball quickly. The right fielder runs quickly to second base to cover the bag. The third baseman covers third base. The shortstop goes into shallow left field ahead of the second baseman, who stays 15 feet behind him. The first baseman runs to the third-base side of the pitcher's mound. The catcher waits at the plate for the throw from the cutoff man. The pitcher backs up the plate. As soon as either the left fielder or centerfielder picks the ball up, he throws a strike to the shortstop, who turns glove-side and throws to the catcher.

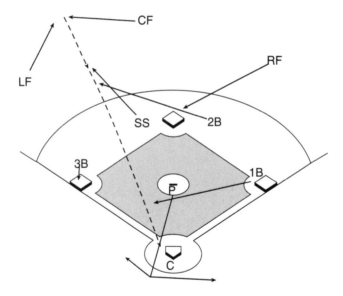

Coaching Points Make sure that once the ball is hit all position players and the pitcher move quickly into their positions. Have your outfielders make the longer throw to the cutoff man if they have a strong arm. If not, move your cutoff man out farther into the outfield.

EXTRA-BASE HIT TO RIGHT-CENTER WITH A RUNNER ON FIRST

Focus To keep a runner at first base from scoring on an extra-base hit to right-center.

Setup All position players take their places on the field, including a pitcher. A runner is on first base. A coach hits long balls to right-center with a fungo bat.

Procedure Once the ball has been hit, the pitcher backs up home plate. The catcher stays at the plate, ready to receive the throw from the double relay. He's also responsible for telling the double relay where to throw the baseball by reading the speed of the base runner and the throw from the outfielder. The first baseman goes near the mound on the first-base side and awaits a possible overthrow from the outfield. The second baseman leads the double relay by going out into right field with his hands up and yells to the outfielder to throw him the ball. The shortstop positions himself 15 feet behind the second baseman to cover an overthrow. The double relay should be in a straight line with the outfielders who are throwing the ball to home plate. The third baseman stays at third base. The left fielder goes to second base. The centerfielder and right fielder converge on the ball and communicate on who will throw the ball to the double relay.

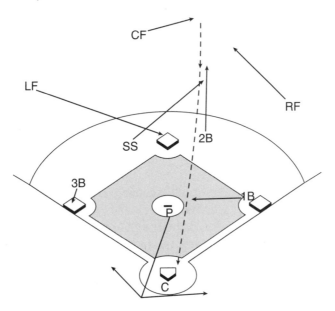

Coaching Points If your outfielders don't have strong arms, move your double relay out further into the outfield. If your outfielders have strong arms, have them try the longer throw.

184 EXTRA-BASE HIT TO THE RIGHT-FIELD CORNER WITH A RUNNER ON FIRST

Focus   To hold the hitter to two bases and the runner on first base to two bases or throw him out at home.

Setup   All position players take their places on the field, including a pitcher. A runner is on first base. A coach hits long balls to the right-field corner with a fungo bat.

Procedure   Once the ball has been hit, the pitcher backs up home plate. The catcher stays at the plate, ready to receive the throw from a middle infielder. The first baseman stays near the line and on the infield grass. The second baseman goes out into the outfield near the right-field line. The shortstop follows the second baseman into right field and positions 15 feet behind him. The third baseman stays at third base. The right fielder goes after the ball. The centerfielder goes to second base. The left fielder backs up third base.

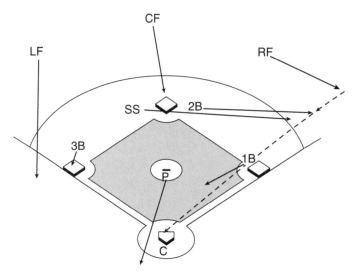

Coaching Points   Emphasize quick, accurate throws to cut down the base runner's time. If your right fielder has a weak arm, move your middle infielders (your relay men) out further down the line. Generally, your right fielder will have the strongest arm on the team. In such a case, let him make the longer throw.

It's a good idea to cover all the cutoff and relay situations at least once a week to keep your players fresh on where they go and what to do in these important situations.

Chapter 18

Game-Situation Drills

Bob Todd and Bob Bennett

Most of the drills in this chapter are team oriented. They are designed to help our players make good decisions in gamelike drills, with the goal that these decisions will carry over into games. We typically allow only 20 to 25 seconds between a pitch and a new situation. As each new situation presents itself, we want our players to be conditioned to analyze and react quickly and successfully.

We found these drills to be most helpful in getting our teams prepared to start the season. Game-situation drills place our players in a setting that is as close to an actual game as possible. The closer we can match the drills to the situations that occur in the game, the better our players will handle game conditions under pressure. It's extremely important for them to refine their skills and elevate to a highly competitive environment as quickly and as often as possible.

In imitating situations that players will confront in a game, one key is to increase the physical and mental energy level of the players during the drills. It's difficult for players to approach a drill with the same level of interest and adrenalin flow they approach a game with. But with proper focus and attention to details, along with establishing and maintaining a disciplined and goal-oriented work ethic, drills can be executed in a gamelike fashion.

We try to make our game-situation drills highly competitive. We want our players to want to win. We want them to develop a competitive familiarity with even the toughest situations. The more tough challenges they can handle, the more confident they become.

For the drills to be as challenging and competitive as an actual game, it's important for the situations to change from inning to inning, play to play, and pitch to pitch. A successful play by the offensive team perhaps evolves into a new set of circumstances for the defensive team. A successful execution of a defensive maneuver might change the situation for the offensive team. In most, if not all, of our game-situation drills, the circumstances change rapidly.

Make your drills as gamelike as possible and your players will be ready on game day.

Focus   To see that infielders respond properly to gamelike base-running situations and make sound decisions under pressure.

Setup   Infielders take their positions. You can use more than one player at each position. All other players run the bases. Use base coaches. One coach hits balls with a fungo bat.

Procedure   The drill starts on the motion of the pitcher to home. Always have a runner starting at home plate. Vary the situations by placing runners at different bases. By changing the number of outs, the inning, and the score, you create different situations that must be played in very specific ways. A coach calls out the situation, the pitcher pitches, and the coach puts the ball into play with a fungo bat.

Infielders react to the hit ball from the coach. They move into their proper positions to make the play. Repeated work on a variety of situations will familiarize them with what occurs in a game and boost their confidence in their ability to make plays. Of course a big part of the infielders' job is to prevent runners from advancing. If that can't be prevented given the circumstances, the primary goal is to at least get an out at first base.

Repeat each situation several times, getting successful responses before moving to a different situation.

Coaching Points   Stress the importance of sound decision making on defense. Tell players to get an out on every ball put in play. Have a coach at third whose job is to instruct base runners and assess their decisions on the bases.

186 BATTING PRACTICE WITH GAMELIKE DEFENSE

Focus   To make efficient use of the total field while taking batting practice; to force players to make gamelike plays defensively.

Setup   Coaches throw batting practice. When not batting or performing another assigned duty, all players take their positions in the field. Put a bucket near first and third for extra balls.

Procedure   Players in the field react to hits by their teammates. Players are hitting batting practice so the ground balls will be live, off the bat, not the fungo. If there's more than one player at a position, rotate players in and out so that everyone gets a turn in the field. Balls hit to the infield are thrown to first; balls hit to the outfield are thrown to third. Each defensive player works on getting a good jump and taking the best route to the ball.

Coaching Points   Both decision making and execution of fundamentals are focal points. Encourage and make corrections to fielders and hitters, as warranted.

Modifications   All ground balls hit to the infielders should be thrown to second base, attempting to turn a double play. Another way to modify the drills is to have infielders play in and throw all ground balls to the plate. This forces quick reactions.

Focus   To practice defensive execution on the sacrifice bunt; to refine proper bunting technique against live pitching.

Setup   Put a defensive team on the field. At least four hitters take turns at bat.

Procedure   Pitchers throw batting practice. The hitter tries to bunt the ball down either baseline. Each hitter gets one strike and then rotates out for the next hitter. Each hitter should repeat this process for four or five at-bats and then rotate to a defensive position. Using good communication, the defensive team fields the bunt and throws to the proper base.

     Another way to run the drill is to use only the pitching position to field the bunt. We allow all players except pitchers to have a ball in hand. Start at home plate. We use a manager or assistant coach to play first base, put one pitcher on the mound and one on call, and have the rest of the pitchers form a single line behind the mound. The pitcher on the mound is solely responsible for getting an out on the bunted ball. Runners at home attempt to roll a perfect bunt and beat the play to first base. It's the pitcher's responsibility to field the bunt and get an out. This challenges the pitchers to be aggressive, while reinforcing the need for the batter to run hard to first base. It's a good idea to time the runners.

Coaching Point   Insist on aggressive play from all players involved. Check that good bunting techniques are practiced. The hitter should not square too early.

Modifications   Try the drill with a drag bunt or push bunt instead of the sacrifice. Put runners on the bases and challenge the defense to get the lead runner on each play.

Focus   To stress the importance of the lead and jump by each base runner.

Setup   Fielders take their positions in the field. Several batters take turns at bat.

Procedure   The defensive team is in the field and defends against the hit-and-run play. This means that one of the middle infielders must hold his ground until the ball is hit or missed and then cover second base if the ball is missed. The runner at first base is running as soon as he's sure the ball is being delivered to home plate. After his third step, the runner looks in at the hitter to see the ball off the bat. Batters swing at every pitch and try to hit the ball on the ground. His job is to advance the runner from first base to second base.

   The base runner should make sure the ball is going home before committing to advance. The runner has protection from the hitter; he must see the ball off the bat. If there's a fly ball to the outfield, the runner gets back to first base before being doubled off. If a line drive is hit, the runner keeps running. The ball might not be fielded or might get through the infield. (He'll be doubled off anyway if the ball is caught.) We encourage our hitters to hit the ball on the ground, not necessarily behind the runner. Any ball hit on the ground will likely advance the runner.

Coaching Points   Emphasize the importance of the hitter swinging and making contact on any hit-and-run situation. Stress leads and jumps and the need to pick up the ball. Encourage hitters to hit the ball on the ground. Stress the defensive responsibilities.

Modifications   (1) Put runners at first and second or at first and third. This challenges infielders to communicate and gives them various situations to practice. (2) Have a base coach give signs to the offensive team. The offense has several options, such as a sacrifice bunt, drag, or hit and run. The different possibilities keep the defensive players on their toes.

189 PITCH AND HIT

Focus   To stress hitting discipline and encourage hitters to swing only at strikes.

Setup   Place a defensive team on the field. The rest of the squad members alternate between live hitting and batting practice in the cage.

Procedure   The hitter at the plate hits against a live pitcher. No runners are on base, and the count is kept. The defensive team reacts to any ball hit. Fungo hitters are stationed on both sides of home plate. They hit ground balls to designated infielders between pitches as time permits. The hitter stays at the plate for amounts to one at-bat in a game.

Each hitter stays for one at-bat. After four or five gamelike at-bats, the hitter rotates to defense or to a batting cage. The pitcher works on throwing strikes.

Coaching Points   The mission for the pitcher is to throw strikes to live hitters. This gets him familiar with hitters in the batter's box. The hitter works on making good contact and gaining plate discipline against live pitching.

Modifications   Add base runners to develop good base-running techniques and to give infielders a variety of situations to defend.

190 THE FAIR MAN

Focus   To hone hitting technique, base-running skills, and defensive execution.

Setup   Divide 16 players into four groups. This gives each group a chance to work on base running, live hitting, fielding, and batting practice in the cage.

Four groups:

SS	3B	SS	3B
2B	1B	2B	1B
OF	C	OF	C
P	OF	OF	OF

Procedure   Put players into equal-size groups. Organize the groups with playing postions as the basis. Players rotate from live hitting and running the bases to two groups playing defense live and one group taking batting practice in the cages. Always start with a runner at first base.

Give each group an equal amount of time to hit. Each group faces a variety of gamelike situations at bat, in the field, and on the bases, as well as getting extra batting practice in the cages.

Coaching Points   Watch for proper base running, defensive execution, solid at-bats against live pitching, and improved batting skills over time.

Modifications   Add the drag bunt, push bunt, and squeeze bunt to the drill. If you use other offensive strategies in the drill, it's a good idea to use base coaches.

191   FULL DEFENSE AND GAMELIKE BASE RUNNING

Focus   To react properly and make good decisions within various gamelike situations on defense and on the base paths.

Setup   A full defense takes the field, including a pitcher. The rest of the players are base runners. Pitchers rotate one at a time to the mound, working a set number of pitches before giving way to the next pitcher. A coach hits balls with a fungo bat.

Procedure   Create as many situations as you have time for. Vary them by placing runners at different bases. Always make sure there's a runner starting at home. Vary the number of outs. Everything starts on the pitcher's motion to home. Decide on and call out the situation before you receive the pitch. You might change situations frequently or stay with one for several repetitions.

Coaching Points   Don't give players a lot of time to think. Give them no longer than 20 to 25 seconds after each play. Quick reactions and good judgment are both important to the success of each play. This a good drill to get across your coaching points. A brief pause in action to evaluate and correct the play of either a base runner or a defensive player, followed by several correct repetitions, pays dividends. This is a good base-running drill and a good conditioner as well.

Focus   To use proper strategy and proper execution within game play.

Setup   This drill requires two teams, base coaches, and a coach or captain for each team. This is the first of a three-part sequence of drills. In this drill, teams play the seventh inning. In the next two drills, the eighth and ninth innings are played.

Over the three drills, the two teams have a total of three innings each and must decide on the best way to use them in order to win the game. Depending on what occurs, one team might be forced to play for a big inning, while the other team might choose to play for one run at a time. Each team will face a variety of challenges, as occurs in a real game.

Procedure   Players play a controlled intrasquad game. An offensive team (visiting team), a defensive team (home team), base coaches, and a coach for each team make up the two competitive units.

This drill is the first inning of a competitive three-inning game beginning in the seventh inning with the score tied and a runner at first base. The three-inning game will be completed in the subsequent two drills.

The visiting team is at bat. A runner is at first base. One of several strategic moves can be made. The bunt is a likely choice to start the inning, but the offensive team may choose another approach. This makes the setting gamelike and requires the defensive team to make decisions, as it would need to do in a real game. The inning evolves, with various situations unfolding. When the visiting team makes three outs, the home team starts their half of the inning with a runner at first base.

Coaching Points   Proper alignment of the defensive players to defend the given situation is an important part of attacking the opposing team's offense. Exploiting the defensive setup is the task of the offensive team. Assess each team on execution and strategy during this and the other two innings of this competitive drill.

Modifications   This drill can also be adapted to accommodate a four-man offensive unit.

193   PLAY THE EIGHTH

Focus   To use proper strategy and proper execution on each play during a game.

Setup   This is a continuation of the previous drill. The same two teams compete into the eighth inning keeping the same score from the end of the last drill.

Procedure   This drill is the second part of a competitive three-inning game that began with the last drill in the seventh inning. The game has now evolved into a situation that challenges each team. With only two innings remaining, each team is compelled to use the strategy that gives it the best chance to win.

     If the score is lopsided, one team will be forced to try to score a lot of runs while the team that leads has a wider array of options. If only one or two runs separate the two teams, both teams will likely employ bunting, stealing, and using the hit and run.

Coaching Points   Each member of the defensive unit must communicate and execute properly. Each member of the offensive unit is assessed on a variety of offensive skills. Each skill can be evaluated under gamelike pressure.

Modifications   You can also run this drill with a four-man offensive unit.

194   PLAY THE NINTH

Focus   To use proper strategy and proper execution on each play during a game.

Setup   This drill is a continuation of the previous two drills. The same two teams compete into the ninth inning keeping the same score from the end of the last drill.

Procedure   We're into the last inning of the game. The challenge for each team is now established. Scoring the number of runs needed to win the game is the challenge for the offensive team. Minimizing the score and winning the game is the challenge for the defensive team. If the game is tied, each team wants to score at least one run and hold the other team to no runs. In any event, playing a sound defensive game makes the job tougher for the opponent to accomplish their objective.

Coaching Points   These last three drills provide each offensive strategist with ample opportunities to make critical decisions concerning whether to bunt or hit with given hitters. These drills are a great opportunity to teach lessons in strategy and to show players the different approaches toward winning that must be used to attain consistent results.

Focus   To execute under pressure and operate effectively using various strategies.

Setup   This drill is a controlled intrasquad game. A defensive team (home team) and an offensive team (visiting team) are required. Each team needs base coaches and a coach or captain.

Procedure   The game is on the line. The score is tied with only one inning remaining. This inning is the only opportunity to win the game. Each team begins its offensive half of the inning with the bases loaded. This puts pressure on both the defense and the offense and creates challenges similar to those faced in real games.

If the visiting team doesn't score, the home team must score only one run to win. Should that occur, the game is over. If the visiting team scores several runs, the home team must respond by scoring one more run than the visiting has earned. If neither team scores, a tie results, and the drill is over.

This drill can provide strategic challenges for both teams. The precise situation is critical to the pitcher's approach and to the alignment of the defense. The offensive team also has a variety of decisions to make that should match the situation. Teams must decide whether to play for one run, which is easier, or to go for several runs, which is harder but makes winning more likely.

Coaching Points   The object of the drill is to execute with poise under pressure, play sound defense, and use a variety of offensive weapons to win a game. This is a chance for your players to impress you with their strategic savvy as well as their athletic skills.

Modifications   Starting the inning with no one on base or with a runner on first and one strike on the batter changes the strategy significantly.

Focus   (1) To advance or score a base runner (offense); (2) to prevent a runner from advancing or scoring (defense).

Setup   A defensive unit competes against an offensive unit. Play in a game-like setting with base coaches and a coach (or captain) leading each team. The offensive team is the visiting team.

Procedure   The offensive team begins its half of the inning with a runner at second base, a tie score, and no outs in the eighth inning of a game. With only two innings left to play, it's extremely important to move the runner to third base. There are several ways for the runner to advance, but the offensive team has its best chance by bunting the runner over or hitting a ground ball to the right side of the infield.

Each team starts its half of the inning with the sixth man in the batting order up to bat. This makes the drill gamelike. The first batter for the visiting team tries to advance the base runner. If he's successful, the next batter tries to score the runner from third base. His best shot at scoring the runner is via a fly ball hit deep enough for the runner to tag and score or via a ground ball hit hard and deep enough to score the runner. If the defense is playing shallow, the best choice for the hitter is to try to hit a fly ball. If the middle infielders are playing back, the options widen to either a fly ball or a hard-hit ground ball toward the middle. If the batter fails to move the runner to the next base, the next batter's job is more difficult. With one out, his objective is either (1) to get a base hit to score the runner and get on base himself so that he might eventually score, or (2) drive the runner in with a sacrifice fly or hard grounder to the right side of the infield. If the hitter fails, the next batter is faced with a tougher situation. There are two outs. Now the objective is to get a base hit (or force an error) to score the runner.

Should neither team score, the ninth inning begins with a runner at second base (the player who made the last out of the inning becomes the runner). The game continues until the final out. If either or both teams score, the play in the ninth inning continues with whatever score now exists. If the game remains low scoring, a certain strategy should be employed; if the score is lopsided, another strategy is necessary.

Coaching Points   Watch for good decision making and proper fundamentals and execution at all positions. Stress the need to make adjustments to deal with the changing competitive challenges.

Modifications   Play only the ninth inning. Start a new inning and switch the home and visiting teams. Start at different spots in the line-up.

Focus   To recognize and apply the best game plan to fit the situation.

Setup   A complete offensive team (visiting team) faces a complete defensive team (home team) to play the middle innings of a game. Assign base coaches and a captain to each team.

Procedure   The two teams begin the fourth inning of a game and play two additional innings. The visiting team begins the inning with a four-run lead. Each team begins its offensive half of the inning with a runner on first base and no outs. Each team proceeds to use the best strategy for the situations that arise.

The home team has a disadvantage and must choose whether to try to play the short game to win the game or try to score a lot of runs in an inning. The defensive team has the advantage of trying to break the game open with a big surge or to add one run at a time.

The defense must also make some critical decisions and adjustments to what the offense decides to do. This could evolve into a game that sees the visiting team take advantage of its lead and play a wide-open offense; meanwhile, the home team might play too cautiously because of the four-run deficit. What occurs over these three middle innings will likely set the strategies for the last three innings of the game.

Coaching Points   Stress the importance of the middle innings and how to deal with and manage a lead. Watch how players operate when they're behind. Do they tighten up or remain loose and confident? Teach strategies that fit each situation, stressing the importance of execution on both defense and offense.

Modifications   Because the score at the beginning of the inning makes a great deal of difference in the strategy for both teams, repeat the drill, alternating the home team advantage. Try starting the fourth inning with fewer or more base runners.

Focus To stress timing, communication, and efficiency on offense and defense.

Setup An offensive unit and a defensive unit are needed for this drill. The offensive unit consists of at least four players and can have as many as nine. There should be one player at each position on defense. If there's more than one defensive player at a position, players should alternate. Every team member becomes an offensive player at some point. Organize all players into functional groups (by full team or by groups of four or more) so they can participate offensively.

Procedure With a defensive team setup to combat the following basic offensive situations, the offensive group or team attacks the defense with the following situations and strategies:

1. Bunt with a runner on first base and no outs. Game is in the late innings.
2. Bunt with runners on first and second base with no outs. Game is in the late innings.
3. Move the runner from second to third with no outs, preferably with a ground ball to the right side.

Each offensive team or group is allotted 10 minutes to attempt these situations in order. Each situation must be done successfully before moving to the next. The team or group with the most successful repetitions is the winner.

This drill offers the defensive unit opportunities to develop the skills and experience to shut down bunt attempts and attempts to advance a runner from third.

Coaching Points For the offense, watch the execution and techniques of bunting, base running, and the ability of your hitters to put the ball into play on the ground to the right side of the infield. For the defense, assess communication, adjustments, and efficiency of execution, all of which are key to combating the short game.

About the ABCA

The **American Baseball Coaches Association (ABCA)** is the largest baseball coaching organization in the world and includes coaches from every U.S. state and hundreds of international members. The association's mission is to improve the level of baseball coaching worldwide. The ABCA assists in the promotion of baseball and acts as a sounding board and advocate on issues concerning the game. In addition, the ABCA promotes camaraderie and communication among all baseball coaches, from the amateur to professional levels. The ABCA also gives recognition to deserving players and coaches through several special sponsorship programs. It is an organization that has grown steadily in membership, prestige, and impact in recent years. The ABCA's headquarters is located in Mount Pleasant, Michigan.

About the Editor

Bob Bennett ended his coaching career in 2002 with a 1,302-759-4 record, ranking him seventh all-time on the Division I win list. In his 34 years as head coach at Fresno State University, his teams had 32 winning seasons, won 17 conference championships, made 21 NCAA Regional Championship appearances, and played in two College World Series. Bennett was awarded 14 Conference Coach of the Year awards and received the NCAA Coach of the Year award in 1988. He coached 32 All-Americans, eight of whom were first-round draft picks. Bennett also served as head coach of the U.S. national team in 1983 and 1986.

Photo by Justin Kase Conder

About the Contributors

Rich Alday has coached at the University of New Mexico since 1990. At New Mexico, Alday has been named Conference Coach of the Year three times and taken his team to postseason play more than any other coach in school history. Before heading up the Lobos, Alday was the head coach at Pima Community College in Arizona for 17 years. In his 30 years of coaching baseball, Alday boasts an 867-587-2 career record.

Rich Alday

    Jim Brownlee began his first year as head coach at Illinois State University in 2003, the very place his baseball career began as a player. In 1969, Brownlee played third base for the Redbirds and helped bring the school an NCAA College Division national championship. Brownlee was head coach for 23 years at the University of Evansville, where he totaled 701 wins.

Jim Brownlee

    Ed Cheff has coached at Lewis-Clark State College since 1977, posting an impressive 1,355-371-2 record and winning 13 NAIA national championships, eight of which occurred in an 11-year span. Cheff has been named NAIA Coach of the Year seven times and was inducted into the NAIA Hall of Fame in 1994. More than 100 of Cheff's former players have gone on to play professional baseball.

Ed Cheff

Jim Dimick was head baseball coach at St. Olaf College in Minnesota for 30 years. While there, his teams won 14 conference championships and were selected to the NCAA Division III Regional Tournament 13 years. Dimick coached the college all-star baseball team in 1989 and was on the staff of the U.S. national baseball team in 1989. He is a former president of the American Baseball Coaches Association and now serves on the board of directors.

Jim Dimick

Pete Dunn has coached at Stetson University since 1980, but he began his baseball career at the school as a player in 1968. His career coaching record stands at 893-529-3, and he has guided his teams to 12 NCAA Tournament appearances in the past 22 years. Dunn has seen 58 of his players go on to play professional baseball. He was inducted into the Stetson University Sports Hall of Fame in 1992.

Pete Dunn

Gordon Gillespie has the most wins of any coach at a four-year college or university and was the first coach to achieve the 1,500-win milestone. Gillespie has been coaching collegiate baseball for 50 years, amassing a career record of 1,630-830. He coached 24 years at Lewis University and 18 years at the College of St. Francis. He's been the coach at Ripon College since 1996. Gillespie's teams have made it to three NCAA Division III playoffs, and he has been named Midwest Conference Coach of the Year four times.

Gordon Gillespie

Rick Jones has guided his teams to more than 700 wins in his 21 years of coaching. Since his arrival at Tulane University in 1994, Jones has led his team to postseason play eight times, including a trip to the College World Series in 2001. He has also captured three Conference USA championships and four conference tournament titles. Before coming to Tulane, Jones was a head coach at Ferrum College in Virginia and Elon College in North Carolina.

Rick Jones

Mark Kingston was named associate head baseball coach at Tulane University in 2003. After playing five years in the Milwaukee Brewers and Chicago Cubs systems, he began his coaching career at Purdue University in the fall of 1996. In his first season, the Boilermakers posted a school-record 17 wins in the Big Ten. Kingston spent the 1999 season at Illinois State, where he helped the Redbirds set a school record for wins, runs scored, RBIs, doubles, hits, and walks. He then became an assistant coach for the Miami Hurricanes, who won back-to-back regional championships in 2000 and 2001 and the national championship in 2001.

Mark Kingston

Photo courtesy of Tulane University Media Relations

Sonny Pittaro has amassed more than 740 wins during his 33 years as head coach at Rider University. His teams have won nine conference titles and attended eight NCAA Regional Tournaments. Pittaro was named Metro Atlantic Athletic Conference coach of the year in 2001. He has also served as president of the American Baseball Coaches Association.

Sonny Pittaro

Photo by Peter G. Borg, Rider University

John Savage became head coach at the University of California at Irvine in 2002 after serving as an assistant coach at the University of Southern California for five seasons. At USC Savage earned *Collegiate Baseball*'s Assistant Coach of the Year award after the Trojans clinched the 1998 College World Series.

John Savage

Photo courtesy of University of California, Irvine

Steve Smith, designated by *Baseball America* as one of the top 10 rising stars in the sport, was named Big 12 Conference Coach of the Year from 1998 to 2000. Since Smith joined Baylor University in 1994 as head coach, he has led the team to its first out-right conference title in 77 years; earned six NCAA Tournament selections; won the most games in the Big 12 from 1998 to 2002; and broke the school's win record, set in 1977, with a 50-15 season in 1999. The Bears were ranked among the top 10 teams nationally during each season from 1998 to 2003.

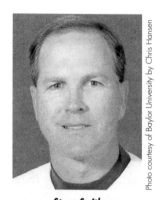

Steve Smith

Jack Smitheran, head baseball coach of the University of California at Riverside, has enjoyed many successes during his 32-plus years of coaching, including eight CCAA titles, nine NCAA Division II West Regional appearances, two NCAA Division II National Championships (1977 and 1982), and eight CCAA Coach of the Year awards. In 1998, Smitheran became only the fifth NCAA Division II coach to reach 900 victories in his career. In 2002, he reached another milestone as he won his 1,000th game, bringing his record to an impressive 1,000-706-3.

Jack Smitheran

Gene Stephenson has won more games in his 26 years as head coach of Wichita State University than any other coach in Division I program. He is ranked first place nationally among active NCAA Division I coaches in winning percentage with a career 1,406-449-3 (.758) record. In May 2003 he became just the third coach in Division I history to reach the 1,400 win plateau. Under Stephenson's tutelage, the Shockers have qualified for NCAA tournament play 21 times in the last 24 years, and claimed the College World Series title in 1989.

Gene Stephenson

Ray Tanner, head coach at the University of South Carolina, won more baseball games during the 2000, 2001, and 2002 seasons than any other NCAA Division I coach, posting a winning percentage of .771. He has a record of 274-113 since joining USC in 1997 and a 15-year winning percentage as a head coach of .700. In six seasons with the Gamecocks, Tanner has sent 35 players to professional baseball and has had 10 players named to All-America teams. Tanner was honored as National Coach of the Year in 2000 and South-

Ray Tanner

western Conference Coach of the Year in 1998 and 2000. He was also an assistant coach for the gold medal–winning U.S. team at the 2000 Olympics.

Bob Todd has coached at Ohio State University since 1987, where he is the winningest coach in 119 years of OSU baseball. He has guided the Buckeyes to a 607-298-2 record, six Big Ten championships, and nine NCAA regional appearances. OSU has been ranked as high as third nationally during his tenure. Todd has been named the Big Ten Coach of the Year an unprecedented four times. Since 1998 he has served on the prestigious NCAA Division I Baseball Committee. Before coming to Ohio State, Todd was an assistant coach at Missouri for nine years and head coach at Kent State for three years.

Bob Todd

Bob Warn has posted an impressive 1068-662-9 record in his 30 years as coach at Indiana State University. He is among the top 30 for all-time victories by a NCAA Division I coach and is in the top 20 among all active coaches. Warn has taken his team to seven NCAA Tournaments and has had nine 40-plus win seasons. Warn is a three-time MVC Coach of the Year (1979, 1983, 1984) and a member of the Indiana Baseball Coaches Hall of Fame and the Iowa Western College Hall of Fame. He is a former president of the American Baseball Coaches Association.

Bob Warn

Jim Wells, head coach of the Crimson Tide at the University of Alabama, currently has the highest winning percentage in the SEC. Wells began his Alabama career in 1995 after five seasons at Northwestern State University in Louisiana, where he led the Demons to two NCAA regionals and was selected as Southland Conference Coach of the Year three times. Since then, he has taken the Crimson Tide to three College World Series, five SEC Tournament Championships, and eight NCAA Regionals. He's also broken the school's single-season winning record. Wells was named SEC Coach of the Year twice (1996 and 2002) and *Baseball America* Coach of the Year (1997).

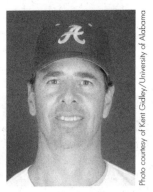

Jim Wells